"Milestone Bridge offers a compelling and useful set of frameworks, tools, and example to help guide the life science entrepreneur through the complex array of choices they face. Every life science entrepreneur and investor should read this very practical and insightful book."

—*Gary P. Pisano, Harvard Business School, USA*

"Onetti and Zucchella provide a powerful framework for designing an effective business model. The focus on life science companies makes it a must-read for all bio-entrepreneurs."

—*Patricia P. McDougall, Indiana University, USA*

"This book is of great help for entrepreneurs and scientists aspiring to create a sustainable business out of research. The use of real life business cases makes the book practical and interesting to read. I recommend it to everybody working in the area of life science startups."

—*Elizabeth Robinson, Nicox Research Institute, Italy*

"Onetti and Zucchella provide a simple but powerful management tool to visualize a company's business model. Their fresh approach to milestone completion allows the business executive to focus on which company resources are best utilized to create value during each stage of growth and development. Their insightful guidance shines a welcome light on the challenging task of executive decision-making."

—*Lisa Conte, Napo Pharmaceuticals, USA*

Business Modeling for Life Science and Biotech Companies

Most books on the biotechnology industry focus on scientific and technological challenges, ignoring the entrepreneurial and managerial complexities facing bio-entrepreneurs. Business Modeling for Life Science and Biotech Companies aims to fill this gap by offering managers in this rapid growth industry the tools needed to design and implement an effective business model customized for the unique needs of research intensive organizations.

Onetti and Zucchella begin by unpacking the often-used 'business model' term, examining key elements of business model conceptualization and offering a three tier approach with a clear separation between the business model and strategy: FOCUS, exploring the different activities carried out by the organization; LOCUS, evaluating where organizational activities are centered; and MODUS, testing the execution of the organization's activities. The business model thus defines the unique way in which a company delivers on its promise to its customers. The theory and applications adopt a global approach, offering business cases from a variety of biotech companies around the world.

Alberto Onetti is Professor of Entrepreneurship and divides his academic career between Italy at the University of Insubria in Varese and Silicon Valley. He is Chairman of the Californian Mind the Bridge Foundation. He is a seasoned serial entrepreneur and business consultant. Twitter: @aonetti

Antonella Zucchella is Professor of Marketing and International Entrepreneurship at the University of Pavia in Italy. She has been Visiting Professor at the Université Robert Schuman—Strasbourg and Université Jean Moulin Lyon 3, France. Her research focuses on innovation and international business. Antonella is author of over 100 articles and several books.

RIOT! Routledge Studies in Innovation, Organization and Technology

For a full list of titles in this series, please visit www.routledge.com

Business Modeling for Life Science and Biotech Companies

Creating Value and Competitive Advantage with *The Milestone Bridge*

Alberto Onetti and Antonella Zucchella

LONDON AND NEW YORK

First published 2014 by Routledge

2 Park Square, Milton Park, Abingdon, Oxfordshire OX14 4RN
711 Third Avenue, New York, NY 10017

*Routledge is an imprint of the Taylor & Francis Group,
an informa business*

First issued in paperback 2018

Library of Congress Cataloging-in-Publication Data

Onetti, Alberto.
Business modeling for life science and biotech companies : creating value
    and competitive advantage with the milestone bridge / by Alberto Onetti
    and Antonella Zucchella.
        pages cm. — (Routledge studies in innovation, organization and
technology ; 35)
    Includes bibliographical references and index.
    1. Biotechnology industries—Management.   2. Entrepreneurship.
I. Zucchella, Antonella.   II. Title.
    HD9999.B442O54   2014
    660.6068′4—dc23
    2013039191

ISBN: 978-0-415-87474-8 (hbk)
ISBN: 978-1-138-61690-5 (pbk)

Typeset in Sabon
by Apex CoVantage, LLC

Contents

Figures

Tables

Acknowledgments

First and foremost we want to thank Charles Versaggi for his inspiration, creative ideation, and editorial guidance. In the last five years we spent a lot of time together discussing the concepts behind *The Milestone Bridge* and the issues entrepreneurs and scientists have communicating their value propositions and identifying their business models. This book reflects a lot of our lively and open-minded discussions.

Also of great help to us was Valeria Lorenzi, who contributed to structuring the business cases. She injected fresh energy into the book project and greatly helped us to bridge our final Milestone, i.e. the book's on-time delivery to the Editor.

A special thank you to two colleagues we have had the honor and pleasure of conducting research with on the topic of business models: Marian V. Jones (Business School, Department of Management, University of Glasgow) and Patricia P. McDougall-Covin (Kelley School of Business, Indiana University).

We are also grateful to all managers and entrepreneurs in the life science and other industries we have had the pleasure of working and collaborating with in the past years. They include Betsie Robinson, Bill Young, Diana Villegas, Elisabetta Bianchini, Germano Ferrari, Giorgio Mosconi, Lisa Conte, Maria Luisa Nolli, Marina Del Bue, Robert Baffi, Robert Spiro, and all the John Murphys with whom we have spent hours discussing how to bridge technology to business. Speaking of John Murphy, a thanks to Paolo Di Trapani, a physicist we helped to spin-off a company from his research work at the university, who graciously accepted to give his face to John.

Last but not least, very special thanks to our amazing research "crew" at the University of Insubria: Alessia Pisoni, Marco Talaia, and Simona Bielli. We wish you happiness and much success[1].

NOTE

1. The book has been jointly written by Alberto Onetti and Antonella Zucchella with the contribution of Valeria Lorenzi. Specifically Alberto Onetti wrote Chapters Two, Three, Four, Five, and Seven; Alberto Onetti and Antonella Zucchella jointly wrote Chapter One. Valeria Lorenzi wrote Chapter Six

and Appendix B, C and D. Appendix A was edited by Marco Talaia and is a partial revised reprint of the article "Internationalization, Innovation and Entrepreneurship: Business Models for New Technology-based Firms" by Alberto Onetti, Antonella Zucchella, Marian V. Jones, and Patricia McDougall-Covin published first online (in 2010) and later (2012) in print in the *Journal of Management and Governance* (16, no. 3 [SI]: 337–368).

Research reported in this book is supported by Ministero dell'Istruzione dell'Università e della Ricerca (MIUR National Research Project) through the PRIN 2010 Project: "Scientific research and competitiveness. Variety of organizations, support systems and performance levels".

1 Introduction to *The Milestone Bridge*

"Man has three main goals in life: seeing the future, amassing wealth and living forever."

—David Watson[1]

1.1 INTRODUCTION

The Milestone Bridge provides entrepreneurs in the life science industry with a simple, but effective, *business-modeling tool* to make informed decisions that create value and competitive advantage. Written especially for the start-up executive, our method will show you how to identify, prioritize, and execute the most important activities of your business plan, and achieve the milestones that are critical to the growth and development of your business. Although much of what we discuss is applicable to entrepreneurial startups, this book is not a how-to manual on starting a life science company.[2] As with other commercial sectors steeped in science and technology, the life science industry is dependent on innovation as a key driver of competitive advantage and commercial success (Burns, 2002). However, innovation—the successful implementation of a creative idea or invention into the marketplace—is dependent upon managerial skills and the successful completion of milestones that create value for the company, its stakeholders, and, most importantly, society.[3]

In the following chapters we will present a managerial tool that helps you organize your key operational activities to make fundamental business decisions with respect to FOCUS—the *strategic relevance and prioritization* of these activities to achieve a developmental milestone; LOCUS—*where* you should geographically conduct these activities; and MODUS—the *way* in which these different activities are executed (Onetti et al., 2012a).

We show you that a successful business is not just about having the right business vision, but it requires the timely completion of milestones. Toward such completion, an accurate planning of activities is key.

The Milestone Bridge will also help you identify and decide which activities are worth building as *in-house operations,* and which activities are best *outsourced*. Especially useful for early-stage life science companies with long product-development cycles (e.g., drug developers), seeing your business within the context of the three dimensions of FOCUS, LOCUS, and MODUS enables you to more effectively manage each stage of product development. For more mature companies with multiple products,[4] our approach may help you to identify the most effective business model for supporting and generating revenues from each product.

For the budding entrepreneur, familiarity with *The Milestone Bridge* may make you reconsider and revise your original business plan, as you realize that not enough thought went into understanding the nature of your activities, which of these activities are milestone-driven, and how they relate to your value proposition and your business model. Most importantly, our approach will help you turn your ideas into a go-to-market plan, identifying the most important activities on which to focus. Additionally, if you have a clear business strategy and business model, you will be all the more effective in engaging prospective investors in all your communications—regardless of whether they be via an email, a two-page executive summary, a slide presentation, or a 200-page document (preferably not this long!). The book will help your business strategy not to sound vague, your value proposition confused, and your investor pitching non-engaging and ineffective. It will give your project a strong chance to get to "due diligence."

The Milestone Bridge embodies several meanings of the concept of "*bridge*." At the highest level it provides a comprehensive overview of your operations akin to the elevated platform on a ship from which the captain can oversee its activities and navigate a course of action—and, if necessary, change it in the face of the many uncertainties inherent in building an innovative life science company. In navigational terms, a ship's direction is its bearing relative to a fixed point, magnetic north or the North Star. Following a specific bearing and course, the ship ultimately reaches its destination.

"Bridge" is also an action verb referring to the objective of our approach: enabling executives to effectively connect their business activities to the achievement of successive *milestones* that not only complete an important developmental event, but ones that signal *value creation* for all the company's stakeholders—especially investors. For development-stage companies backed by venture capital, these so-called *value inflections* are milestones associated with funding events that are critical to both company valuation and survival. They may include the completion of a medical device prototype, pre-clinical drug testing in animals, proof of concept of a new therapy, the issuance of a major patent, the formation of a strategic alliance, or the regulatory clearance and launch of a new medical product.

And finally, "bridge" is a reference to our approach as a means for facilitating a company's activities into the *innovation ecosystem* that helps drive entrepreneurship, innovation, and globalization in the life science industry.

Often treated separately, these three processes need to be linked,[5] and our book helps you do that.

1.2 OUR SCOPE

Although applicable to any business enterprise, the scope of our book is the global life science industry and the growing convergence of enabling technologies that produce commercial applications of the biological sciences. This includes the healthcare sector—developers of pharmaceutical and biological therapies, diagnostics, medical devices, and healthcare information technology. While biology and medicine remain centerpieces of the life science industry, the industry includes applications of molecular biology, nanotechnology, systems biology, and genomics beyond healthcare—the use of living organisms and bioprocesses to produce a myriad of products from agricultural as well as industrial applications that include bioremediation and alternative fuels.[6]

Business models have been a topic of perennial debate in the life science industry, especially in light of how both the pharmaceutical and biotechnology sectors continue to redefine their business models and value-chain participation in today's rapidly changing global market (Onetti et al., 2012b). The global financial crisis—which is likely to continue for several more years—is compounding this value chain, as the need for increasing cost efficiency has become the operational "new normal" for life-science product development. Although in 2009 the global biotechnology industry was able to weather the worldwide economic turmoil reaching profitability for the first time in history, according to Ernst & Young's global biotechnology report, the gap between the "haves" and the "have nots" in the biotechnology sector continues to widen, posing new challenges for emerging companies in accessing the capital needed for R&D.[7]

Technological innovation is making it more and more difficult to define any industry with well-defined boundaries and sectors. Consider the melding of the pharmaceutical and biotechnology sectors, as innovations in one sector are utilized by another in drug discovery, development, and commercialization. Thus the life science industry is more a *meta-industry* (Onetti and Zucchella, 2008) where technologies are cross-platforms that are transversal and pervasive—all the more reason why in this book we shift the business focus from industry to the *company:* what matters most is not to what industry a company belongs, but the *business strategy, business model, and corresponding revenue model* it has chosen in order to succeed.

Due to the heterogeneous nature of this evolving meta-industry, the activity mix chosen by a company is increasingly at the intersection of different industries and markets. Thus a company's business model decisions also provide the seeds for innovation and new industry generation, which of course, is how the life science industry continues to evolve and innovate into new applications and market sectors.

1.3   OUR AUDIENCE

Our book is written not only for entrepreneurs and entrepreneurial executives, but also for business managers, investors, financial analysts, and academics—anyone who wants to get a better understanding of the operational complexities of life science companies.

For business managers, *The Milestone Bridge* provides a vehicle for aligning day-to-day management decisions to the company's long-term strategy, and communicating to employees and third parties what the company is doing.

It also supports *managers* in preparing budget allocations to different operational functions and departments, keeping the company's strategy and objectives aligned and on track. *The Milestone Bridge* also helps to focus, and if necessary to balance, the company's resource allocation—e.g., research and technology development with marketing and commercialization.

For *investors* and *analysts,* our approach provides a simple blueprint to check whether and how their portfolio companies are executing the best strategy for achieving a return on investment. Although risks still exist, investors are able to better understand how their investment is tracking against the activities of a company and its completion of milestones critical to creating value.

For *academics* seeking a better understanding of the life science industry, our approach provides them with a practical conceptualization of the business model construct. Providing the reader with real-world case studies, our business modeling approach helps them merge theory with practice.

Although our discussion is confined to the life science industry, our construct can be applied to other high-tech sectors where the proactive management of complex business activities is required to successfully deliver a company's value proposition to customers in an increasingly complex and dynamic global market.

For those seeking to find the "ideal business model" for forming, funding, and operating a profitable life science company, we offer no monolithic answer to the uncertainties of science-based businesses—particularly with respect to risk management, integration, and learning.[8] Nor are we arguing for any particular business model or degree of vertical integration for biotechnology companies engaged in the drug-development value chain—e.g., the Fully Integrated Pharmaceutical Company (FIPCO) at the top of the chain versus the Research-Intensive Pharmaceutical Company (RIPCO) at the bottom (Burns, 2002).[9] While one company may find that *operational integration* is competitively advantageous, another may choose to *"disintegrate"* its operations and outsource some of its activities to achieve optimal operational synergy in the value creation process. The so-called

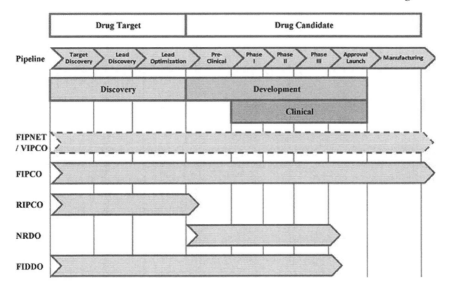

Figure 1.1   Biotechnology Companies by Degree of Vertical Integration

Source: Authors' elaboration from www.discoverymanagementsolutions.com/from-fipco-to-fipnet-to-vipco-%E2%80%93-say-what/

Virtually Integrated Pharmaceutical Company (VIPCO) or Fully Integrated Pharmaceutical Network (FIPNET) are ones where virtually all key activities— R&D, preclinical support, clinical development, manufacturing, sales, and distribution—are outsourced to contract service providers. This allows a company to access complementary assets outside the firm by contracting extensively activities at any point(s) in the value chain, while maintaining control of the whole product development process and defer the point at which they plug into the value chain.

Rather than arguing for a generic business model per se, *The Milestone Bridge* enables one to make managerial decisions focused on specific activities that impact the *degree of vertical integration that's best for the individual company based on its core competencies*. Should the company strengthen its capabilities in and around its position in the industry value chain, or should it move downstream to control more of product development, manufacturing, marketing, and selling? For life science entrepreneurs, scientific skills, managerial experience, intellectual property rights, and access to capital are the resource limitations that drive business model design and adoption (Sammut, 2005):

- Where are the points of greatest value creation?
- Can the company participate in those points effectively?
- What resources are needed to participate?
- Are those resources available?

Nor do we believe, as some critics have said, that "the biotechnology business model" is broken (Pisano, 2006). They argue that the combined revenues generated by the industry are overshadowed by the combined profits being at or below zero, ignoring the fact that most of the companies are early-stage companies that consume rather than produce capital. The big difference between discovery in the oil industry and the biotechnology industry is the length of time it takes to learn the well is "dry." Biotechnology companies may not discover that their well is "dry" until their drug candidate has completed Phase 3 clinical trials, and this can be 8–12 years from start. "Unfortunately, in biotechnology, product development cannot run in parallel. Just as you cannot put two 4 1/2-month pregnant women together to get a baby—some things just require time."(Shimasaki, 2009)

But the life science industry encompasses more than drug development. We envision the life science value chain eventually becoming a *fully integrated innovation ecosystem* of producers, suppliers, and service providers. This is certainly the trend for the medical device sector where microelectronics has revolutionized medical practice (Kruger, 2005). Thus, our approach may help to elucidate these issues: our concept of an *activity-focused* business model may help to define a company's position in the market's value chain. As Wharton senior fellow Stephen Sammut aptly states, "Genes and business models must each be reengineered. . .business models must adapt—discretely or continuously—to shifts within value chains" (Sammut, 2005).

1.4   OUR READING COMPANIONS

Before starting reading the book, we would like to introduce you to our "reading companions."

They are companies we had the chance to analyze through *The Milestone Bridge*. Their experience will surely help you understand better the business model concept (and its building blocks) and specifically how to identify and execute your own business model.

They are all real companies, except for Biomagen. The latter is a fictional spin-off company where we put together all our years of experience (and all the challenges and issues we encountered) working with startups in the biotech/biomedical field. Also, its founder, Dr. John Murphy, is a fantasy character, though he has a real "soul" and a concrete challenge: decide whether it makes sense or not for him to leave the laboratories and enter into the entrepreneurial arena. He ideally represents all the techno-entrepreneurs and wanna-be entrepreneurs who are struggling to find commercial applications for their research and identify a viable business model.

Below you can find a short introduction of our travel companions.

Table 1.1   The Companies

Napo Pharmaceuticals	**Areta International**
Country of origin: California (US)	Country of origin: Italy
Headquarters: California (US)	Headquarters: Italy
Year of foundation: 2001	Year of foundation: 1999
Activity: Development and commercialization of proprietary pharmaceuticals for international markets.	Activity: Contract development and manufacturing of innovative biological drugs and advanced therapy medicinal products.
Partners' locations: California (US), China, India, North Carolina (US).	Partners' locations: Canada, France, Italy, UK.
MolMed	**Nicox**
Country of origin: Italy	Country of origin: France
Headquarters: Italy	Headquarters: France
Year of foundation: 1996	Year of foundation: 1996
Activity: Research, development, and clinical validation of innovative therapies to treat cancer.	Activity: Development and commercialization of nitric oxide-donating drugs primarily for inflammation and cardio-metabolic diseases.
Partners' locations: Belgium, Italy, Japan, UK.	Partners' locations: Canada, France, Italy, New York (US), Spain, Switzerland.
Quipu	**OXiGENE**
Country of origin: Italy	Country of origin: Sweden
Headquarters: Italy	Headquarters: California (US)
Year of foundation: 2010	Year of foundation: 1994
Activity: Products and services in high-tech diagnostic and preventive medicine.	Activity: Research and development firm in the area of oncology and ophthalmology.
Partners' locations: Estonia, France, Germany, Greece, Italy, Romania, Spain, Turkey, UK.	Partners' locations: Arizona (US), Florida (US), Massachusetts (US), New York (US), Sweden, Texas (US), UK.
Neurosilicon	**Biomagen**
Country of origin: Canada	Country of origin: California (US)
Headquarters: Canada	Headquarters: California (US)
Year of foundation: 2005	Year of foundation: 2012
Activity: Develops novel brain-computing interfaces to expand the scientific understanding of the human brain and to improve the effectiveness of drug discovery.	Activity: Development of therapeutics to treat osteoporosis.
Partners' locations: Connecticut (US), Germany.	Partners' locations: California (US).

THE "SOUL"

John Murphy: John was born in 1972 in Boston and grew up with a deep passion for science and art but with a sort of "dislike" for anything that was business-related (his father was a violinist and his mother a researcher in the cardiovascular field). After graduating in biology from Cornell University and from medical school at Stony Brook, he moved to California where he received his internal medicine training and completed his endocrinology fellowship at UCSD. In 2007, he moved to UCSF Medical Center and, after a few years, opened his own new venture, Biomagen.

1.5　HOW TO READ THIS BOOK

The life science entrepreneur should read the chapters of this book consecutively. Chapter 2 clarifies some basic business concepts. Chapter 3 goes deep into the business model concept and provides an overview of the key concepts underpinning its logic. Chapter 4 introduces *The Milestone Bridge*'s approach and shows you how to identify and prioritize your ACTIVITY LIST and explains the three business-model drivers, FOCUS, LOCUS, and MODUS, with examples on how to effectively set up a business model. Chapter 5 reviews how to manage the most common issues in the business model building process, in a form of a Q&A with a techno-entrepreneur (John Murphy). Chapter 6 provides some real case studies, which are analyzed in depth in order to illustrate how *The Milestone Bridge* works in practice. In Chapter 7 (Conclusions) we wrap-up the main concepts and provide a check list. In addition, you will find at the end of each chapter a small summary of the "blocks" of knowledge you are supposed to have learned. If some of them do not sound familiar, you can go back and check what you have missed.

In this book we apply a "hyperlink" approach (which represents quite an innovation for a printed book). At the end of the volume, we added four Appendixes with the goal of providing a deeper understanding of the main topics we discussed in the first seven chapters: Business Model, Biotechnology, Entrepreneurship, and Internationalization. These four topics are the conceptual backbones of the book. Therefore, for each of them, we provide you with a comprehensive overview and literature background, which is some further reading for those who need and/or want it.

Along with achieving the three main goals in life—seeing the future, amassing wealth, and living forever, our goal is to empower life science executives with the necessary vision to make informed decisions; achieve prosperity for their companies, their employees, and their investors; and especially to fulfill the promise of an improved quality of life for society. For the price of this book, two and a half out of the three is a bargain.

Table 1.2   Learning Blocks—Chapter 1

Value Inflection	Operation Integration	FIPCO
RIPCO	VIPCO	FIPNET

NOTES

1. Quote by David Watson (2005).
2. The authors recommend Peter Kolchinsky's (2004) guide to run a biotech startup.
3. Quoting Foster and Kaplan (2001): "Two factors determine the level of innovation: how new the innovation is and how much wealth it generates."
4. Later stage companies and specifically diversified companies are not the main target of this book. However, the main principles we discuss are applicable also to these firms.
5. Nowadays, as suggested by Onetti et al. (2012b), entrepreneurship, innovation, and internationalization are deeply intertwined. This poses novel challenges for a firm's survival and success. The context in which business decisions are taken is far more complex than in the past and requires entrepreneurs and managers to assume a systemic view of the firm and its environment (Jones, 1999; Golinelli, 2010) and to adopt adequate managerial tools.
6. Refer to Appendix B for a more comprehensive view about life sciences and biotechnologies.
7. *Beyond Borders: Global Biotechnology Report.* 2010. EYGM Limited.
8. Gary P. Pisano. *Science business: The promise, the reality, and the future of biotech.* (Boston, MA: Harvard Business School Press, 2006).
9. Please note that, as shown in Figure 1, other variants are possible, such as the No Research, Development Only Company (NRDO)—that originates around an in-licensed drug candidate—and the Fully Integrated Drug Discovery and Development Organization (FIDDO) that represents the evolution of a successful RIPCO that may decide to add capabilities as the research ideas progress and the company evolves with the goal of partnering or licensing the drug to a FIPCO. And there will likely be additional acronyms created that fill the needs of different audiences.

REFERENCES

Burns, Lawto 2002. *The Health Care Value Chain.* San Francisco, CA: Jossey-Bass.

Ernst and Young. 2013. "Beyond Borders: Global Biotechnology Report." Report, EYGM Limited.

Foster, Richard N., and Sarah Kaplan. 2001. *Creative Destruction: Why Companies That Are Built to Last Underperform the Market—and How to Successfully Transform Them.* New York: Random House.

Golinelli, Gaetano M. 2010. *Viable Systems Approach (VSA). Governing Business Dynamics.* Padova: Cedam.

Jones, Marian V. 1999. "The Internationalization of Small High-Technology Firms." *Journal of International Marketing* 7, no. 4: 15–41.

Kolchinsky, Peter. 2004. "The Entrepreneur's Guide to a Biotech Startup." Report, Evelexa. www.evelexa.com/resources/egbs4_kolchinsky.pdf.

Kruger, Kurt. 2005. "The Medical Device Sector." In *The Business of Healthcare Innovation,* edited by Lawton R. Burns. New York: Cambridge University Press.

Onetti, Alberto, and Antonella Zucchella. 2008. *Imprenditorialità, internazionalizzazione e innovazione. Il business model delle imprese biotech.* Roma: Carocci.

Onetti, Alberto, Antonella Zucchella, Marian V. Jones, and Patricia McDougall-Covin. 2012a. "Internationalization, Innovation and Entrepreneurship: Business Models for New Technology-based Firms." First online 2010 (doi:10.1007/s10997–010–9154–1). Print version *Journal of Management and Governance* 16, no. 3 (SI): 337–368.

————. 2012b. "Guest Editor's Introduction to the Special Issue: Entrepreneurship and Strategic Management in New Technology Based Companies". First online 2010 (doi:10.1007/s10997–010–9153–2). Print version *Journal of Management and Governance* 16, no. 3 (SI): 333–336.

Pisano, Gary P. 2006. *Science business: The promise, the reality, and the future of biotech.* Boston: Harvard Business School Press.

Sammut, Stephen M. 2005. "Biotechnology business and revenue models: the dynamic of technological evolution and capital market ingenuity." In *The Business of Healthcare Innovation,* edited by Lawton R. Burns. New York: Cambridge University Press.

Shimasaki, Craig. 2009. *The Business of Bioscience.* New York: Springer.

Watson, David. 2005. *Business Models.* Petersfield, Hampshire: Harriman House, Ltd.

2 Bridging the Gaps

"Pessimism and optimism are slammed up against each other in my records, the tension between them is where it's all at—it's what lights the fire."

—*Bruce Springsteen*[1]

2.1 IMPORTANCE OF MILESTONES

Widely used by road-builders in the Roman Empire, a *milestone* was originally one of a series of numbered stone markers placed along the road to tell the traveler how far they had traveled (the first Roman milestones appeared on the Appian Way). They are *reference points* to reassure the traveler that the proper path is being followed, and to indicate either distance traveled or the remaining distance to a destination. This destination is represented by the *business objective*—what will you achieve in your business and by when.

> MolMed's business objective is to get its product TK marketable in 2014.
>
> OXiGENE's objective is to increase the potential value of its leading compound Zybrestat.

Accordingly, *business strategy* is the "how"—how will you achieve the objective you have set? As we define it, business strategy is the *directional plan of action* you take to grow and develop your business (Porter, 1980, 1985; Treacy and Wiersema, 1995). "Where are we now?"—"Where do we want to be?"—"How do we get there?"—thus *business milestones* are distance markers that signal the completion of a significant stage in the growth and development of your enterprise. In line with previous examples:

> MolMed's strategy for getting TK marketable in 2014 is to use TK's Orphan Drug designation to get a faster Conditional Marketing Authorization from the European Authority.
>
> OXiGENE's business strategy for increasing Zybrestat's potential value is to FOCUS on ovarian cancer as one of its lead indications.

Strategy belongs to the upper level of the business decision process, since it selects the business/businesses with which to compete (*corporate strategy*) and defines how to position for each of them (*business strategy*) (Cotta Ramusino and Onetti, 2013). The design of a business strategy is thus necessary.

Although, for successful execution, it requires a *business model*[2] to support the comprehensive set of decisions that jointly determines and shapes the company's business activities. The business model logically is presented at operational level, since it defines how to execute the strategy, representing the firm's underlying core logic and strategic choices. In particular, the business model here is defined by the company's activities architecture, based on the prioritization and timely completion of milestones that create value and competitive advantage—namely, the generation of sustained profits that exceeds the average for a given industry sector.

Not all activities will necessarily do this—"What *activities* are needed to achieve our objectives?" "How do we reach our next milestone on time?"—Within this framework what matters most is the business model a company has chosen—especially the activities it decides to conduct (FOCUS), and the location (LOCUS) and manner (MODUS) in which it decides to operate each activity in order to deliver its value proposition.

Using *The Milestone Bridge* to organize their key activities, companies can assess where their current business models stand in relation to their potential and then define appropriate next steps for the further improvements of those models.

In line with that, *business model innovation* is increasingly identified by the literature as the real differentiator in conceiving and delivering novelty to the market (Chesbrough, 2010). We don't think that a business model in itself can generate innovation. While you can identify a novel value proposition and build an innovative strategy, it is definitively rarer to create innovation through a business model. This does not make the business model less important. Actually it is quite the opposite. Innovation needs to be realized in order to create value. The business model allows you to make innovation happen and exploit the innovation potential.

INDUSTRY OUTLOOK

A few decades ago, pharmaceutical companies started to understand that the blockbuster drug business model was becoming prohibitively expensive. The large market segments were saturated, the costs of R&D was rising steeply, and the failure rate had been disappointingly high. Future markets would have to be smaller and highly targeted (and effective), and this new approach would require different processes to develop and launch drugs successfully. The complex and massive biotechnology revolution made many pharma companies change their business objectives, strategies and, consequently, their business models.

The business model is what enables the company to deliver the innovative value proposition to the market and give execution to the innovative strategy. And a good execution is as critical as a brilliant idea.[3] In such a perspective the business model becomes the real differentiator in conceiving and delivering novelty to the market. Companies rarely lack ideas. Most of the time they simply lack focus; i.e., a business model. "Knowing where to focus creativity changes the dynamics of idea generation"[4] and the chance of success of the company.

A company has as much value to gain from executing a novel strategy as from developing an innovative new technology (Chesbrough, 2010). Indeed, few life science companies understand their business model well enough— the premise behind its development, its natural interdependencies, and its strengths and limitations. So, they don't know when they can leverage their core business and when success requires them to change their business model altogether (Christensen, Grossman, and Hwang, 2008).

A company's business strategy and business model will also inform its *revenue model—how* it makes money. Thus a company's business strategy (plan of action) informs its business model (milestone-driven activities that create value) to make money (revenue generation). Generally, biotech companies and startups are not able to generate a positive cash flow during the early years of activity. Thus the revenue model is replaced by the financing model— i.e., how the business model's activities are or may be financed/funded—until the new venture does not reach a certain product/technology maturity and becomes ready for entering revenue generating agreements and/or deals (e.g., out-licensing, co-development, asset sale, etc). The objective of any business is, of course, to keep the costs of your business activities low, while creating high value for your customer, maximizing profit and generating cash.

The challenge for technology-based companies, life science or otherwise, is that there is no permanently fixed point against which to gauge their direction—markets are dynamic and constantly changing.[5] In response to changing market conditions managers may need to adjust their company's business strategy, business model, and revenue model. Although strategy is a long-term commitment, adjustments are frequent for companies. In certain extreme cases (quite recurrent within the start-up arena) a radical change in strategy or business model (*"pivoting"*) is required to avoid further loss of time and money.

During its initial growth, to help fund the development of its lead product, a biopharmaceutical company may decide to out-license a portion of its intellectual property or provide geographical marketing rights to a future product for upfront payments and backend royalties. This change in activity enables the company to continue focusing on achieving a critical milestone; for example, completing animal testing of its lead product, or change the FOCUS of its product development altogether because of a negative experimental outcome.

As we will explain further in Chapter 3, business strategy, business model, and revenue model are three distinct—but extremely interrelated—concepts.

Notwithstanding, they are instead too often treated synonymously or ill defined. Table 2.1 provides an example of the differences between the three concepts taken from OXiGENE's business case. As you may appreciate, the level of detail is quite high.

The Milestone Bridge will show you how to choose the most appropriate business strategy, business model, and revenue model relative to your company's development stage within the context of FOCUS, LOCUS and MODUS. As we will discuss later on, there is no "right" business model for all life science companies—biotechnology, medical device, diagnostics, etc.—in fact, there are multiple alternative business models available for each company. Your company is required to arrive at its own unique business model relative to its developmental stage and market milieu. This book is intended to help and inform companies in their business model choice.

Typically, the business objectives and business strategy are described in the *business plan*. In fact, your business plan documents and justifies how you will execute your business model and explains the steps needed to effectively perform the activities related to that model.

Below you can find the "conventional" structure of a business plan. More than the index of a real document (if you really write down something that long, nobody will likely read it; additionally—since information ages really fast—a long document is almost impossible to maintain and keep up-to-date), it represents the list of all the potential questions you may be required to answer while pitching an investor, having a job interview with a key employee to be hired, negotiating a strategic agreement with a potential partner, discussing a growth opportunity, or working capital line with a bank.

The real value of drafting a business plan is not in having the finished product in hand; rather the value lies in the process of writing it, which requires you to think things thoroughly, to perform further research if unsure of the facts, and review critically all the assumptions. It could absorb time now, but could avoid costly, sometimes fatal, mistakes later.

Recently there has been a lot of debate regarding the utility of structured and medium-term business planning, specifically for early-stage companies. People and investors are growingly skeptical of startups with plans. Quoting Steve Blank, "no one besides venture capitalists and the late Soviet Union requires five-year plans to forecast complete unknowns" (Blank, 2013). The conventional wisdom is that detailed plans are "generally fiction" because everything is just going to change anyway.

A methodology called the *lean startup approach* (Ries, 2011) specifically favors experimentation over elaborate planning, and customer feedback over intuition ("No plan survives first contact with customers"), and iterative design over traditional "big design up front" development. Concepts such as "*minimum viable product*" and "*pivoting*" have quickly taken root in the start-up world, and business schools have already begun adapting their curricula to teach them. And despite the methodology's name, in the long term some of its biggest payoffs may be gained by the large companies that decide to embrace it.

Table 2.1 Differences between Business Strategy, Business Model, and Revenue Model

Business Objective	Business Strategy	Milestones	Business Model Activities	Revenue Model
Increase ZYBRESTAT's potential value	Focus on ovarian cancer as one of our lead indications of ZYBRESTAT	Phase 2 trial of ZYBRESTAT in combination with bevacizumab	Patient Recruitment Treatment-Randomization into two arms Quality Check-Progression-Free Survival Quality Check-Safety, Overall Survival and Objective Responses	This trial is being conducted under the sponsorship of CTEP of the National Cancer Institute. The trial is also being done in collaboration with Genentech, the manufacturer of bevacizumab, who, along with Oxigene, supplies the drugs for the study in addition to providing some of the trial's funding. While Oxigene pays for some costs related to this trial, CTEP bears most of the cost of the trial.
		Phase 2 study of ZYBRESTAT in combination with weekly paclitaxel	Patients Enrollment Treatment-One-To-One Randomization Quality Check-Progression-Free Survival Quality Check-Safety, Overall Survival, Objective Response Rate and Ca125 Response Rate	This trial is dependent on having sufficient funding from collaborating partners
		Phase 1b/2 study of ZYBRESTAT in combination with pazopanib	Patients Enrollment Treatment-Three-Way Randomization	This trial is dependent on receiving funding from an externally funded collaboration
	Pursue the commercialization of ZYBRESTAT in Europe for the treatment of ATC	Commercialization	Regulatory Approval Marketing Authorization Business Development	Distribution agreement: Azanta Danmark A/S, is responsible for all regulatory activities necessary to distribute and sell ZYBRESTAT on a compassionate use basis for the treatment of ATC within the specified territories. There is no transfer of ownership of intellectual property rights for ZYBRESTAT to Azanta under the terms of the agreement
Bring OXi4503 to Phase 2	To continue to support the ongoing investigator-sponsored Phase 1 trial of OXi4503	…	… … …	…

Table 2.2 Sample of a Business Plan for a Biotechnology Company

BIOTECH BUSINESS PLAN OUTLINE

Executive Summary	The opportunity
	The company
	Business model
	Intellectual property
	Use of proceeds
	Exit strategy
Market Opportunity	An unmet medical need, or a way to break into a market without infringing another company's patents
	Disease incidence, survival statistics, patient demographics
	Market size and growth for each indication
	Market segments, if any
The Company	Background
	Management
	Directors
	Scientific Advisory Board and research collaborations
Product Development	Indications for the product
	Explain company's science in terms of filling the unmet medical need
	What is known about product's safety and efficacy
	Plan for preclinical development
	Plan for Phase 1 clinical trials
	How much money will plans require
Competitive Analysis	Company's competitive advantages, including potential for orphan drug status
	Current competing drugs for this indication
	Competing drugs now in clinical trials
	Advantages of company's route of administration vs. how competing drugs are delivered
	How the company will be reimbursed by the government or insurers vs. reimbursement for competing drugs
	Consider doing a SWOT analysis (Strengths, Weaknesses, Opportunities, Threats)
Intellectual Property	Include an explanation that your company's IP will not infringe anyone else's
Financial Overview	Capitalization (money raised to date)
	Use of proceeds to be raised with this business plan

(Continued)

Table 2.2 (Continued)

Exit Strategy	One possible approach to ROI calculations: Give examples of how much other drugs or companies sold for after successful Phase 1 trials. From these figures calculate how much investment money it is possible to obtain and deliver to investors a 3-fold, 5-fold, and 10-fold return in 5 years.
Risk Management	Technical risks of preclinical development and alternative approaches
	Management risks
	Business risks
	Regulatory risks
Appendix	Collaborations with other companies
	Mechanism of action
	Glossary of scientific terms
	Audited financials
	Scientific bibliography or selected papers
	Media coverage and press releases

The idea has already started to aggregate many followers among young startups, business schools, and other institutions. Professors at important universities think that this new approach may be able to boost innovation and incredibly decrease the risk of failures for new entrepreneurial firms. The concept underlying the process comes from the lean manufacturing process, fine-tuned in Japanese factories decades ago and focused on eliminating any work or investment that doesn't produce value for customers.

In line with this goes the emphasis on rapid development, small teams, and constant improvement. One of the problems in a science-driven industry is that entrepreneurs sometimes set up their own business just because they want to see their "baby" grow up. And they invest time, energy, and resources for achieving this goal. But if they are not creating something with a potential market that buys it, they are condemned to fail very soon. Not because the technology doesn't work, but because what you want to do is not in line with the customers' needs.

A very good example of the application of the lean approach is Dropbox. When they first launched the software, it was very simple and basic in its features, but extremely efficient in solving the pain points of the users. Then, through continuous experiments and new updates, the company has been able to capture and monitor the market response and change the product consequently.

We think that the lean methodology can really help in improving the business planning process and making business modeling more effective.

The Milestone Bridge is conceived as a milestone-based process. A business model has to be revised after every milestone and, if required, also along the journey.

But we are still strongly convinced that having a detailed plan is key. Adopting a lean approach does not mean that aspirations may replace plans. Quoting Peter Thiel (entrepreneur and venture capitalist, co-founder of Pay-Pal, and first outside investor in Facebook), "there are some cases where things work despite the lack of a plan. But there is an awful lot of failure there too. Winning without a plan is hitting the jackpot, and most people do not hit the jackpot. Since you want to have as much mastery over things as possible, you need to plan."

And *The Milestone Bridge* may help you to structure it in a smart and lean way.

2.2   OUR CENTRAL THESIS

Keeping the previous key concepts in mind, *The Milestone Bridge* is conceived to be used as a decision-making tool aimed at helping the life-science manager:

- FOCUS on what business activities demand priority, resources, and attention;[6]
- Determine the best geographical LOCUS for conducting these activities;[7] and
- Identify the MODUS in which these different activities are executed to achieve critical milestones during a company's growth and development.[8]

Our central thesis is that a business model supports milestone completion by manipulating your operational activities and resources, choosing which ones are the most profitable as in-house value-building activities, and which are best outsourced to a more cost-effective activity provider.

How you structure the execution of your activities to complete a specific milestone is more than just a business decision—it is a *business model decision*. The value of our approach is that it helps you think about your business in a systematic way.

Firstly, it brings you to consider your business activities as a related series of pivotal milestones that need to be completed to achieve your business objectives. Secondly, it helps you think of milestone completion within the strategic framework of your company's business model, rather than as an isolated activity. And finally, as you identify operational activities that are milestone-driven, you will see that *business model sustainability* is a function of how you complete your milestones within the three-dimensional framework of FOCUS, LOCUS, and MODUS. Therefore, business model and milestone completion are inextricably related, and function together as essential elements for successfully delivering your company's strategy and value proposition and sustaining its competitive advantage.

A key differentiator of our approach is that our business-model framework emphasizes the location of operational activities, as well as what activities to focus on, and the selection of value partners for these activities (Onetti et al., 2012b). Our contribution makes a clear distinction between the business strategy and the business model, and underscores the relevance of *location decisions*—where do we place our activities, and where do we locate our company? These are critical decisions not fully addressed by extant literature on business models.[9]

Companies today have to be international from day one—"*born global*" (Oviatt and McDougall-Covin, 2005). Globalization and capital efficiency are forcing companies to cross their national boundaries and spread their activities in different countries where knowledge and resources best serve their business strategy. Today, the management of time, space, and network relationships has become the key variable for business model design. Although these three dimensions are well represented in the international literature on entrepreneurship, they have not yet been fully incorporated into the practical application of business model design (Onetti et al., 2012a).

Table 2.3 Learning Blocks—Chapter 2

Business Objective	Business Strategy	Business Plan
Business Activities	Milestones	Lean Startup
Revenue Model		Business Model Innovation

NOTES

1. By Bruce Springsteen, Paris press conference of "Land of Hope and Dreams" (in *Wrecking Ball*).
2. As Alex Osterwalder frequently points out: "Strategy is about doing the right things, while Business Model is about doing things right" (Osterwalder and Pigneur, 2010).
3. Quoting Guy Kawasaki, Alltop co-founder and entrepreneur: "Ideas are easy. Implementation is hard." Similarly Michael Dell (Dell chairman and CEO) points out: "Ideas are commodity. Execution of them is not."
4. Tweet by Alex Osterwalder on June 28th, 2013.
5. In the current scenario, change is the norm also for non-high-tech businesses. Peter Drucker defines it as the "age of discontinuity," while Toffler defines it as the "third phase of civilization" and Rifkin as the "age of access." Continuously changing market conditions make it difficult for companies (all, not only the ones operating in innovative or emerging markets) to define their strategy and stick with it (Drucker, 1968; Toffler, 1970, 1980; Rifkin, 2000).
6. We refer to the selection of activities on which the company's efforts should be concentrated (Prahalad and Hamel, 1990; Amit and Schoemaker, 1993;

Daley, Mehrotra, and Sivakumar, 1997; Wernerfelt, 1984; Feeny and Willcocks, 1998).

7. We refer to decisions re: the location of activities (i.e., local versus foreign-based activities, inward–outward relationships with space, entry modes, and local embeddedness) (Dunning, 1988; Porter, 2000).

8. The relationships with other players and about organizational boundaries (i.e., insourcing and outsourcing of activities along social and inter-organizational ties, inward–outward relationships with other players, strategic alliances) (Glick, 2008).

9. Our literature review established that Mitchel and Coles (2004) offer the only definition that includes location decisions in its business model constituents.

REFERENCES

Amit, Raphael, and Paul J. H. Schoemaker. 1993. "Strategic Assets and Organizational Rent." *Strategic Management Journal* 14, no. 1: 33–46.

Blank, Steve. 2013. "Why the Lean Start-Up Changes Everything." *Harvard Business Review* 91, no. 5: 63–72.

Chesbrough, Henry. 2010. "Business Model Innovation: Opportunities and Barriers." *Long Range Planning* 43: 354–363.

Christensen, Clayton, Gerome H. Grossman, and Jason Hwang. 2008. *The Innovator's Prescription: A Disruptive Solution for Health Care.* New York: McGraw Hill.

Cotta Ramusino, Enrico, and Alberto Onetti. 2013. *Strategie d'impresa*, 4th ed. Milan: Il Sole 24 Ore.

Daley, Lane, Vikas Mehrotra, and Ranjini Sivakumar. 1997. "Corporate Focus and Value Creation. Evidence from Spinoffs." *Journal of Financial Economics*, 257–281.

Drucker, Peter F. 1968. *The Age of Discontinuity.* New York, NY: Harper & Row.

Dunning, John H. 1988. *Explaining International Production.* London: Allen & Unwin.

Feeny, David F., and Leslie P. Willcocks. 1998. "Core IS Capabilities for Exploiting Information Technology." *Sloan Management Review* 39, no. 3: 10.

Glick, Leslie J. 2008. "Biotechnology Business Models Work: Evidence from the Pharmaceutical Marketplace." *Journal of Commercial Biotechnology* 14, no. 2: 106–17.

Mitchell, Donald W., and Carol Bruckner Coles. 2004. "Business Model Innovation Breakthrough Moves." *Journal of Business Strategy* 25, no. 1: 16–26.

Onetti, Alberto, Antonella Zucchella, Marian V. Jones, and Patricia McDougall-Covin. 2012a. "Internationalization, Innovation and Entrepreneurship: Business Models for New Technology-based Firms." First online 2010 (doi:10.1007/s10997–010–9154–1). Print version *Journal of Management and Governance* 16, no. 3 (SI): 337–368.

———. 2012b. "Guest Editor's Introduction to the Special Issue: Entrepreneurship and Strategic Management in New Technology Based Companies." First online 2010 (doi:10.1007/s10997–010–9153–2). Print version *Journal of Management and Governance* 16, no. 3 (SI): 333–336.

Osterwalder, Alexander, and Yves Pigneur. 2010. *Business Model Generation: A Handbook for Visionaries, Game Changers, and Challengers.* New York: Wiley.

Oviatt, Benjamin M., and Patricia P. McDougall-Covin. 2005. "Defining International Entrepreneurship and Modeling the Speed of Internationalization." *Entrepreneurship Theory and Practice* 29, no. 5: 537–554.

Porter, Michael E. 1980. *Competitive Strategy: Techniques for Analyzing Industries and Competitors.* New York: Free Press.

———. 1985. *Competitive Advantage: Creating and Sustaining Superior Performance*. New York: Free Press.

———. 2000. "Location, Competition, and Economic Development: Local Clusters in a Global Economy." *Economic Development Quarterly* 14, no. 1: 15–34.

Prahalad, Coimbatore K., and Gary Hamel. 1990. "The Core Competence of the Corporation." *Harvard Business Review* 68, no. 3: 79–91.

Ries, Eric. 2011. *The Lean Startup: How Today's Entrepreneurs Use Continuous Innovation to Create Radically Successful Business*. New York: Crown Business.

Rifkin, Leremy. 2000. *The Age of Access*. New York: Putnam Books.

Toffler, Alvin. 1970. *Future Shock*. New York: Bantam Books.

———. 1980. *The Third Wave*. New York: Bantam Books.

Treacy, Michael, and Fred Wiersema. 1995. *The Discipline of Market Leaders*. Reading: Addison Wesley.

Wernerfelt, Birger. 1984. "A Resource-Based View of The Firm." *Strategic Management Journal* 5, no. 2: 171–180.

3 Milestones to Go before I Sleep[1]

> *"The safest road to hell is the gradual one—the gentle slope, soft under-*
> *foot, without sudden turnings, without milestones, without signposts."*
>
> —C. S. Lewis[2]

Despite the growing importance and adoption of the business model concept, there is still a lack of a generally accepted definition of what a business
model is. Similar concepts are instead too often treated synonymously or ill
defined. The aim of this chapter is to help you to navigate through all these
different concepts and provide some guidance in understanding what they
really mean and where and how they differ.[3]

3.1 FROM BUSINESS MODEL TO REVENUE/PRICING MODELS

What's a *business model*? Guided by a passionate vision and clear business
objectives, informed by a well-thought-out strategy, a business model is a
collection of *prioritized activities* focused on achieving clear milestones critical to delivering the company's value proposition. The business model is the
company's *milestone engine,* and like any engine it must be efficient with the
fuel it burns to produce value for its customer in the form of a product or
service—while maximizing profit. But this is where the metaphor ends: no matter how efficient, real engines don't *create* energy. This is the magic of building
a company—the ability to transform a vision into reality that has value. And
milestone completion is at the heart of this transformational process.

In order to approach each milestone effectively, firms must identify their
potential competitors and build an appropriate strategic positioning within
the industry environment. An accurate analysis of those aspects contributes
to the definition of revenue and pricing models, which helps the company to
identify how to make money to support the financing of its lead product or
product line. Revenue models at the very beginning of a company's life (the
so-called *pre-revenue* phase) are usually identifiable as financing models.

Actually, entrepreneurs must not forget that their actions are and will
always be observed and evaluated by external stakeholders. Particularly,

financial investors of any type should be taken in special consideration, given their pivotal role in many companies' growth and success at any time of their life and not just at the beginning. Unfortunately, just a few companies have the luxury of not needing third parties' money.

3.1.1 Strategic and Competitive Positioning

Strategic positioning, a concept fully developed by Michael Porter (a leading Harvard authority on corporate strategy and competitiveness), aims to achieve sustainable competitive advantage by preserving what is distinctive about a company. It means performing *different* activities from rivals, or performing *similar* activities in different ways, which are well integrated and reinforce one another (Porter, 1996). When company's activities mutually reinforce each other, competitors can't easily imitate them. As we discuss in subsequent chapters, strategic positioning often requires a company to make informed decisions about what activities *not* to do. The Silicon Valley maxim "You can't be all things to all people" is a hard lesson for many companies, not just startups.

In line with Nicox's strategic positioning in the ophthalmic space, the research platform of the company is now focused on ocular diseases where nitric oxide has been shown to play an important role. A specialized team in Nicox's Italian research subsidiary is pursuing targeted projects also in partnership with external research centers. This will enable Nicox to enhance its knowledge about application of nitric oxide (NO) in ocular diseases and leverage its long-standing expertise in the therapeutic application of NO-donating compounds.

Strategic positioning informs both the business model and value proposition. The *business model* concerns a company's unique operational strategy, and is about creating a proper fit among its activities to deliver products and services (the *value proposition*). The latter is a marketing function that underlies branding and brand identity, and concerns how the customer perceives the sum total of these activities through the company's product/service delivery as "uniquely different" from its competitors.

In October 2012, Nicox unveiled a new visual identity as it also announced a new product called AdenoPlus, a test for acute conjunctivitis. The new logo represents Nicox's new positioning as an international late-stage development and commercial ophthalmic group, as shown in Figure 3.1.

Figure 3.1   Nicox's Logo Before (Left) and After (Right) the Rebranding
Source: www.nicox.com

Originally a concept applied to consumer goods (Ries and Trout, 1981), *competitive positioning* was redefined by Regis McKenna as a strategic approach to differentiate high-technology products (McKenna, 1986). Later this became the foundation for the insights of Geoffrey Moore (a colleague of Regis McKenna) for elucidating the technology adoption life cycle and the high-tech marketing model that is common to most high-tech marketing campaigns today (Moore, 2001). Together, the seamless integration of strategic positioning and business model—*strategic fit*—creates sustainable competitive advantage (Figure 3.2). For technology-based companies, the addition of intellectual property (IP strategy) adds yet another competitive layer. As we further explain in Chapter 4, operational activities uniquely aligned with strategic fit—aimed at the timely completion of milestones— are the essence of the business modeling and the basic units of competitive advantage.

Strategic Positioning

Mission Our purpose	**Vision** What we want to become	**Business Objectives**

Value Proposition

Values Core Beliefs	**Positioning** Mindshare
Behaviors Actions w/ Stakeholders	**Identity** Visual, Verbal, Feel

Business Strategy

Strategic Fit

Business Model

Basic Research	Product Development	Manufacturing	Information Technology	Product Service Delivery

Figure 3.2   Strategic Fit as Integration of Strategic Positioning and Business Model
Source: Authors' elaboration

3.1.2 Revenue Model

The concepts of *business model* and *revenue model* (or revenue stream) are sometimes used interchangeably. And, although related, a revenue model is not synonymous with pricing model (or pricing strategy). The business model, as we define it, is a company's operations focused on the timely prioritization and completion of milestones that create value and competitive advantage, while a company's *revenue model* describes *how* it makes money selling its products (monetization).

Companies generate revenue through one or more of the following:

- *Asset sale*—selling ownership rights to a physical product.
- *Usage fee*—charging for the use of a particular service, e.g., phone or TV cable service.
- *Subscription fee*—selling continuous access to a service, e.g., online newsletter, exercise gym.
- *Lending, renting, leasing*—providing a temporary right to use a product or service, e.g., cars, tools, housing.
- *Licensing*—giving a customer the permission to use protected intellectual property in exchange for a fee, e.g., technology licensing. Franchising is a license to use a company's successful business model in exchange for a direct stake in the business.
- *Professional services fees*—selling services on a "time and material basis" or based on a mutually agreed upon "statement of work" (SOW).
- Support fees—providing support on licensed or sold products typically in exchange for a recurring fee, e.g., annual maintenance and support fees for software products.
- *Transactional or brokerage fees*—intermediation services performed on behalf of two or more parties, e.g., stock brokers, real estate agents, mortgage lenders.
- *Advertising*—selling "mind space" for a fee on TV, in print, online or through another medium.
- *Revenue Sharing*—taking a percentage of revenue ("royalty") generated from your customer companies; it is quite typical for OEM (Original Equipment Manufacturing) deals, i.e., deals where the customer company embeds your product and/or service into its own offering.

Life science companies often combine more than one revenue model during their development as a way to support the financing of their lead product or product line. A therapeutics company may grant an exclusive or non-exclusive license to another company to sell its product or technology in a secondary geographic region, while maintaining the right to sell in a preferred region. A medical device company may provide manufacturing, marketing, or distribution rights to another company in exchange for upfront payments and royalties on sales. A medical instrumentation company may (1) sell an instrument; (2) rent the use of the instrument; (3) license the instrument's technology exclusively or non-exclusively; and (4) provide customer support either for a flat fee or a scaled fee from limited to full-service pricing.

> Napo Pharmaceuticals granted an exclusive license to Glenmark in 2005 for completing the product development and marketing the product in 140 countries.

3.1.3   Pricing Model

Each of the foregoing revenue streams will have different pricing mechanisms, ranging from fixed to dynamic pricing. How a life science product is priced—it's *pricing model* or *pricing strategy* is dependent on macro and micro factors in each market sector (e.g., drugs, medical devices, diagnostics, health care services, and so on), and whether or not a product is subject to insurance reimbursement and/or specific regulations. The pricing and brand management of life science products are beyond the scope of this book, but several excellent texts have been written on the subject (Simon and Kotler, 2009).

> Starting with the back end and working their way to the customer, Neurosilicon is optimizing its build of materials, focusing on cost of goods sold and pricing. The goal is to create a pricing model that would support early adoption of the new technology while maintaining high production quality.

3.2   FROM BUSINESS MODEL TO FINANCIALS: OPERATIONS, FUND RAISING, AND EXIT

3.2.1   The "Exit" Strategy

One of the very first decisions entrepreneurs must make is to decide whether they want to build a *lifestyle business* without plans to sell it in the future, i.e., one that you'll spend the majority of your life in, or one in which you build equity to transform into cash for you and your investors (the so called *GBF,* "*Get Big Fast*"). Needless to say, professional investors are not interested in investing in lifestyle companies. Whether angel or venture capitalists, investors typically seek a return on their investment within three to five years—the sooner the better. Thus when you start a new business, or as you develop strategies and plans to grow your existing business, you need to think about your most critical milestone—your *exit strategy*.

Realizing an exit strategy and building a sustainable profitable business are not mutually exclusive objectives. Both objectives are synergistic in the value creation process. You can't have a bone fide exit strategy unless you are truly building a sustainable business.

Designing the exit strategy (which of course will be continuously evolving along the company's life cycle) is an important part of a company overall strategy decision. Being able to outline a clear future value for the company and its technology as well as to collect and keep track of early success (such as key partnerships, licensing deals, and early sales) will serve to increase the number of interested partners for potential sales deals while also increasing the company's overall potential value and final sale price for prospective buyers.

The completion of Phase 2a is identified by Biomagen founders as the trigger for a possible acquisition from a big pharma company.

Too often, entrepreneurs and investors have a myopic focus on the exit strategy, failing to realize that the purpose for establishing the business in the first place is to profitably serve customers. An alternative to building a real business is to engage in a fraudulent Ponzi scheme or similar pyramid scheme where money trades hands without any real value being created in the process. Although named after Charles Ponzi, a notorious Italian immigrant in 1920s, this fraudulent investment scam probably goes back several hundred years. More recently, Bernard Madoff is now the most infamous admitted operator of a Ponzi scheme that is considered to be the largest financial fraud in U.S. history.

3.2.2 Funding Process and Milestone Completion

Depending on your goals and the type of business and the business model you choose to grow, your business plan should be aligned with your end-game objectives, i.e., the exit strategy. And how will those objectives be met? You guessed it—by completing your milestones!

The completion of milestones is, therefore, a "do or die" proposition: if you fail to meet your milestones in a timely fashion, you lose the support of investors and it's time to flip hamburgers until your next venture (if you're lucky). It's one thing to fail to meet a major milestone because the experimental data did not support the therapeutic objective (the value promise), rather than fail because you focused on what you realized later

Milestone Completion

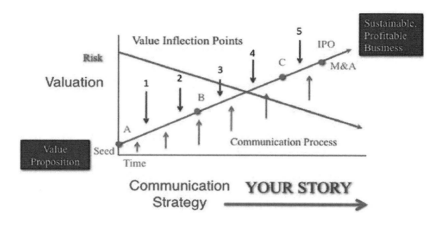

Figure 3.3   Milestone Completion is the Lifeblood of a Company
Source: Courtesy of Charles Versaggi

was the wrong operational activity. While the former is the high-risk nature of development-stage bio-business, the latter is inexcusable.

Figure 3.3 presents how the completion of milestones drives the valuation process of a development-stage life science company. Starting with seed financing, successive milestone completion increases the company's stock valuation through various "up rounds" of venture financing from Series A, to Series B, to Series C and other eventual subsequent rounds, and eventually, to the Initial Public Offering (IPO) of common stock or an acquisition (M&A)—the highly anticipated event for which founders and investors have waited years. While the slope of the valuation curve is shown ideally to increase over time, a company's stock value will not always be incrementally positive, as it can (and often will) be subjected to the ill winds of laboratory failures, patent hurdles, regulatory delays, market fluctuations, fickle investors, and other risks well known to experienced CEOs and veteran investors.

Alternatively, such events can flatten the curve or push it in the opposite direction—valuation "down rounds" that dilute stock ownership, waste hard earned "sweat equity," or in the worst case, close operations altogether.

Founding entrepreneurs have to be prepared for a long road. Fast exits are rare in any sector, and even rarer in the life science industry.

Some recent research shows how the median time from first financing to a significant M&A[4] or an IPO event is over six years (as shown in Figure 3.4). This number needs to be read carefully. First of all, it refers to the period from the first financing to the exit. And the holding period is not the same thing as the time from founding to an exit event. These data suggest that

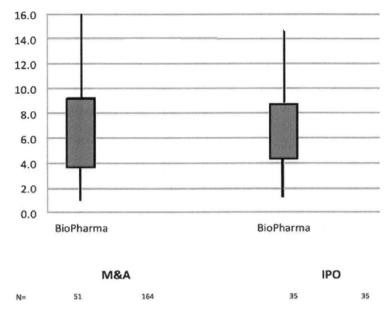

Figure 3.4 Time (Years) from First Financing to Exit
Source: Dow Jones Venture Source, May 2013

founders of life science companies should expect to hammer away for the better part of a decade before liquidity. And, differently from other tech businesses, the valuations of these companies typically stay near cost or at very modest step-ups for years in the private markets (~2x or less) since these companies remain pre-revenue for a longer period of time compared to the software and other technology sectors. This is why funding for life science companies typically passes through syndicates that can go all the way to an exit and tranche the financings over many years.

Anyway, building great life science companies takes time. But frankly, the real issue is that the same goes for building mediocre ones.

3.2.3   Value Inflection Points

Milestones critical to corporate and product development in an early-stage life science company are called *value inflection points* (Figure 3.3, numbers 1–5). These include the issuance of a patent, the completion of a clinical trial, the signing of a strategic alliance, and a product marketing approval, among others. Note the inverse "*Risk*" slope: in the early stages of corporate and product development, financial risk is highest and matches the risk profile of early investors who will get larger returns on their investment, compared to the return on investment of those who choose to invest later in the company's development when risk is lower. Anyway, until a product actually reaches the customer, and the company reaches the stage of a sustainable, profitable business, the value proposition is more a value promise.

For publicly traded companies, stock valuation is linked to the P/E ratio (or "multiple"): a measure of the share price relative to the annual net income or profit earned by the firm per share. A higher P/E ratio means that investors are paying more for each unit of net income, so the stock is more expensive compared to one with a lower P/E ratio. Thus the stock valuation of a publicly traded life science company without earnings is a *perceived stock valuation*, often governed by vague intangibles rather than quantitative financial metrics based on product sales.

But long development cycles with a focus on achieving milestones specific to product development, financing, patent filings, or strategic partnerships often cause executives to lose sight of what should be the intended goal of any solid business venture: *a sustainable, profitable business.*

For years analysts have argued that early-stage life science companies should achieve earnings as soon as possible, closing the gap between perceived value and real value. Focusing on perceived value could cost the business loss of confidence among investors, especially if the company takes "too long" to deliver the value proposition. When public markets are impatient, for private venture-backed startups the strained values of their public counterparts can contribute to the poor valuations of their own fledgling operations. This is all the more reason why it's so important for an early-stage company to complete its development milestones as soon as possible.

3.2.4 Entrepreneurial Efficiency

The timely completion of milestones directly impacts how long a company takes to generate revenues and become profitable. Figure 3.5 shows how invested capital, time to profits, and profitability define *entrepreneurial efficiency*.[5] The area under "*Loss*" is the total amount of capital (accumulated losses) a company burns before achieving breakeven. The area under "*Profit*" (accumulated profits) represents the amount of net profit a company earns after paying expenses. The more the breakeven point moves further to the right on the expense line, the more losses continue to accumulate and the longer it will take for the company to become profitable. Conversely, as the breakeven point moves further left of the expense line, revenue growth outpaces expenses, and the company will rely less on investor capital as it becomes profitable to provide a return on investment.

For venture-backed companies it is quite common to cumulate significant losses before turning the company into cash-flow-positive. Obviously investors are available to bridge the company all the way through the area under "Loss" if—and only if—the area under "Profit" promises to be huge enough to remunerate (with a big multiplier) the capital they poured into the company and the risk they assumed.

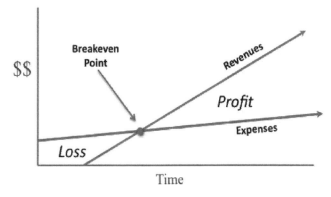

Figure 3.5 Bridging to Breakeven
Source: Authors' elaboration

3.2.5 Capital Efficiency

From the eyes of an investor, entrepreneurial efficiency is all about *capital efficiency*—how much return on capital the entrepreneur is able to achieve. The return is often measured by how much growth and development ("bang for the buck") is achieved to reach a critical milestone or value inflection point—the most important of which is the return on investment that comes from realizing that most sacred of all events investors seek: the exit strategy. As explained before, the most common exit strategy is the sale of equity to someone else through either an initial offering of common stock to the public (IPO), or through the sale of your business to a strategic buyer (merger or acquisition—M&A). In case of lifestyle companies, the return on investments is reached through distributions (dividend payments) of the net income produced annually by the company.

3.2.6 Operational Effectiveness

Operational success is defined by how well a company performs particular activities more efficiently than its competitors. If a company has the same costs as competitors, it will have the same profits. The goal is to determine the best activities that lower costs and generate superior profits. Whether you are a startup with a product in development, or a well-established company with products on the market, how well you perform your operational activities will directly impact capital efficiency and entrepreneurial efficiency. Therefore, the winning move is to identify and prioritize those operational activities that result in the lowest-cost business model than that of the competition. As we will see, *The Milestone Bridge* is a modeling tool that allows you to identify and prioritize what those activities should be to achieve entrepreneurial efficiency, capital efficiency, operational effectiveness, and hopefully a successful exit strategy for you and your investors.

For life science companies, especially those involved in drug development, operational effectiveness is contingent on how successful you are at producing a succession of positive results and outcomes, from research and development through product manufacturing, sales, and marketing. While operational effectiveness includes operational efficiency, such as controlling costs and maximizing productivity, it also includes how well a company applies its core competencies to develop better products faster.

At Areta, the lean design of the Gerenzano GMP facility contributes to maintaining the high flexibility and efficiency of the manufacturing process. The GMP's staff has solid experience in the field of research and development of innovative pharmaceuticals and is regularly trained as required by the Areta's internal Quality System.

3.3   COMMUNICATION: TURN YOUR VALUE PROPOSITION INTO A STORY

3.3.1   The Value Proposition

The lifeblood of a development-stage company is inextricably linked with the completion of milestones that enable it to deliver its *value proposition*— the bundle of products, services, and benefits that creates value for the customer by solving a problem or serving an unmet need. But unless life science companies—especially developers of therapeutics with a long product-development process—achieve a sustainable, profitable business, and actually deliver products to the customer, their value proposition is really a *value promise*. The value promise is not only to prospective patients or health-care providers that may benefit from the company's future product, but for employees, investors, strategic partners, university research centers—all the stakeholders in the company's business during the span of product development. Thus during early-stage development, the concept of "customer" is more that of "*value recipient*," a useful concept that is fully explored by management consultant Anders Sundelin (2009). To make it clear, let's take as an example Nicox's value proposition:

"... to create a different scale of specialty ophthalmic company, which combines international reach in the key markets of North America and Europe while remaining close to the medical community and patients." (Nicox)

Of course, the company must also translate its value proposition into concrete "fuel for the engine." Until the value proposition is realized in the form of earnings, the company's primary measure of value will be the price of its capital stock—its *stock valuation.* The milestone completions that add to the company's stock valuation are deemed *value inflections.* This is what boards of directors expect, what makes investors restless, what keeps CEOs awake at night, and why everyone with employee stock options comes to work in the morning—if they even left the building at all the night before.

3.3.2   The Story: Communicating Your Vision

The previous Figure 3.3 also shows how cash flow, valuation, and effective corporate communications are directly linked to a life science company's success, especially during the early stages of development and the completion of mission-critical milestones (the arrows along the valuation slope). From seed, through successive financing rounds, to the IPO or M&A, the quality of communications to the financial community and other influencers in the market infrastructure can impact a company's stock valuation. In the absence of a product and a demonstrable value proposition, the value promise is best communicated as the company's *vision*—a vision of how the world will be a better place thanks to the company's future products or services.

Companies need compelling answers to overarching questions that are at the heart of a company's strategic plan and business model: "*Why* should I invest in you?" "Why should I do a deal with you?" "Why should I work for you?" "Why should I write about you?" And most importantly—"Why should I buy your product or service?" The answers to these perennial business questions are conveyed effectively in "*The Company Story.*" Ask any investor, and you will hear they invest in people . . . and "The Story." More often than not, successful companies are managed by CEOs who are successful communicators.

> Napo Pharmaceuticals' CEO Lisa Conte is an extraordinary communicator and networker. Since 1989 she has raised over $200 million in funding, the majority of which came from wealthy individuals who believed in her idea. "Where are the patients?" Lisa Conte told us the first time we met. "In emerging countries. There is where we go." Napo's strategy is built around a simple but really clear key statement. That's the *vision.*

Armed with the foregoing concepts, let's now examine the key elements of *The Milestone Bridge,* and how they enable you to decide on the appropriate business model to execute your business objectives and strategy, and to identify and prioritize the key activities that drive the completion of value-creating milestones.

Table 3.1   Learning Blocks—Chapter 3

Revenue Model	Pricing Model	Strategic Positioning
Competitive Positioning	Value Proposition	Vision
Exit Strategy	Funding Process	Milestone Completion
Entrepreneurial Efficiency	Operational Effectiveness	Capital Efficiency

NOTES

1. An allusion to Robert Frost's classic poem: "*Stopping by Woods on Snowy Evening.*"
2. Clive S. Lewis, *The Screwtape Letters* (England: Geoffrey Bles, 1942).
3. In the Appendix A you can find a more in-depth literature background about business model definitions.
4. Estimated at over 25 million dollars.
5. *Entrepreneurial efficiency* is based on three variables: invested capital, time to profit, and size of profits. Fueled by invested capital, the timely completion of milestones directly impacts how long a company takes to generate revenues and become profitable (Kolchinsky, 2004).

REFERENCES

Kolchinsky, Peter. 2004. *The Entrepreneur's Guide to a Biotech Startup*. Report, Evelexa. www.evelexa.com/resources/egbs4_kolchinsky.pdf.

Lewis, Clive S. 1942. *The Screwtape Letters*. England: Geoffrey Bles.

McKenna, Regis. 1986. *The Regis Touch: New Marketing Strategies for Uncertain Times*. New York: Basic Books.

Moore, Geoffrey A. 2001. *Crossing the Chasm: Marketing and Selling Disruptive Products to Mainstream Customers*. New York: Harper Business Essentials.

Porter, Michael E. 1996. " What is Strategy." *Harvard Business Review* 74, no. 6: 61–78.

Ries, Alf, and Jack Trout. 1981. *Positioning—The Battle for Your Mind*. New York: McGraw-Hill.

Simon, Francoise, and Philip Kotler. 2009. *Building Global BioBrands: Taking Biotechnology to Market*. New York: Simon and Schuster Inc.

Sundelin, Anderson. 2009. "What Is a Value Proposition." Report, The Business Model Database. http://tbmdb.blogspot.com

4   Avoiding the Bridge to Nowhere[1]

*"Given all that lies beyond my control, I obsess about the few things
I can control."*

—*Andre Agassi*[2]

Most business plans provide a detailed explanation of a huge market need
(*The Problem/Opportunity*), how a proprietary technology and/or product/
service meets that need (*The Solution*), the key steps in order to reach the
market (*The Go to Market Plan*), a financial plan to support a competitive
business through the point of profitability (*The Ask*)—and, most importantly, why management is qualified (*The Team*) to achieve a successful exit
strategy and return for prospective investors (*The Exit Strategy*). However,
the company's business model is often barely addressed, if considered at
all. Although value-critical milestones may be identified, the key activities needed to complete these milestones may not be well-thought-out or
prioritized. Worse yet, some critical activities are overlooked and not even
considered. Moreover, an *operational plan* to execute the company's strategy is given short shrift, as these decisions are often postponed until funding
is completed. When the operational plan is finally considered, little thought
may be put on the prioritization of these activities, what's the best use of the
company's skills and resources to successfully complete these activities, and
whether or not they should be conducted in-house or outsourced.

4.1   SO WHAT'S THE BIG IDEA?

Whether you are an entrepreneurial startup or a well-established company,
your *raison d'être* is to develop your product/service and get it to the customer
(*The Market*) as soon as possible, at the lowest cost with superior profits. Your
job as the chief executive officer is to identify, prioritize, and decide which of
your *operational activities* result in the lowest-cost structure to achieve this
objective. These activities need to be focused on the completion of milestones
that create value and competitive advantage as fast and efficiently as possible
(think *operational effectiveness* and *capital efficiency,* see Chapter 3).

As anticipated in Chapter 1, some of these activities are best outsourced, either to a service provider (e.g., a contract research organization), or as part of a strategic alliance (e.g., a pharmaceutical partner). The degree of vertical integration (i.e., how many operational activities are done in-house) is, therefore, a key consideration in the design of your business model and the value-driven milestones that drive its execution. The factors that guide these "IN or OUT" executive decisions are governed by whether or not the company is capable of participating in the points of greatest value creation based on its brain power, technology, labor, and capital, and where it wants to position itself in the industry value chain. The same logic should inform decisions about the acquisition of strategic assets or technologies (BUY-IN).

Entrepreneurial executives may not give much thought to their business model; drug development, for example, follows a "standard" path of execution—from target identification to molecular design and proof of principle, to preclinical studies, and to Phases 1, 2, and 3 clinical trials. Although the scientific method drives the process, and regulatory requirements for patient safety and efficacy must be strictly adhered to, depending on your financial and human resources, there's a multitude of ways you can execute each stage of drug development as defined by your business strategy. However, business model decisions need to be made in the business planning stage, not after you've begun operations. One can have a sound business strategy, but a poorly executed business model based on inappropriate or wrong decisions that can lead to "the bridge to nowhere." This is what *The Milestone Bridge* helps you avoid.

At this point, let's reiterate the distinction between business goal, business strategy, and business model (Figure 4.1). Developing a new drug may be your overall goal, but how you develop and commercialize it is your business strategy (e.g., seeking an exit at the end of Phase 2a clinical trials), and the business model (the activity set) you choose is the vehicle for realizing this business strategy.

For example, repurposing an old drug for a new indication is a business strategy that can have several business models. The value proposition is the synthesis of all these decisions.

Once you have decided on your business goal and business strategy, your first objective is to identify and prioritize which activities are required to

Figure 4.1   The Relationship of Business Goal, Business Strategy, and Business Model to Value Proposition

Source: Authors' elaboration

execute your business strategy. Subsequently, you need to organize and prioritize these activities into *achievable milestones* within the context of the company's core competencies. Each company will have its own set of activities and corresponding milestones to complete that fulfill its business strategy at a specific stage of development.

Note that as you complete each milestone, your business model and the *unique way* your company delivers its value proposition to customers is defined by the way you collectively prioritize and structure these activities. Thus, if an activity is the basic unit of a milestone, we need a *navigational tool* to help us make decisions on how to effectively execute these activities toward successful milestone completion. *The Milestone Bridge* is designed to do just that.

4.2 OVERVIEW OF *THE MILESTONE BRIDGE*

Figure 4.2 provides an overview of the key elements of *The Milestone Bridge*. What you see is an *"activity matrix"* to help you make business model decisions regarding your company's activities to complete a specific milestone that executes your business strategy and delivers your value proposition. First, you'll see each milestone will be guided by the following parameters:

- *Milestone Statement:* the outcome of highest completion priority.
- *Relevance:* how the milestone relates to the company's overall business strategy.
- *Financial Prerequisite:* the budget required to complete the milestone.
- *Timeframe:* when the milestone needs to be completed.

	ACTIVITY LIST	FOCUS *(Strategic Importance)*	LOCUS *(Location of Activity)*	MODUS *(Mode of Execution)*
Activity A	Which activities are required to execute the overall strategy?	How much to allocate?	Where?	In-House or Third Parties? Capital or labor-intensive? How tech-intensive?
Activity B				
Activity C				
...				

Figure 4.2 Overview of *The Milestone Bridge*
Milestone #1: The outcome of highest priority we need to complete
Overall Strategy: What is our long-term objective?
Financial Prerequisite: How much money is needed to complete the milestone?
Deadline: When does the milestone need to be completed?

Source: Authors' elaboration

Looking at the matrix above, one point needs to be made: the amount of money (what we called Financial Prerequisite) and the time (Deadline) required to complete the next Milestone depend on the business model decisions you will make. Almost always there are alternative options regarding the way you structure your company's activities (i.e., different business models) that have diverse execution time and financial need. It is frequent that a manager is requested to present alternative plans before being assigned a budget. This applies to start-up companies, which negotiate with investors the amount of money to be used for funding their growth (the size of the financing round), as well as established companies, which make budget allocations to projects/departments based on the overall company objectives.

Conversely, depending on the available budget, certain business models may prove to be executable, while others may not. Therefore business model decisions, besides being *milestone based,* are *budget constrained.*

Therefore, designing a business model is not a one-way process, but an iterative process, where you break your overall strategy into milestones, identify some temporal deadlines, assume to have a certain amount of financial resources (the Financial Prerequisite), and make an operational plan (activity by activity). While working on the plan, you may be required to modify the deadlines and/or the financial prerequisite.

4.2.1   The ACTIVITY LIST

On the far left of the activity matrix is the ACTIVITY LIST of operational activities that you have identified and prioritized that are needed to support the completion of a specific milestone (and, in general, the overall strategy). The list of activities will be different depending on your overall business objective and business strategy. The ACTIVITY LIST will designate a specific milestone under research, product development, manufacturing, sales, marketing, business development, and so on.

The design of the ACTIVITY LIST (in terms of number of activities) is strictly a *firm-specific* exercise. Depending on the level of detail you need to apply in your business modeling, you can have a longer or shorter activity list as well as you can identify activities in a broader way or articulate them in really detailed sub-activities.

In our experience we have seen different companies use different ACTIVITY LISTs even if aiming for similar milestones.

For example MolMed, in order to complete Phase 3 (NGR-h TNF technology), has identified five key activities: analytical methods, fill finish, toxicology, clinical trials, and testing. Conversely Nicox, to reach the same milestone (Phase 3), identified a single activity to be performed: testing their drug with large patient groups to assess efficacy and safety.

At the end of the game, there are just a few basic guidelines you need to follow while structuring your ACTIVITY LIST:

- List all the activities that are strictly required to reach your next milestone and do it in a really analytical way.
- Group activities when there are no substantial differences in terms of FOCUS, LOCUS, and MODUS, and keep them separate if there are.
- Include activities required to complete other subsequent milestones also if they are not strictly required for completing the next immediate one. This way you always know what's coming next.

As you can see, the message we are trying to convey to you here is to focus on the next milestone but never forget about the overall strategy (i.e., the final destination of your journey).

Note that corporate development activities—such as finance, G&A, patent prosecution, human resources, and IT—are *support activities*. They do not define the company's business model. While these activities enable the company to operate (and they are really critical), they don't directly drive milestone completion to generate the company's value proposition. Support activities just service the operational activities that are the ones strictly required to bridge the company to the targeted milestone. They have a key role but are ancillary to the business model. They help the company stay alive and work properly.

How you decide to execute these activities depends on the FOCUS, LOCUS, and MODUS decisions (the columns to the right of the ACTIVITY LIST): *each milestone will have this trio of decision parameters*. Moving from left to right, for each activity one needs to make decisions with respect to FOCUS—the *relevance and prioritization* of the activity to achieving a fundamental milestone; LOCUS—*where* you should geographically conduct these activities; and MODUS—the mode, or *way,* in which the activity is executed. At the business model level, the FOCUS, LOCUS, and MODUS of your activities represent the company's output—the unique way in which a business executes its strategy to the market.

4.2.2 FOCUS

FOCUS decisions concern the strategic importance and allocation of a company's resources to specific milestone-related activities—i.e., where to *invest* additional resources vs. from where to *divest* resources. The key decision process here is to prioritize which activities to focus on during a specific stage of growth and development. By definition, often prioritization will be guided by determining the order of importance each activity has in relation to the next milestone. After all, you can't build a house without first laying the foundation, followed by the first-story frame, the second-story frame, and so on. But, before deciding what's important, one has to identify *all* of the possible activities that are required. Moreover, one has to decide which ones are naturally related to support a critical milestone before moving on to the next series of related activities that support the next pivotal milestone. By going through this decision exercise, you may discover that your milestone needs to be broken into smaller "sub-milestones." Again the decision criterion here is to split a milestone into sub-milestones anytime you see that the FOCUS for some of the relevant activities changes before the deadline assigned for the completion of the milestone.

In theory, for a linear process this should be as easy as seeing that A, B, and C are completed before moving on to D, E, and F. But in practice, the business of growth and development is obviously more complex. Some milestone decisions are not necessarily linear or longitudinal, and are basically informed judgment calls that may require input from an advisory board or outside consultants. Consider the decision of whether or not to conduct a Phase 1 clinical trial for a drug that's being repurposed for a new indication. Assuming a similar projected dose range for the new indication, regulations of the U.S. Food and Drug Administration (FDA) may allow a drug developer to bypass Phase 1 toxicity studies as long as the drug was already proven to have no major adverse drug reactions. As a result, Phase 1 data from the original indication can be resubmitted in support of the new indication. However, it may behoove the developer to repeat some of the Phase 1 studies to reassure the medical establishment or the company's investors that the drug is, indeed, safe.

Similarly, a medical device developer may have a case to support an FDA 510(k) submission for marketing clearance that does not require clinical trial data to demonstrate safety and efficacy because, by regulatory definition, the product is substantially equivalent to another FDA-cleared product. However, the medical device company may still choose to conduct a clinical trial to demonstrate the product's safety and efficacy to the medical community and patients to foster product usage and acceptance.

Another example is marketing activities. For a company in the early stage of the drug development process (such as Phase 2), they could be considered low priority activities since the company's FOCUS is obviously on clinical tests. By anticipating these activities and conducting market research for understanding which is the best way the drug could be delivered to patients (nose inhalations versus Band-Aid dosing versus syringe injections) a company could modify the product development process and save some time later on.

The discussion above supports the relevance for a company to draw the full activity list from the very beginning. It is important to identify all the activities required by the company to deliver its product/service to the market and not to restrict the activity list to only the activities required to reach the next immediate milestone. Although the ladders are key, a comprehensive view of the whole activity list can help the management to better strategize the process and identify the better business model, milestone by milestone.

Obviously and almost certainly, the FOCUS for each activity will change over the life of the company, as it moves from milestone to milestone.

4.2.3 LOCUS

LOCUS decisions are those that concern in which geographical areas or industrial clusters to locate the company's value-adding activities. From our literature review, we were not able to find a single definition that includes location in considering the elements that define a business model. For young and new technology-based companies, location decisions are among the most relevant ones for milestone management. From our perspective, location choices are among the company's primary differentiators (Onetti et al., 2012a). That's why we included the LOCUS dimension in the three key decision parameters.

When we speak of "LOCUS," we do not merely refer to decisions such as what market to address, but also to decisions like: Where do we locate our company? Where do we locate our operational activities? These decisions can make the difference in terms of a company's ability to access key local resources, develop distinctive competencies, create a network, and thus excel in the ability to execute a successful strategy of innovation.

Location decisions are not neutral in terms of the company's operations and performance, since it has multiple options for locating different activities with different cost/quality implications. Deciding to conduct basic research in Europe versus Asia is a decision that is not irrelevant both in terms of costs as well as the way such activity can be performed.

A multi-localization approach is possible both for different activities as well as for the same activity. For example, basic research can be located in a different place than manufacturing, while the same company can have research and development conducted in more than one country. Thus at the business model level, LOCUS decisions determine the geographical configuration of the company's *internal and external value chain*.

Just to provide you with an immediate example how location decisions are relevant for life science companies, let's look at the two following charts (Figures 4.3 and 4.4).

In the first one you see a representation of the location of the eight companies we used as business cases. We built this map based on the places where they were born and have put their headquarters. They cover only three countries over two continents.

But if we extend the analysis and look at where their key activities are located (both with a direct presence and through strategic partners), you will get a totally different picture: our eight companies are active in approximately 20 countries over three continents.

As you may notice, LOCUS decisions are not just about where the company is based, but also where the company's key activities take place. And where to locate key activities is a relevant business model decision that needs to be carefully planned.

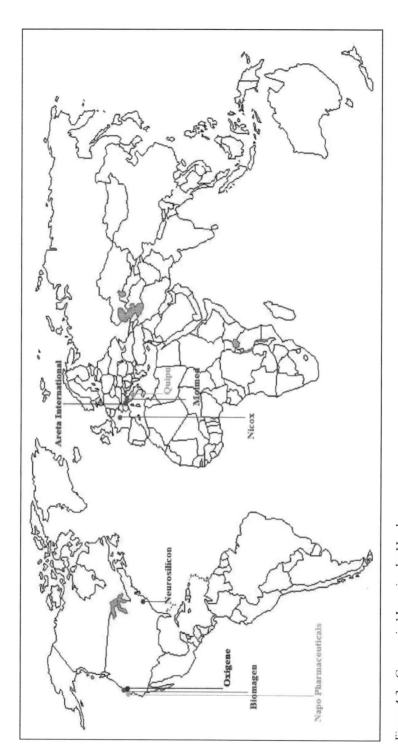

Figure 4.3 Companies' Location by Headquarter

Source: Authors' elaboration from www.freeusandworldmaps.com/html/World_Projections/WorldPrint.html

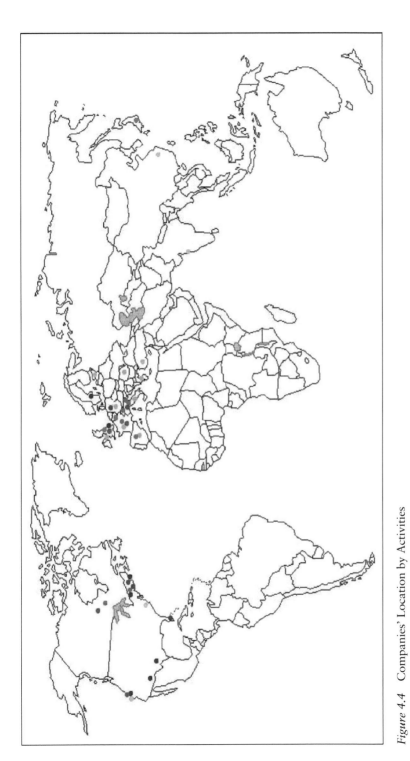

Figure 4.4   Companies' Location by Activities

Source: Authors' elaboration from www.freeusandworldmaps.com/html/World_Projections/WorldPrint.html

4.2.4   MODUS

MODUS decisions are closely related to LOCUS decisions. They concern the mode, or method of operation (*modus operandi*), you choose to conduct the milestone-focused activity—whether it's managed *in-house* or *outsourced* to another provider. MODUS and LOCUS decisions are the result of evaluating the company's core competencies and the cost-efficiency of conducting an activity in-house versus outsourced. Rare is the life science company that does not outsource some of its activities. And for some companies, the virtual company (VIPCO or FIPNET as we discussed in Chapter 1) is the business model of choice in which the majority of core activities are outsourced.

Contract research is the most common outsourced activity for companies involved in drug development. Some of them are also experimenting in the externalization of the full R&D or large portions of that. For medical device developers, contract manufacturing is another common activity that's outsourced. For the early-stage medical device developer, contract manufacturing is a more cost-efficient choice compared to the cost of scaling-up its own manufacturing. In this case the outsourced vendor must be carefully selected, and the level of involvement in the company relationship must be well defined—e.g., should there be a long-term collaborative agreement with stable partners, or a short-term project-based transaction?

Decisions involving internationalization and cross-border or foreign market entries are *business model decisions* where the MODUS decisions are closely intertwined with LOCUS decisions.

For activities performed in-house, the business model defines how the company should approach these activities from among the different options available. An activity can be alternatively performed in terms of intensive *capital technology* or *labor*, and, in the latter case, the quality and skills of the work force is another key decision (what we define as *brain* intensity).

For activities that have been outsourced, the vendor has to be selected, and the level of company involvement in the relationship also has to be defined (should there be a long-term collaborative agreement with stable partners or a short-term market-transaction? What kind of involvement should the company have in this business relationship?) (Onetti et al., 2012b).

Now that we've provided an overview of *The Milestone Bridge*, it's time to move deeper into the process.

4.3   *THE MILESTONE BRIDGE:* PRAXIS

Let's take a look at how we can now apply the basic elements of *The Milestone Bridge* to a practical example of a startup deciding how to organize its activities into pivotal milestones that need to be completed.

Figure 4.5 shows the activity matrix for Biomagen, an early-stage biotech company based in the San Francisco Bay Area developing therapeutics

ACTIVITY LIST	FOCUS	LOCUS		MODUS		
				Brain intensity	Technology intensity	Labor intensity
Basic Research						
1-Target Validation		San Francisco	OUT	9	7	2
2-Cell Studies	4		IN	8	2	4
3-Proof Principals			OUT	7	5	3
Preclinical Development						
1-Medicinal Chemistry	5	Hercules	JOINT	8	6	4
2-Animal Model	9	Hercules	JOINT	5	2	2
3-Animal Efficacy	6	Hercules	JOINT	5	6	7
IND Application	4	Burlingame	JOINT	TBD	TBD	TBD

Figure 4.5   The Milestone Bridge for Biomagen—The Milestone #1 Activity Matrix
Milestone #1: Complete Preclinical Development and submit IND application to FDA
Overall Strategy: Complete a pivotal Phase 2a clinical trial and target an alliance/M&A with a pharma company
Financial Prerequisite: $5M
Deadline: 18 months
Source: Authors' elaboration

to treat osteoporosis. The goal of *Milestone #1* is to complete Preclinical Development for the company's lead small-molecule drug, and to submit an Investigational New Drug (IND) application to the FDA. The IND milestone is critical to the company's overall strategy toward completing a pivotal Phase 2a clinical trial, demonstrating drug efficacy, setting the stage for either a strategic alliance with a pharmaceutical partner—or best case, having the company be acquired to fulfill an exit strategy and return on investment for its investors. The company's planned Series A of $5 million (Financial Prerequisite) provides the budget to support the milestone within a timeframe of about 18 months (Deadline). The completion of this first major milestone is pivotal for both getting a regulatory green light for patient testing, but also for setting the stage for the company's Series B round of financing.

Using the activity matrix as a decision tool, the CEO John Murphy shows that the majority of the basic research on the drug has already been completed (e.g., target validation, in vitro cell efficacy, and proof-of-principle studies) at the University of California San Francisco (UCSF). This is because the drug (from the FDA's perspective, a *New Chemical Entity,* or NCE) was exclusively licensed (BUY-IN[3]) from the university in exchange for upfront and milestone payments, as well as royalties on sales, assuming the drug will be approved by the FDA and reaches the market. Although some basic research will need to be further verified, and some work on preparing the Investigational New Drug application is underway (e.g., some cell studies), the CEO decides that the primary FOCUS of the company is *Preclinical Drug Development*—additional medicinal chemistry, lead optimization, and dose efficacy in a disease animal model.

The foregoing is a decision the CEO made because his research team evaluated all of the possible activities that were required to reach this point of drug development, making sure nothing was overlooked in terms of the drug's basic science and therapeutic rationale. The level of strategic importance—and the dedication of human and physical resources—is, therefore, high as represented by the "intensity bars" under FOCUS. Qualitative in nature, these intensity bars are used to show the relative relevance of one activity to another. As we will go into more detail in Chapter 5, we use numbers between 0 and 10 to better visualize the relevance of different activities. We will also do the same for the MODUS. As a first reference, 0–3 means somewhat not relevant, 3–5 not that much relevant, 5–7 relevant but not key, while 8–10 are key and completely relevant.

Next, management needed to decide how it would execute the Preclinical Development activities based on its core competencies and resources. Are these activities best conducted in-house, or should they be done back at UCSF under a research agreement? Or should some of the studies be done by a contract research organization (CRO)? Is it more cost-effective to conduct the studies locally, out of state, or overseas?

After careful analysis of all the cost-benefits, the decision was made to conduct the majority of the studies by a CRO based in the San Francisco Bay Area. Although the CRO will conduct the studies, Biomagen will work together with the CRO, but analyze the data in-house, and subsequently, submit the IND application to the FDA. This LOCUS decision was informed by related MODUS decisions regarding *how* to conduct the activities and *what* resources would be required, depending on the company's core skills and competencies. As shown on the activity matrix, MODUS decisions are informed by answers to three categories of resource questions with their corresponding qualitative "intensity bars" (ranging between 0 and 10) showing the relative degree of importance. Are the activities:

- *Brain intensive*—do they require a specialist to conduct, i.e., a high-level Ph.D. or a mid-level technologist? A person with a deep experience in the field or a junior?
- *Labor intensive*—do they require large teams of people, or a small group, or just one person?
- *Technology/capital intensive*—is specialized and expensive equipment needed to conduct the activities, or is low cost equipment enough? May these activities be automated?

Note that the company's level of integration, its internal R&D structure, and its external network architecture (its value-chain approach) will be determined by these MODUS decisions: make (IN), buy (OUT), or make-together (JOINT). How you manage such activity decisions enables you to create unique relationships with potential collaborators that will have an impact (hopefully positive!) on the company's strategic positioning.

Using the activity matrix, management would use the same decision process for completing subsequent milestones.

ACTIVITY LIST	FOCUS	LOCUS		MODUS		
				Brain intensity	Technology intensity	Labor intensity
Phase 1: Safety and Toxicology						
1-Patient Safety Trial	9	Hercules	OUT	6	2	8
2-Formulation/Dosing	7	Hercules	OUT	5	6	4
3-Data Analysis	5	Burlingame	JOINT	8		2

Figure 4.6   The Milestone Bridge for Biomagen—The Milestone #2 Activity Matrix
Milestone #2: Complete Phase 1
Overall Strategy: Complete a pivotal Phase 2a clinical trial and target an alliance/ M&A with a pharma company
Financial Prerequisite: $25M
Deadline: 6 months after completion of Milestone #1
Source: Authors' elaboration

The second milestone is to complete a Phase 1 Patient Safety trial based on a larger follow-up financing round (Biomagen is planning a $25 million Series B). The key objective of the clinical trial is to show there are no adverse side effects to the drug over a prospective dosage range (Figure 4.6).

Although the clinical trial is the major FOCUS of this *Milestone #2,* formulation, dosing, and subsequent data analysis are also key activities that must be completed in order to achieve the milestone. Examining the company's core competencies in view of the brain, technology, and labor requirements, the CEO decides that the clinical trial should be conducted by a CRO located locally. Moreover, data analysis will be jointly conducted with a regulatory consultant to ensure FDA compliancy. However, the CEO identified a CRO in San Diego as best suited for drug formulation of the small molecule. Once data analysis is completed, the decision will be made to move the drug to Phase 2a, thereby setting up the activity list for *Milestone #3* (Figure 4.7). Completion of Phase 2a will put the company in a position to form a strategic partnership with a big pharma to further test and develop the drug—and a possible acquisition. It is anticipated that the completion of Milestone #3 will require a follow-up financing round of approximately $15/30 million.

ACTIVITY LIST	FOCUS	LOCUS		MODUS		
				Brain intensity	Technology intensity	Labor intensity
Phase 2a: Efficacy						
1-Patient Recruitment	6	Hercules	OUT			8
2-Dosing Efficacy	7	Hercules	OUT	5	6	2
3-Clinical Trials	9	Burlingame	JOINT	6	10	8
4-Data Analysis	5	Burlingame	JOINT	7		2
Initiate Phase 2b	3	TBD	TBD	TBD	TBD	TBD

Figure 4.7   The Milestone Bridge for Biomagen—The Milestone #3 Activity Matrix
Milestone#3: Complete Phase 2a and initiate Phase 2b
Overall Strategy: Complete a pivotal Phase 2a clinical trial and target an alliance/ M&A with a pharma company
Financial Prerequisite: $15/30M (preliminary estimate)
Deadline: 12 months after completion of Milestone #2
Source: Authors' elaboration

4.4 BRIDGING MILESTONES TO THE BUSINESS MODEL

By now it should be obvious that *how* you execute your milestone is not just a "business decision," but more importantly, a *business model decision:* business model design and milestone completion are best approached by manipulating your operational activities and resources, choosing which are the most profitable as in-house value-building activities, and which are best outsourced to a more cost-effective activity provider. Business growth and development are concerned with more than just completing milestones. Rather than as an isolated activity, the completion of one milestone must be bridged to the next milestone—all within the framework of your company's strategy (Figure 4.8). While the strategy defines your overall business goal, milestones are intermediate objectives to reach your goal.

Each milestone will be completed with its own *cost structure* and contribution to the company's *revenue model.* For development-stage companies, until sufficient revenue is generated (the so called *pre-revenue* or *cash-negative* companies), the revenue model needs to be either replaced or complemented by the company's *financing model.* The company has to gather financial resources to fund the operations until the company turns from cash burning into cash generating. There are alternative funding sources available for development-stage companies, ranging from research grants to bridge or convertible loans to equity investments.

As you identify which operational activities are milestone-driven, you will see that *business model design* is a function of *how* you complete your milestones within the three-dimensional framework of FOCUS, LOCUS, and MODUS. Our business model framework underscores the location of

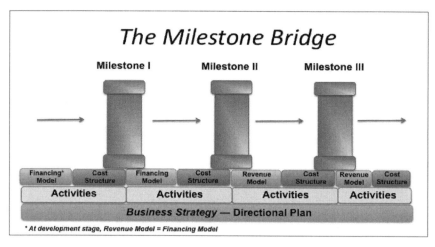

Figure 4.8 Bridging Milestones to the Business Model
Source: Authors' elaboration

operational activities, as well as what activities to focus on, and the selection of value partners for these activities. *The Milestone Bridge* makes a clear distinction between the business strategy and the business model, and underscores the relevance of location decisions. Thus, business model design and milestone completion are inextricably related, and function together as essential elements for successfully delivering a company's value proposition and sustaining its competitive advantage.

Your business strategy should not change, but sometimes it may change because of the unknowns and risks of running a science-based business like drug development. Alas, sometimes you can't avoid "the bridge to nowhere." *The Milestone Bridge* can't guarantee a successful drug or medical product. On one hand it can help to mitigate the development risk by getting you to fail sooner rather than later. On the other hand, an earlier failure may get you sooner to success.

4.5 COMMUNICATING THE BUSINESS MODEL THROUGH THE VALUE ARCHITECTURE

While *The Milestone Bridge* approach can help identify, prioritize, and manage a company's activities toward the completion of milestones, the system also provides a way to characterize the output of a company into what we call its *VALUE ARCHITECTURE* (Figure 4.9). Representing a high-level snapshot of the company's business model, the VALUE ARCHITECTURE summarizes the key elements of FOCUS, LOCUS, and MODUS—the three-dimensional output of your business model decisions at a particular stage of company growth and development. The VALUE ARCHITECTURE in Figure 4.9 shows our example company (Biomagen) at Milestone #1 is focused on outsourcing its preclinical research, and about to begin Phase 1 clinical trials—both brain and labor intensive activities, localized in the San Francisco Bay Area.

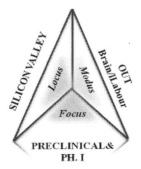

Figure 4.9   The VALUE ARCHITECTURE for Biomagen

Source: Authors' elaboration

The VALUE ARCHITECTURE can be a visual tool for managers to better understand the current position of the firm, and the implications of new decisions they are requested to make. For the industry or academic analyst, the VALUE ARCHITECTURE can be helpful for high-level comparison of the business models of a group of companies at relative stages of development.

The VALUE ARCHITECTURE can also help entrepreneurs and managers to better communicate company-specific positioning. Being able to communicate what your company does is important for all companies. It is key for life science and high tech companies that are not easy to pitch given the complexity of their products and activities.

The Milestone Bridge helps you to analyze in detail how the company actually works. Through the VALUE ARCHITECTURE, it also helps you to wrap-up the company's business model and communicate it in an effective way.

Table 4.1 Learning Blocks—Chapter 4

Business Model	ACTIVITY LIST	FOCUS
LOCUS	MODUS	VALUE ARCHITECTURE
	The Milestone Bridge	

NOTES

1. We refer to any ill-conceived and poorly-executed project costing inordinate amounts of time and money leading to nothing gained.
2. Quote by Andre Agassi (2009).
3. Acquisition and exclusive licensing are ways to internalize an asset or technology. We refer to them as BUY-IN to distinguish from internal development (IN).

REFERENCES

Agassi, Andre. 2009. *Open: An Autobiography*. New York: Random House.
Onetti, Alberto, Antonella Zucchella, Marian V. Jones, and Patricia McDougall-Covin. 2012a. "Internationalization, Innovation and Entrepreneurship: Business Models for New Technology-based Firms." First online 2010 (doi:10.1007/s10997–010–9154–1). Print version *Journal of Management and Governance* 16, no. 3 (SI): 337–368.
———. 2012b. "Guest Editor's Introduction to the Special Issue: Entrepreneurship and Strategic Management in New Technology Based Companies." First online 2010 (doi:10.1007/s10997–010–9153–2). Print version *Journal of Management and Governance* 16, no. 3 (SI): 333–336.

5 Bridging Theory to Practice

"Failure is not going to kill you, but not trying is worse than anything you can imagine."

—Seth Godin[1]

After a full chapter spent to walk you into the logics behind *The Milestone Bridge* and explain how it works, we expect a lot of questions coming from the audience (particularly from scientists who wish to become entrepreneurs), the most important one being: it looks interesting, but how can I turn my business idea/research into a structured business model? How can I apply *The Milestone Bridge* to my business?

In this chapter you will find some answers. In the next pages we are going to explain how to design your own *Milestone Bridge*. We will show you how to map your ACTIVITY LIST, assign priorities to the different activities (FOCUS), understand where to locate them (LOCUS), and the best way to perform them (MODUS). We will walk you step-by-step to put you in condition at the end of this chapter to do your homework and build the business model of your company, whether you are an entrepreneur looking for help in writing the business plan, a manager looking for assistance in giving execution to the business plan, or an interested party, i.e., an investor or financial analyst, trying to find a blueprint for understanding how a company is using its money.

To make this discussion less theoretical and more practical, we will do a sort of "reverse-engineering" of the business model of Biomagen. Specifically, we will show you how we helped John Murphy, the techno-entrepreneur behind Biomagen, to identify and structure it.

John Murphy, as we mentioned in Chapter 1, is a fictional character. Actually just the name is fictional, because he is a real person, and we spent some time in the past working as advisors for him. In order to make him not recognizable, we changed a bit of his story and slightly modified his business venture. And we made him ask questions, the same questions he asked, and we are pretty sure you too would ask us.

John Murphy is your Virgil, he will walk you through *The Milestone Bridge* bringing his own business story that—like all business stories—is full of excitement, challenge, fear, doubt, and mistakes. This books aims at helping John, and you, to make a business story a business fact. This book is not an entrepreneurial machine—we do not create ideas and inspiration. That's not our job; that's John's and your job. But we can help John and you to turn the idea into a sustainable business model and articulate it into a business plan.

But first of all, let us introduce John Murphy to you.

5.1   INTRODUCING JOHN MURPHY

John Murphy was born in 1972 in Boston from a well-off family. Carl, his father, was a gifted violinist, who, despite his enormous talent, was not able to become a professional musician (his performance in public was negatively impacted by a mix of stage fright and performance anxiety). Margaret, his mother, was a scientific pioneer at the University of Boston, where she conducted innovative research in the cardiovascular field, focusing on the prevention of unwanted clots and their consequences (thromboembolism and peripheral arterial occlusion).

John grew up with a strong empathy with science and art and a sort of mild dislike for anything that was business related.

After graduating from Cornell University in biology and then Stony Brook Medical School, John moved to California where he received his internal medicine training and completed his endocrinology fellowship at UCSD. In 2007, he was recruited to the UCSF Medical Center, where—in line with his tendency to push the boundaries of his own limits—he rapidly became an osteoporosis specialist and clinical scientist in the Clinical Research Center. His research focused on the causes of osteoporosis and how a particular hormone and statins work to treat osteoporosis.

During his work at the California Medical Center, John identified the potential of existing patents at UCSF as a possible opportunity for seeding a

John Murphy

company. Thanks to his personal network over there, he was in a position to get an exclusive license from the university to seed the technology platform for a new company, Biomagen. His goal was to repurpose a drug for a new application, in this case an inhibitor of cholesterol synthesis for osteoporosis treatment. He was able to persuade five among his colleagues and friends to jump on board Biomagen.

With an idea and a team, John needs funding. And investors love ideas, but they also ask for a business model. And here John comes to us for help in developing Biomagen's business model and plan.

5.2   LET'S GET STARTED: IDENTIFY THE STRATEGY AND THE MILESTONES

Q: John, where's the opportunity?

A: *The technology and opportunity is the repurposing of a class of drugs known as statins. Statins have been used to prevent the build-up of cholesterol. Originally isolated from oyster mushrooms, statins lower cholesterol by inhibiting the enzyme HMG-CoA reductase, which is the rate-limiting enzyme of the mevalonate pathway of cholesterol synthesis.*

Q: Wait, John, we are losing you . . . we will have time to go into scientific details later on. Please state the opportunity you see, possibly in a few short sentences.

A: *There have been multiple studies to show that there is a secondary, positive effect of statins on bone formation. Therefore, they could be repurposed for use as a therapeutic to treat osteoporosis.*

Q: Now it sounds clearer. Let's move from technology to business. What's your strategy? What's your long-term vision?

A: *I want to produce a new pharmaceutical drug to treat osteoporosis.*

Q: That's a good statement and the right way to start our work together. Now tell me John, where does your idea come from?

A: *Recent discovery of statins as bone anabolic agents has spurred a great deal of interest among both basic and clinical bone researchers. In-vitro and some animal studies suggest that statins increase the bone mass by enhancing bone morphogenetic protein-2 (BMP-2)-mediated osteoblast expression.*

Q: Ok. But it looks like there is nothing innovative. There may be other firms already working on similar projects.

A: *Well, this is correct, but incomplete. Actually, although a limited number of case-control studies suggest that statins may have the potential to reduce the risk of fractures by increasing bone formation, other studies have failed to show a benefit in fracture reduction. So randomized, controlled clinical trials are needed to resolve this conflict.*

Q: Have you thought about why previous tests presented such discrepancies in the results?

A: *One possible reason for the discrepancy in the results of preclinical, as well as clinical, studies is the liver-specific nature of statins. Considering their high liver specificity and low oral bioavailability; the distribution of statins to the bone microenvironment in optimum concentration is questionable. To untie their exact mechanism and verify a positive action on bone, statins should reach the bone microenvironment in optimal concentration. Dose optimization and use of new controlled drug delivery systems may increase the bioavailability and distribution of statins to the bone microenvironment.*

Q: That is very clear. So this is the story now. . . . According to your scientific point of view, the discovery of bone-specific statins or their bone-targeted delivery offers great potential in the treatment of osteoporosis.
   But John, how are you going to do this—i.e., what's your business model?

A: *My business model is to repurpose statins for use as a therapeutic drug to treat osteoporosis.*

Q: John, that's the opportunity you see; that is not a business model. We need to understand how you are going to exploit the opportunity.

A: *Oh, I will go through Phase 1, 2, and 3, etc.*

Q: John, these are the phases you must go through for any drug development. Getting the FDA approval and putting the drug on the market is neither a strategy nor a business model. That's the generic destination for any entrepreneurial journey in the biotech and pharmaceutical sea.
   But you still need navigation to get there. And it's the activities that you define that can make the difference. It means that you need to identify milestones (i.e., intermediate ports) and decide where your priorities are, i.e., what activity to FOCUS on now, which activities to postpone, which activities not to do.
   What is your first immediate milestone?

A: *Get funded.*

Q: No, fundraising is a support activity. Support activities, although really important, do not characterize your business model. As Tim O'Reilly (O'Reilly Media founder and CEO) used to say: "Money is like gasoline during a road trip. You don't want to run out of gas on your trip, but you're not doing a tour of gas stations." Let's then focus on your trip. What's the first place to be visited, metaphorically speaking?

A: *I think the first result we need to reach is to complete Preclinical Development for our lead small-molecule drug, and to submit an Investigational New Drug (IND) application to the FDA.*

Q: Great, that will be your Milestone #1 in your *Milestone Bridge*. What's the next step?

A: *The IND is critical for completing both Phase 1 and Phase 2. Thereafter we will be ready to move into Phase 3.*

Q: Ok, that's way too fast. Probably we need to identify some intermediate milestones.

A: *Well, actually completing a Phase 1 Patient Safety Trial could be the second main goal.*

Q: Good, Phase 1 will be your Milestone #2. What's next?

A: *Obviously, Phase 2.*

Q: Is the completion of Phase 2 a monolithic target or can it be split into some intermediate milestones?

A: *Right, actually Phase 2 is really a large objective. We should focus initially on dosing efficacy. When successful with that, we should be well positioned to complete Phase 2, probably in partnership with a large pharmaceutical company.*

Q: Got it—therefore Milestone #3 could be the completion of Phase 2a. As you will reach that point, you should be in position to enter into a strategic alliance with a pharmaceutical partner or, even better, be acquired.

A: *An early exit. . . . I hadn't thought about that. It wouldn't be that bad. Should I then just focus on completing Phase 2a and then try to sell the company?*

Q: No, companies are acquired, not sold. You can't plan a company sale. You should have a plan for bringing Biomagen all the way through the end of your journey (i.e., putting your product on the market). But, at the same time, you must be ready to take any valuable exit opportunity that could materialize along the journey. Don't target a sale, but be prepared for that.

Ok, we have now defined the first three milestones. Let's spend a few moments to understand a bit more the financial prerequisites and deadlines for each of them. How much time and money do you need to complete the Preclinical Development (Milestone #1)?

A: *With the current team it will take from 3 to 5 years.*

Q: It is quite a long period of time. Is it not possible to reduce it?

A: *Oh yes. If I got some funding, I could speed up the process significantly. I estimated that with a $5 million investment we could complete Preclinical Development in 18 months at maximum.*

Q: Ok, a Series A of $5 million will be the Financial Prerequisite for Milestone #1, with an estimated completion time of 18 months. What about Phase 1 (Milestone #2)?

A: *Difficult to say at this time. To complete Phase 1, a larger financing round (approximately $20/30 million) could be required. This way we could complete it in 6–9 months.*

Q: And what about Phase 2a (Milestone #3)?

A: *I definitely need to do more analysis here, but the completion of Milestone #3 may require an additional $15/30 million dollars and one additional year time period.*

Great, now we have a plan. We have identified the main milestones together with some preliminary estimates in terms of capital required and time of completion. Now what you need to do is to map the activities you are required to run. This analytical work will help you understand in much greater detail how much fuel (money) you need, how much time, and how many resources. Business success is all about having enough time and money, not just the right idea. We cannot guarantee that your idea will work. Where we can help you is to get there and not to remain short of fuel in the middle of the ocean.

5.3   BUILDING YOUR ACTIVITY LIST

The first step is to understand what activities you need in order to run your business and reach your next milestone.

Each company has a different ACTIVITY LIST, because companies frequently point to different destinations (i.e., they have different strategies and, as a consequence, different business models) and, even when they share the same strategy, they may choose different ways to get to the same destination (i.e., companies that have similar strategies perform differently because they have different business models). Companies are uniquely characterized by the decisions they make (both at strategic and business model levels). Thus, the first thing to be done by a company is to list the activities required to run its business.

While defining your ACTIVITY LIST, you have to think about all the activities—i.e., what are all the activities that are required to get to your final destination. As we discussed above, the strategy points to your destination, but the activities provide the multiple ways to reach your destination. When you define your ACTIVITY LIST, think as broadly as possible. This way you will have in your scope all the possible ways to reach your destination.

In our experience we see companies make two typical mistakes when asked to identify the ACTIVITY LIST.

The first common mistake they make is just to think about the activities they want to perform. We call it *"narrow-minded thinking."*

Frequently, entrepreneurs and managers consider their own way of doing things as the universally accepted way of doing things, and also identify the market with their own product. Sometimes this magic coincidence happens, but more frequently it doesn't. Or, although it does for a certain period of time, after a while, it is no longer true. This happens because the market needs evolve, or because new alternative technologies emerge. If companies are not able to anticipate these trends, they go off road. Home delivery of ice is no longer the way of choice for conserving food in your house, although it represented a successful business model for quite a long period of time.

Too often, you focus on one activity thinking that's your business, when in fact you have a multitude of activity options to achieve your value proposition. You need to have an open mind in mapping your ACTIVITY LIST, trying to think as broadly as possible.

Therefore initially you have to identify all activities that may be required for running your business. Entrepreneurs think about some activities, while forgetting there are others. So the point here is to look at the big picture, determine all the required activities. Don't limit the land of opportunities with your own business idea. The danger of this is that you don't have the full view of what you need to do.

What if you aren't able to identify all the activities first-hand? You need to do some research, maybe talk to a consultant or related entrepreneur. This may cost you some dollars, but it can save you a lot of dollars later on.

But what kind of activities are we talking about? As discussed in the prior chapter, we refer mostly to the *operational activities* that are required to deliver and execute the value proposition to the customer (i.e., research, development, manufacturing, sales, etc.). *Support activities* (human resources, IT, etc.) and *corporate development activities* (finance, IP prosecution) do not define the business model of the company, they just enable the company to operate and survive.

When we ask entrepreneurs, not only in startups, but also in established companies, "What's your business model?", we frequently receive this answer: "Fundraising; we need to close the series X; we need to have access to seed financing." We are not implying that raising money is not an important activity, but this does not characterize the business model. Rather, it enables the business model by providing the company with the required financial resources (we call it The Financial Prerequisite).

Another common mistake is called "*short-term sighting.*"

When you map your activities, you have to think long-term, about all the business cycle of your company. If, for example, you decide to stop product development/testing at Phase 2, you still need to know Phase 3 and 4 activities, and so on, from the perspective of the prospective pharmaceutical partner or potential acquirer.

So you have to produce your ACTIVITY LIST. Let us state a generic caveat: "*Don't be afraid to go analytical.*" Again, *The Milestone Bridge* is a tool that is supposed to help you to come out with a high-level picture of your business. But in order to get this result, you need to get into the details first. You need an analytical planning tool for moving from the details to the broader picture.

We can't provide you with a "standard" ACTIVITY LIST. This is going to be different and unique for each company. Every company has a value chain, i.e., a process of interconnected value-adding activities on the basis of which it may derive its source of competitive advantage: for instance, basic research, applied research, manufacturing, sales, and so on. The value-adding ACTIVITY LIST is strictly firm-specific. It changes not only from business to business, but also from firm to firm and thus it has to be identified case-by-case. Basic/applied research and development, manufacturing, marketing, distribution, sales—these are generic categories of activities. There is no longer a one best way to do things. And you need to identify the many ways to do things before choosing your own way. Now let's come back to John Murphy.

Q: John, let's walk through the ACTIVITY LIST of your company.

A: *Ok, as of today, we are working to complete the Preclinical Drug Development.*

Q: Ok, what are the main activities here you need to complete?

A: *We need to do additional medicinal chemistry, lead optimization, and dose efficacy in an animal model of disease. And obviously submit an Investigational New Drug (IND) application to the FDA. This is the key prerequisite for Phase 1.*

Q: What activities are required to complete Phase 1?

A: *We need first to complete a patient safety trial to show that there are no adverse side effects to the drug over a prospective dosage.*

Q: So is this the only activity required for this phase?

A: *No, we need also to know the best dosage for bone formation efficacy. One can't assume that the cholesterol dosage will be the optimal for bone efficacy. Formulation, dosing, and subsequent data analysis are other key activities.*

Q: Ok, it looks you refer to dosing and formulation as single activity.

A: *Right, but how can I know when to break activities into sub-activities?*

Q: Well, let us list some criteria that can help you to decide when it makes sense to do it.

- Difference: you can group similar activities, as long as they are not too different. In the latter case it is better to keep them separate.
- Relevance: do not merge activities that have different strategic importance.
- Geography: as we will see later on, keep separated activities that are performed in different places.
- MODUS: treat separately activities that require to be performed in different ways.

Obviously this is an iterative process. You may be required to come back and change your ACTIVITY LIST after having fully analyzed and also understood the LOCUS and MODUS of your business. If later on we determine that these activities are performed in different ways and maybe in separate locations, then it could make sense to split the activities in separate categories.

A: *Ok, dosing and formulation can be grouped. They have similar relevance and will be performed by the same vendor. Additionally there are operational synergies between them.*

Q: Ok, then we have our ACTIVITY LIST for Phase 1. What about Phase 2?

A: *Well, for sure dosage and formulation and probably studies about efficacy.*

Q: You did very well going analytical as we asked you to do. Then "safety," "toxicology," "efficacy studies," and "formulation" are part of your ACTIVITY LIST. The first two refer to Phase 1, while the others are subphases of Phase 2 ("Efficacy" and "Dosage and Formulation"). But we think there is more than that. Your ACTIVITY LIST starts with Phase 1; what about R&D?

A: *Well, I'm repurposing an existing drug; therefore these activities have been already done, at least to some extent.*

Q: You should not assume that activities that are already done are no longer important. This is not necessarily true. What you have done in the past is a building block of your company and could be a key differentiator. We also need to add those activities to the ACTIVITY LIST because they contribute to characterize in an unique way your business model.

   You mentioned "Safety and Toxicology," "Efficacy studies," and "Dosage and Formulation"; what are you expected to do after that?

A: *I haven't yet thought about it at this stage, it is way too far from where I'm now . . .*

Q: It's definitely time to do it.

A: *Ok, I assume it will be a multi-trial efficacy for Phase 3 and then regulatory approval.*

Q: And what thereafter?

A: *Market tests (the so called Phase 4), and, if everything works ok, manufacturing and sales.*

Q: Very good, now we have completed the map of the activities for Biomagen. You can find your ACTIVITY LIST represented in the chart below. By now, as a first immediate outcome, you should have a better picture of the items you need to address with your consultants, in order to ask the smart questions and evaluate one consultant's recommendations versus another. Now it should also be easier for you to deal with your consultants and possibly save some time and money.

ACTIVITY LIST
Basic Research
1-Target Validation
2-Cell Studies
3-Proof Principals
Preclinical Development
1-Medicinal Chemistry
2-Animal Model
3-Animal Efficacy
IND Application
Phase 1: Safety and Toxicology
1-Patient Safety Trial
2-Formulation/Dosing
3-Data Analysis
Phase 2a: Efficacy
1-Patient Recruitment
2-Dosing Efficacy
3-Clinical Trials
4-Data Analysis
Phase 2b: Dosage and Formulation
Phase 3
Regulatory Approval
Phase 4: After Market
Manufacturing
Sales

Figure 5.1   The ACTIVITY LIST of Biomagen
Source: Authors' elaboration

5.4 DEFINING THE FOCUS

After having listed all the activities required to run a company's business, now we need to understand what activities are more important, i.e., which activities the company must focus on. Defining the FOCUS means defining the relevance that you attribute or give to the different activities that are required to do your business. Running a business means to make choices. Focusing is likely the most difficult business model decision. The ability to execute the strategy and the final strategic positioning of the company is the result of such decisions.

In our experience we have met many executives who are reluctant to make decisions, i.e., focus the company in a specific direction. There is in companies a widespread fear of commitment because taking a direction means abandoning others. And it is hard to seemingly give up revenue opportunities. But this is the cardinal sin of the entrepreneur—the inability to focus. If you postpone choices or, even worse, do not make decisions, you lose time and cash and you may prevent your company from reaching the milestones required to succeed. Focus is everything, although it may be tough to make choices.

Focus is especially relevant for companies that have a long path, i.e., life science companies and pharma companies. You don't have the luxury of time. Time is money, and today, since some companies are playing across multiple industries, you cannot dominate all these technologies and be on the edge for all the activities. You have to decide your core specialization. You have to decide what technology and activities to focus on. You cannot be a leader in everything. Focus is a matter of deciding what to do and what not to do. And, as Michael Porter points out (Porter, 1996), the toughest choice is not what you decide to do; it's what you decide not to do. That could be tough as we said, but, quoting Steve Jobs, "it is crucial, every now and then, to roll the dice and bet the company on some new idea or technology." That is exactly the risk he took on a new product called the iPod. "I had this crazy idea that we could sell just as many Macs by advertising the iPod. In addition, the iPod would position Apple as evoking innovation and youth. So I moved $75 million of advertising money to the iPod, even though the category didn't justify one hundredth of that. That meant that we completely dominated the market for music players. We outspent everybody by a factor of about a hundred" (Isaacson, 2011).

FOCUS decisions should all be about completing milestones and getting to the market as soon as possible. The base of your decisions is your strength: where I have distinctive core competencies, where I'm better than my competitors—that's the place I have to be. If you have trouble making decisions, concentrate on what you're really good at. Rarely will you be proven wrong.

Don't forget that when you focus on something, you're giving an identity to your company and a clear perception of what it does. That's really important not only for established companies (a well-defined corporate identity helps to better market the products and services), but also for technology companies that haven't yet a product on the market and are looking for capital. Investors prefer properly focused ventures.

A point important to make at this stage of the discussion is that when we talk about FOCUS, we mean the *current* FOCUS. You have to focus on activities that are important to reach your next milestone. As we discussed in Chapter 3, the business model decisions are milestone-based. And the importance of the various activities must be assessed in terms of their relevance to completion of the next incoming milestone.

The FOCUS of the company may change as the company evolves. This is typical for life science firms that change FOCUS as their research moves from early to later phases. Other companies do not (the so called "satellite" companies, such as CROs) since their business model is anchored to a certain FOCUS over the time.

But let's go back to John Murphy.

Q: John, it's now time to define the relevance of the activities we identified earlier in order to execute your next milestone. Which activities is Biomagen currently focused on?

A: *Well, today we are particularly focused on Preclinical Drug Development. Currently we are mainly concentrated on verifying some results of basic research in a disease animal model.*

Q: Ok, John, this is a very good start. And what about the other activities? Are they also important to Biomagen?

A: *Of course they are. The activities I have listed are now the core of the company's life and the basis for future development. But also many activities have been important in the past. For example, Medicinal Chemistry was our main FOCUS months ago, but is still relevant. Everything is, has been, or will be important very soon.*

Q: Here you go John! You addressed the problem perfectly. We know that you consider vital all your activities, but what we are asking you is how much you are investing in each of them right now. Today. The relevance will probably change during the next few quarters or years, but this is exactly what a business model should provide: a good picture of the present situation. So tell us, at this moment, how much effort and resources are you dedicating to each of these activities? Give us a number between 0 and 10 for defining the relevance of each activity (0–3, not relevant or barely; 3–5, not very relevant; 5–7, relevant but not key; and 8–10, key activities). The valuation, as we pointed out above, has to be done looking at today's situation, with reference to the next milestone.

A: *Hum, it is difficult to give values here.*

Q: Totally understood, but we need a way to visualize your FOCUS. Ballpark figures are okay. These are semi-quantitative assessments that can incorporate gut feelings. But assigning values helps greatly in describing your company as it works today.

A: *All right then. Now the concept is clearer in my mind. Let's say that, on a 1 to 10 scale, Preclinical Development activities (lead optimization and dose efficacy) are a 9. We are almost all concentrated on it, even as we are already preparing the ground for the following steps, in particular for the IND Application that is a 4. Medicinal Chemistry is almost completed; it could be a 5.*

Q: Very good. And what about the Basic Research? Is there anyone performing some studies at that stage?

A: *Well . . . not now. I mean . . . of course there is always a person on our team who is doing some studies on new potential applications of what we want to develop here, but is not our main FOCUS currently.*

Q: But you are still doing that. It is written down in your ACTIVITY LIST!

A: *Yes, it is. In fact, it is something that we do, just not so much right now. Well, let's say a 4 for research activities right now.*

Q: Good. Let's look a bit forward. What about the activities listed in Phase 1 and Phase 2?

A: *That will be the next big thing. But now we are not spending so much effort on them. I would say a 3 for Patient Safety Trial and a 2 for Formulation/Dosing. Nothing for Data Analysis at this point. Regarding Phase 2a, on a 1 to 10 scale, it is no more than a 2 now.*

Q: Ok John. But, if you are doing such evaluations, it means that you are already using resources to look for potential partners. And, if you are not, you may discover too late that outsourcing was the most suitable option. So, if you learn to plan in advance the best option according to your strategy, you save time and resources that may be applicable to other more important and urgent activities. But we will talk about it later. Let's go back to the FOCUS intensity. What about Phase 2a, Phase 3, and Regulatory Approval?

A: *We just had a meeting with a patent consultant in New York in order to gain some more detailed information of what we should expect and how will be better to proceed with the Regulatory Approval. So I think a 1 is the right weight for this activity. Regarding Phase 2a and beyond, we still need to look around a bit and see if there is someone that can be hypothetically a good partner. On a 1 to 10 scale, it is no more than 1 at this stage.*

Q: What about the very last activities in your list?

A: *We still don't know anything about what to do for the manufacturing and sales. We will decide that as soon as we see the improvements in the development phases.*

ACTIVITY LIST	FOCUS
Basic Research	
1-Target Validation	
2-Cell Studies	4
3-Proof Principals	
Preclinical Development	
1-Medicinal Chemistry	5
2-Animal Model	9
3-Animal Efficacy	9
IND Application	4
Phase 1: Safety and Toxicology	
1-Patient Safety Trial	3
2-Formulation/Dosing	2
3-Data Analysis	
Phase 2a: Efficacy	
1-Patient Recruitment	2
2-Dosing Efficacy	2
3-Clinical Trials	1
4-Data Analysis	
Phase 2b: Dosage and Formulation	1
Phase 3	1
Regulatory Approval	1
Phase 4: After Market	
Manufacturing	
Sales	

Figure 5.2 The FOCUS of Biomagen (Current)
Source: Authors' elaboration

5.5 GEOGRAPHY MATTERS

The international entrepreneurship/internationalization literature is grounded on the assumption that location matters. Moreover, particularly for young and new technology-based companies, location decisions are among the most relevant ones. In fact, for these firms (a.k.a. *born global companies* and *global startups*[2]), internationalization is not just one of the possible growth options, but is a natural prerequisite for doing business: what really makes the difference is the capacity to make fast and appropriate decisions regarding the most suitable locations for different activities (access to resources and knowledge, sales, etc.) jointly with the system of modalities related to them (make, buy, partner). As we anticipated earlier, with "location decisions" we refer not just to choices regarding the destination markets but also to decisions like "where do we place our activities and where do we locate our company?" These choices can make the difference in terms of the company's ability to access resources, develop competencies, create a network, benefit from knowledge spill-overs and therefore excel, innovate, and implement its strategy. In our definition of business model, we emphasize these kinds of decisions in the "LOCUS" dimension.

Let's go back to John to understand where he is planning to carry out Biomagen's activities.

Q: John, let's talk a bit about the "LOCUS" of Biomagen. Where is your company based?

A: *We are located in Foster City, California.*

Q: Are you telling me that all the activities we listed before are performed in Foster City?

A: *Well, actually no. They are quite scattered . . . Hercules, San Francisco, Burlingame, and San Diego.*

Q: Ok, let's go through them one-by-one.

A: *As I mentioned before, Basic Research has been performed at UCSF San Francisco, whereas we selected a CRO in Hercules for most of the activities in Preclinical Development, Phase 1 and—likely—Phase 2.*

Q: Which activities exactly are performed in Hercules?

A: *We are conducting the whole Preclinical Development in partnership with this CRO. We are planning to outsource to the same company also most of the Phase 1 activities, with the exception of the Data Analysis that we will do in-house and "Formulation/Dosing" that we will contract out to a CRO based in San Diego.*

Q: Why did you choose this CRO in Hercules?

A: *Well, my team is composed mainly of clinical researchers. Hal Steger is our guru. He knows everything about statins, and it is key that he is actively involved in the CRO day-to-day work. Therefore, partnering with a CRO that is close to us helps a lot.*

Q: What about the CRO in San Diego? How did you find this organization?

A: *The owner was a colleague of mine during my internal medicine training at UCSD. Anytime I need competencies we don't have in-house, I first look at my personal contacts. The same happened for the consultant who is helping us for the IND Application. He was recommended to me from a friend at Cornell.*

This is a very common way to identify new business opportunities. Never forget to leverage and nurture your personal network. Also, attending conferences and meeting with other colleagues increases the chance of finding interesting people within the network of friends and acquaintances. If there is a win–win situation, usually people don't mind suggesting a valuable friend's name!

Q: Now John, what about the other activities beyond Phase 1?

A: *Yes. We are considering outsourcing the Phase 2a activities to the same company in Hercules. And I think that for Phase 2b and Phase 3 we could partner again with UCSF San Francisco.*

Q: Why do you say that?

A: *Well, I am looking for a strategic partner but I can't find one. Also because I don't know anybody else in the country who can conduct such activities. So I prefer to find an organization in this area in order to be able to control and monitor its work more closely.*

Q: It is very good to go back to your personal network for finding potential partners, but it could be limiting if this remains the only source for scouting partners. And, most importantly, you cannot limit yourself to a certain territory just because you have potential issues in managing multiple locations.

A: *But, what if I select a company for example in Cambridge, UK? How can I manage the relationship from so far? How can I control how they are conducting Phase 3?*

Q: John, you can't eliminate your potential best option simply because it is located on the other side of the ocean. If, in the Cambridge area, there are key resources and competences for the success of your venture, you need to find a way to exploit them. Either through partners or, eventually, opening an entity or a lab over there. There are always technical solutions to problems. But don't exclude valuable options just because they are not easy to realize.

A: *This makes sense. However, it is difficult for me to trust people I don't know. . . . I'm not sure other partners can work as we do, because they are not motivated and involved as we are. So, being close to them helps me to better control the process. But I feel that this is not the right approach to do things. . . . More than once, people on my team have told me we should probably hire a general manager to do all the "business stuff."*

Q: Don't worry John. No one is going to judge you here. Conversely, we are trying to help you to see things from different perspectives. The ultimate goal is to help Biomagen to grow better and faster! A lot of science

ACTIVITY LIST	LOCUS
Basic Research	
1-Target Validation	San Francisco
2-Cell Studies	Foster City
3-Proof Principals	San Francisco
Preclinical Development	
1-Medicinal Chemistry	Hercules
2-Animal Model	Hercules
3-Animal Efficacy	Hercules
IND Application	Burlingame
Phase 1: Safety and Toxicology	
1-Patient Safety Trial	Hercules
2-Formulation/Dosing	Hercules
3-Data Analysis	Burlingame
Phase 2a: Efficacy	
1-Patient Recruitment	Hercules
2-Dosing Efficacy	Hercules
3-Clinical Trials	Hercules
4-Data Analysis	Burlingame
Phase 2b: Dosage and Formulation	San Francisco? Cambridge?
Phase 3	San Francisco? Cambridge?
Regulatory Approval	New York?
Phase 4: After Market	TBD
Manufacturing	TBD
Sales	TBD

Figure 5.3 The LOCUS of Biomagen (Current)
Source: Authors' elaboration

entrepreneurs underestimate the importance of management principles or sometimes they learn them too late. But don't worry, compared to biochemistry, management and business administration are much easier! And you have already started to get familiar with them.

As we can see, Biomagen does not operate only in the Bay Area, but has a virtual network architecture that goes all across the US and potentially abroad. Through the business model, the company enlarges its boundaries and structures its "value network"—which includes customers, suppliers, partners, distribution channels—that extend the company's proprietary resources.

5.6   CHOOSING THE MODUS

A company has multiple options for performing its activities. One of the biggest mistakes companies make is to assume that they have to do all the activities internally. That's not true. Outsourcing and strategic partnership are viable alternative options.

Partnerships allow the company to access the resources, expertise, and experience it may require. As with contractors, partners must be chosen wisely to ensure that the company gains the specific competitive advantages it requires to move forward without giving away too much in the process. In a "cash-strapped" economy where investors are holding onto investment capital tightly, partnerships are emerging as a solution both for large and established companies as well as SMEs and startups for leveraging resources and enabling further growth and innovation.

When negotiating partnerships in the life sciences arena—whether they are outsourcing, licensing, joint development deals, or other activities—it is key to involve from the beginning a trusted lawyer. It is vital to write down clear contractual agreements where every single term is defined in order to protect your IP, future results, and enterprise value.

Before deciding what to do in-house and what to contract out, you need to understand exactly how each single activity works, and assess your strengths and weaknesses.

The "MODUS" dimension of *The Milestone Bridge* helps you understand and design the way a company operates, activity by activity. More specifically, it identifies:

- Which activities to manage in-house (IN).
- Which ones to outsource (OUT).
- Which ones to manage through strategic partners (JOINT).

For activities to be run in-house, the business model also defines how the company is going to perform these activities in terms of intensity of:

- *Capital/technology* (i.e., level of investments in capital and technology).
- *Labor* (i.e., headcount).
- *"Brain"* (i.e., quality, experience, and skills of the work force).

For activities that have been outsourced, key critical decisions refer to:

- Vendor selection.
- Length of the relationship (long-term transactions versus short-term deals).
- Level of company involvement in the relationship (pure outsourcing/market-transactions versus strategic partnership/collaborative agreements).

Q: We are almost there John. Your business model is gradually taking shape! From our prior discussions, it looks like Biomagen tends to outsource the majority of its activities, is that correct?

A: *Yes, we just started the company and we don't have either the capabilities or the money to do many things internally. This is why we tend to go through partners.*

Q: So are you planning to become a sort of "virtual company?"

A: *Yes, we can define it this way; although we are fully involved in all the activities of the Preclinical Development. We work closely with the CRO in Hercules, and my team spends a lot of time monitoring how our contractors are doing the job and discussing the results.*

Q: Then this is not pure outsourcing. You are actually working together with this CRO since your own resources are strongly involved in the performance of these activities. To highlight this situation, in *The Milestone Bridge* we will mark all the activities related to the Preclinical Development Phase as "JOINT." The costs absorbed by these activities go beyond the fees paid to the CRO. There are actually internal costs, too, that need to be considered. If you don't, you risk underestimating the effort required to complete the milestone.

In terms of "how" you perform these activities, how would you rate them in terms of brain, technology, and labor intensity (from 1 to 10)?

A: *All Preclinical Development activities are mostly labor intensive; I would say a 7 (except Medicinal Chemistry—that is a 4). They need skilled people (5 for brain intensity, except for Medicinal Chemistry that requires higher specialization) and also specialized equipment (approximately a 6 in technology intensity, with the exclusion of Animal Model, which is definitively lower).*

Q: Ok, let's move to Phase 1.

A: *We will outsource most of them, except for Data Analysis, which will be done in-house. Patient Safety Trial requires a lot of highly skilled people, while Formulation/Dosing is more technology intensive.*

Q: What about Efficacy (Phase 2a)? Is it technology based?

A: *Yes, it is mostly technology based . . . they will use DNA Diagnostic System for testing Statin Efficacy. Slightly different is Patient Recruitment, which is mostly a labor intensive activity.*

Q: And for the Dosage and Formulation (Phase 2a)?

A: *This is definitely more brain intensive. Similar to R&D, Phase 2b involves activities where the scientific knowledge and experience weight more. We will probably look for a partner, but we need to be strictly involved in the process. This way we will increase our competence and expertise, and eventually internalize that activity at a certain point.*

Q: Very good, John. We drafted your ACTIVITY LIST and identified the current FOCUS intensity for each of them. Additionally, we specified the geographical location and the modus operandi for the different activities. Now we are ready to put all the pieces together, i.e., the business model of Biomagen. Below you can find the analytical representation of *The Milestone Bridge* with regard to the first milestone.

The analysis we performed can bring about alternative representations.[3] Below you can find an alternative—less analytical—representation of the current business model of Biomagen. This could be useful for status update presentations to the Board of Directors or Investors or in corporate high-level presentations.

The business model is the combination of many decisions. Tomorrow something new or unexpected may happen, and you will be required to

ACTIVITY LIST		MODUS		
		Brain intensity	Technology intensity	Labour intensity
Basic Research				
1-Target Validation	OUT	9	7	2
2-Cell Studies	IN	8	2	4
3-Proof Principals	OUT	7	5	3
Preclinical Development				
1-Medicinal Chemistry	JOINT	8	6	4
2-Animal Model	JOINT	5	2	7
3-Animal Efficacy	JOINT	5	6	7
IND Application	JOINT	9		5
Phase 1: Safety and Toxicology				
1-Patient Safety Trial	OUT	6	2	8
2-Formulation/Dosing	OUT	5	6	4
3-Data Analysis	JOINT	8		2
Phase 2a: Efficacy				
1-Patient Recruitment	OUT			8
2-Dosing Efficacy	OUT	5	6	2
3-Clinical Trials	OUT	6	10	8
4-Data Analysis	JOINT	7		2
Phase 2b: Dosage and Formulation	TBD	5	4	6
Phase 3	TBD	4	3	8
Regulatory Approval	OUT?	8		3
Phase 4: After Market	TBD	7		4
Manufacturing	TBD	2	8	8
Sales	TBD	7	1	6

Figure 5.4   The MODUS of Biomagen (Current)

Source: Authors' elaboration

ACTIVITY LIST	FOCUS	LOCUS		MODUS		
				Brain intensity	Technology intensity	Labour intensity
Basic Research						
1-Target validation		San Francisco	OUT	3	7	2
2-Cell studies	4	Foster City	IN	8	2	4
3-Proof principals		San Francisco	OUT	7	5	3
Preclinical Development						
1-Medicinal chemistry	5	Hercules	JOINT		6	4
2-Animal model	3	Hercules	JOINT	5	2	7
3-Animal efficacy	2	Hercules	JOINT	5	6	7
IND Application	4	Burlingame	JOINT	9		5
Phase 1: Safety and Toxicology						
1-Patient safety Trial	3	Hercules	OUT		2	
2-Formulation/Dosing	2	Hercules	OUT	5	6	4
3-Data Analysis		Burlingame	JOINT	7		2
Phase 2a: Efficacy						
1-Patient Recruitment	2	Hercules	OUT			8
2-Dosing Efficacy	2	Hercules	OUT		7	
3-Clinical Trials	1	Hercules	OUT	6	9	8
4-Data Analysis		Burlingame	JOINT	7		2
Phase 2b: Dosage and Formulation	1	San Francisco? Cambridge?	TBD	5	4	6
Phase 3	1	San Francisco? Cambridge?	TBD	4	3	8
Regulatory Approval	1	New York?	OUT?	7		3
Phase 4: After Market		TBD	TBD			4
Manufacturing		TBD	TBD	2	8	
Sales		TBD	TBD	7	1	6

Figure 5.5   The Milestone Bridge for Biomagen—Detailed Activity Matrix
Milestone #1: Complete Preclinical Development and submit IND application to FDA
Overall Strategy: Complete a pivotal Phase 2a clinical trial and target an alliance/M&A with a pharma company
Financial Prerequisite: $5M
Deadline: 18 months
Source: Authors' elaboration

ACTIVITY LIST	FOCUS	LOCUS		MODUS		
				Brain intensity	Technology intensity	Labour intensity
Basic Research	4	California	IN/OUT		5	3
Preclinical Development	8	California	JOINT	6	5	6
IND Application	4	California	JOINT	9		5
Phase 1: Safety and Toxicology	3	California	JOINT/OUT	6	3	5
Phase 2a: Efficacy	2	California	JOINT/OUT	5	4	5
Phase 2b: Dosage and Formulation	1	California? Massachusetts?	TBD	5	4	6
Phase 3	1	California? Massachusetts?	TBD	4	3	8
Regulatory Approval	1	New York?	OUT?	7		3
Phase 4: After Market		TBD	TBD			4
Manufacturing		TBD	TBD	2	8	8
Sales		TBD	TBD	7	1	6

Figure 5.6   The Milestone Bridge for Biomagen—Streamlined Activity Matrix
Milestone #1: Complete Preclinical Development and submit IND application to FDA
Overall Strategy: Complete a pivotal Phase 2a clinical trial and target an alliance/M&A with a pharma company
Financial Prerequisite: $5M
Deadline: 18 months
Source: Authors' elaboration

modify or revert one or more decisions you have planned so far. Nothing to be surprised or worried about. This is absolutely normal, and it happens more frequently than you probably imagine.

What's really important is to keep in mind that, since the business model is the result of multiple intertwined parameters, modifications in one or some of them will probably impact others and trigger further changes.[4] To avoid losing your direction, don't forget to refer to your final destination, i.e., your strategy and business goals.

Unplanned events happen all the time. *The Milestone Bridge* is about planning and managing your company's evolution and not be driven by events. Have a safe and successful navigation!

NOTES

1. Quote by Seth Godin (TED Conference, Monterey Conference Center, Monterey, California (USA), March 7–10, 2007.
2. For further readings on the topic, the authors suggest the following articles: McDougall et al., 1994; Oviatt and McDougall, 1994; Hordes et al., 1995; Preece et al., 1998; Onetti et al., 2010; Rialp et al., 2005; Presutti et al., 2008; and Jones and Coviello, 2005.
3. In Chapter 4 we presented Biomagen's business model limited to the first three identified milestones. Please note that in that case the FOCUS has been evaluated not based on Milestone #1 (i.e., the relevance of the activities as of today), but on the current milestone (i.e., the relevance of the activities for each milestone).
4. For example, as will be described with more details in Chapter 6, let's look how the business model of Neurosilicon Inc. has changed over time. The change in the activities' FOCUS had implications in terms of LOCUS and MODUS.

REFERENCES

Hordes, Mark, Anthony Clancy, and Julie Baddaley. 1995. "A Primer for Global Start-ups." *Academy of Management Executive* 9, no. 2: 7–11.

Isaacson, Walter. 2011. *Steve Jobs.* New York: Simon & Schuster.

Jones, Marian, and Nicole E. Coviello. 2005. "Internationalization: Conceptualizing an Entrepreneurial Process of Behavior in Time." *Journal of International Business Studies* 36: 284–303.

McDougall, Patricia P., Scott Shane, and Benjamin M. Oviatt. 1994. "Explaining The Formation of International New Ventures." *Journal of Business Venturing* 9, no. 6: 469–487.

Onetti, Alberto, Marco Talaia, Vincenza Odorici, Manuela Presutti, and Sameer Verma. 2010. "The Role of Serial Entrepreneurs in the Internationalization of Global Start-Ups. A Business Case." *Journal of Strategic Management Education* 6, no. 1: 79–94.

Oviatt, Benjamin M., and Patricia P. McDougall. 1994. "Toward a Theory of International New Ventures." *Journal of International Business Studies* 25, no. 1: 45–64.

Porter, Michael E. 1996. "What is Strategy." *Harvard Business Review* 74, no. 6: 61–78.

Preece, Stephen B., Grant Miles, and Mark C. Baetz. 1998. "Explaining the International Intensity and Global Diversity of Early Stage Technology Based Firms." *Journal of Business Venturing* 14, no. 3: 259–281.

Presutti, Manuela, Alberto Onetti, and Vincenza Odorici. 2008. "Serial Entrepreneurship and Born-Global New Ventures. A Case Study." *International Journal of Entrepreneurship Education* 6: 255–278.

Rialp, Alex, Josep Rialp, and Gary A. Knight. 2005. "The Phenomenon of International New Ventures, Global Start Ups and Born Globals: What Do We Know After a Decade (1993–2002) of Exhaustive Scientific Inquiry?" *International Business Review* 14: 147–166.

6   *The Milestone Bridge*
Case Studies

"The risk not taken is more dangerous than the risk taken."

—*Andry Dunn*[1]

Chapter 6 shows how we applied *The Milestone Bridge* to some life science and biotech companies like Napo Pharmaceuticals, MolMed, OXiGENE, Neurosilicon. We put together quite a heterogeneous and diversified group of companies in terms of geography (from the "vieux continent" to the New World), size (start-up vs. public company), business (single business vs. diversified company), and technology (drug compound vs. medical equipment, product company vs. service provider). Therefore you should be able to find some real-life examples that are somewhere close to what you are currently doing or planning to do.

Through *The Milestone Bridge* we analyze and compare the business models of these firms. Additionally we see how they have modified and changed their business models both in response of strategic changes and/or business and demand evolution.

As of today, all of them have reached crucial milestones and built relevant enterprise value, which we hope they will manage with wisdom and leadership.

NAPO PHARMACEUTICALS

Napo Pharmaceuticals Inc. is venture-backed company based in South San Francisco that focuses on the development and commercialization of proprietary pharmaceuticals for the global marketplace in collaboration with local partners. The company was founded in 2001 by Lisa Conte (a serial entrepreneur with an BA in Biochemistry from Dartmouth College and an MS in Physiology/Pharmacology from the University of California at San Diego, beyond an MBA from the Amos Tuck School, Dartmouth College).

The company's IP is based on a patent technology originally developed by Shaman Pharmaceuticals, Napo's precursor. The company strategy is to bring this IP from Phase 2 to the market, completing phases 2 and 3 and passing regulatory approval. To do that Napo initially raised 15 million dollars from private investors and angels, then an additional $22 million dollars in 2006 through an IPO in London and an additional 30 million in 2007–2008 (following the delisting decision). Well over half of the 85 million of capital raised went to implement clinical trials since the company ran close to one million simulations on its historical data. Napo also invested a lot of its cash in patent filings (in different countries) and manufacturing equipment. This was because the company wanted to enter Phase 3 trials with the compound ready for manufacturing and sales.

Napo's overall mission is to develop, manufacture, and distribute life-improving drugs on a global basis, mindful of risk management criteria and investment return.

Currently the company counts 24 employees and many important collaborating partners all over the world.

Main Product

The company's first product, Crofelemer (CRO-HIV) is a compound derived from the latex of Croton lecheri, a tree that grows along the Napo River in South America. It targets a symptom related to HIV/AIDS and the D-predominant irritable bowel syndrome (D-IBS). The patent and development work (through a Phase 2 trial) was acquired by Napo in 2001, after Shaman filed for bankruptcy.

THE BUSINESS MODEL FOR THE CLINICAL PHASE

Running preclinical and early clinical activities would have required too many resources. This explains the decision to acquire the IP from another company (BUY-IN) and focus the company's effort on completing Phase 2 and—thereafter—moving into Phase 3 and registration. Phase 2 activities are highly labor and technology intensive. Therefore there were 100 people initially working for Napo in South San Francisco, and the majority of them were concentrated on optimization of the preclinical work, supporting clinical trials, assessing quality, and managing Phase 2-related activities.

After completion of Phase 2 in 2006, the company focused on supporting the activities related to Phase 3 and Pilot Manufacturing. Napo decided to partner with research organizations, although maintaining support activities in-house. Consequently the team has been downsized. This is represented in the MODUS part of *The Milestone Bridge* that highlights for Phase 3 a high brain and technology intensity but a lower labor intensity than in Phase 2.

In parallel with clinical activities, Napo started to create a global network of partners.

The goal of business development activities was to find partners responsible for drug approval, sales, and marketing in their own countries. "The value of these partnerships is the speed with which we can do things because we are partnering with someone that knows the local environment and culture" says Lisa Conte. "We know our product. We look for local companies in particular territories."

Specifically, they partnered with an Indian company based in Mumbai (Glenmark Pharmaceuticals Ltd.). The vision was to have central manufacturing in India managed by Glenmark and different partners responsible for drug approval and sales in the various regions/countries. Consequently, activities related to Pilot Manufacturing and Tech Transfer to partners have been assuming growing relevance.

ACTIVITY LIST	FOCUS	LOCUS		MODUS		
				Brain intensity	Technology intensity	Labor intensity
Preclinical		California	BUY-IN	8	7	6
Phase 1		California	BUY-IN	6	7	6
Phase 2	5	California	IN		2	4
Phase 3	10	California	IN	7	5	3
Pilot Manufacturing / Tech Transfer	7	California	IN	5	5	6
Registration		California	JOINT		1	6
Business Development	4	California	IN		2	6
Manufacturing		TBD	TBD	1	5	6
Sales		TBD	TBD	3	2	

Figure 6.1 *The Milestone Bridge:* Napo Pharmaceuticals (2001–2010)
Source: Authors' elaboration

TODAY: A GLOBAL NETWORK OF PARTNERS

Having completed Phase 3 and Tech Transfer to Glenmark, Napo's FOCUS is currently on completing the registration process and starting manufacturing and sales. The MODUS decision is to work closely with partners. Specifically, Napo licensed its product to:

- Glenmark for production and distribution of Crofelemer in India and other 145 developing countries.
- Salix Pharmaceuticals, based in Raleigh (North Carolina), for sales in the US, Europe, and Japan.
- Luye Pharma Group, based in Yantai, for distribution in China.

All partners are supposed to be responsible for the regulatory approval in the countries where they have sales exclusivity.

In December 2012 Salix got the approval from the U.S. Food and Drug Administration for one indication (Fulyzaq/Crofelemer to relieve symptoms of diarrhea in HIV/AIDS patients taking antiretroviral therapy) on the US market. The approval process in other countries and for other indications is ongoing.

The current business model is based on partnerships (JOINT) with companies all over the world. The LOCUS is almost global since activities are performed through partners in the US, India, China, and Europe. The main FOCUS is on Business Development ("We don't do sales, we do development and coordinate partners," as Lisa often says) and support of the regulatory approval, while some internal resources are still involved in preclinical and clinical research to identify new products and indications.

ACTIVITY LIST	FOCUS	LOCUS		MODUS Brain Intensity	Technology Intensity	Labor Intensity
Preclinical	2	California	BUY-IN	10		4
Phase 1	3	California	BUY-IN	8	7	2
Phase 2	3	California	IN	4	7	8
Phase 3	2	California	IN	2	2	1
Pilot Manufacturing/Tech Transfer	5	California	IN	5	5	8
Registration	8	US, India, Europe, Japan, China	JOINT	6	1	6
Business Development		California	IN	3	2	6
Manufacturing	4	India	OUT	3	5	6
Sales						
	6	US	JOINT	3	2	8
	6	India	JOINT	3	2	8
	6	Europe	JOINT	3	2	8
	6	Japan	JOINT	3	2	8
	6	China	JOINT	3	2	8

Figure 6.2   The Milestone Bridge: Napo Pharmaceuticals (Current)
Source: Authors' elaboration

ARETA

Areta International was founded by Maria Luisa Nolli in autumn 1999 as a spin-off of Cell Biology and Immunology Laboratories of Lepetit Research Center, part of multinational group of Dow Pharma (Merrell Dow, Marion Merrell Dow, and Hoechst Marion Roussel). Maria Luisa holds a degree in Biological Sciences from the University of Pavia and a Ph.D. from the Université Libre de Bruxelles. She has more than 20 years' industrial experience as a scientist and group leader working at the Lepetit Research Center.

Areta's goal was to turn the excellent basic research base of Lepetit Research Center into new potential biodrugs. The business insight and entrepreneurial initiative of Areta's management team, combined with in-depth scientific expertise, have led the company to become a market leader in providing customized research and development projects and R&D contract manufacturing.

Areta employs 20 highly skilled people (90% hold a master's degree in science and 50% a Ph.D.), 70% of whom are women. Currently, revenue is around 3 million euros, 30% of which was generated from foreign customers.

Core Product/Technology

Areta's technological platform is based on methods developed in-house and efficient techniques for the generation of new monoclonal antibodies (starting from any kind of antigen) and the production of dedicated batches of purified monoclonal antibodies, recombinant proteins, and cells (with special attention paid to the adaptation of all cell types to the most appropriate serum-free medium).

FROM 2000 TO 2003: EXPLOITING THE R&D BASE

Areta was founded as a research and development company for biotechnological products, leveraging its experience gained in the generation of monoclonal and polyclonal antibodies and ELISA (enzyme-linked immunosorbent assay) tests.

In Figure 6.3 below, you can see the initial full ACTIVITY LIST at the beginning of the company life cycle. The dominant FOCUS is on R&D, Quality Control, and Quality and Regulatory System, activities characterized by a high brain and technology intensity.

This strategic positioning of Areta has been supported by its commitment to continuous investment in R&D. Since its foundation, Areta dedicates about 30% of its budget to participating in funded research projects, both at national and EU level. The high qualification of its team is another key enabler.

This approach allowed the company to develop a unique know-how in the field of biodrugs and diagnostic solutions. The result of this continuous investment is a portfolio of first-class collaborations with academia, research institutes, IRCCS (scientific institutes for research and hospitalization), and Italian and foreign companies, with which Areta has been cooperating in several funded projects.

Company activities are spread between Lombardy (Gerenzano, close to Varese) and Tuscany (Siena, within the local life science park). The main partners (MolMed, a biotechnology public company focused on research, development, and clinical validation of novel anti-tumour therapies, and Toma Advanced Biomedical Assays) are located in Lombardy, quite close to the Gerenzano company site.

ACTIVITY LIST	FOCUS	LOCUS	MODUS		
			Brain intensity	Technology intensity	Labor intensity
R&D					
1-Product Development and Purification	10	Italy	IN	8	9	6
2-Manufacturing	9	Italy	IN	5	8	7
Quality Control	6	Italy	IN/OUT	8	7	4
Quality and Regulatory System	6	Italy	JOINT	6	3	7
Business Development	3	Italy	IN	8	2	3

Figure 6.3   The Milestone Bridge: Areta (2000–2003)
Source: Authors' elaboration

2004–2009: THE STRATEGY SHIFT

Nine years ago, Areta started its GMP facility, authorized by AIFA (Italian Medicines Agency), to produce and release biopharmaceuticals for clinical trials.

In 2004, the company was authorized to produce cells for cell therapy, and in 2009 the authorization was extended to become multipurpose, enabling the company to manufacture different types of biodrugs (cells, proteins, immunological products, and plasmids for DNA-based vaccines), as well as to execute aseptic filling, final lyophilisation, and release of finished products. The Gerenzano facility has been expanded and renewed.

Therefore, Areta has been able to work at all stages of development of biodrugs and products for innovative therapies, offering its services in the field of process optimization, manufacturing, aseptic filling, development of new analytical methods, quality control testing, and batch release and stability studies, while also offering highly qualified consultancy for quality and regulatory requirements. The facility (and the company's know-how) allowed Areta to simultaneously manage projects that differ one from the other, both in terms of product categories and quantity of the finished product. Areta processes are simple, GMP compliant, highly personalized and easily scalable—according to the customer needs.

The authorization represented a relevant change in the Areta's strategy (it became an R&D and GMP contract manufacturer, from process development to support of clinical trials) and consequently in business model.

As you can see from Figure 6.4, the main FOCUS of the company during this phase is on GMP-related activities. Construction of cell lines is highly intensive in terms of technology and brain, while the production of cell banks is a medium technology and high labour intensive activity. The FOCUS on R&D and quality activities also remains high during this phase.

In 2007, Areta spun-off part of its competences into HO.p.e., a new company created together with a group of pharmacologists of the University of Milan with strong expertise in studies on the control of the hypophysis hormone secretion and HGH (human growth hormone). The new company's mission is to develop diagnostic kits for detection of HGH and related molecules in biological fluids of athletes. Areta brings to the company the expertise of monoclonal antibodies generation and production and ELISA tests set up. HO.p.e. is co-located at Areta's headquarter in Gerenzano.

ACTIVITY LIST	FOCUS	LOCUS		MODUS		
				Brain intensity	Technology intensity	Labor intensity
R&D						
1-Product Development and Purification	10	Italy	IN	9	6	6
2-Manufacturing	4	Italy	IN	5	8	7
GMP						
GMP Construction of Cell Lines for Biologists	10	Italy	IN	4	10	2
GMP Production of Cell Banks for Cell Therapies	10	Italy	IN	2	4	5
GMP Production of Cell Banks for Clients	30	Italy	IN	3	4	6
Quality Control	8	Italy	IN/OUT	4	7	4
Quality and Regulatory System	6	Italy	JOINT	6	3	7
Fill & Finishing	3	Italy	IN/OUT	5	8	7
Line Batches Release	6	Italy	JOINT	7		
Business Development	3	Italy	IN	8	2	4

Figure 6.4 The Milestone Bridge: Areta (2004–2009)

Source: Authors' elaboration

TODAY: NEVER CHANGE A WINNING BUSINESS MODEL!

In the last years Areta's business model hasn't changed that much. This is not due to the lack of "proactiveness" of the firm, but rather because the business model adopted since 2004 worked effectively. And still does today.

But there are also some small changes in the business model that need to be highlighted.

Areta modified its LOCUS, by closing the unit located in Siena devoted to GMP production of recombinant proteins and DNA. This decision was made in order to optimize the company's resource allocation.

At the same time it expanded the network of partners internationally, entering into R&D collaborative agreements with some companies such as the following:

- Abmedix, a Canadian company mainly involved in licensing and development of new products.
- Accuro Biologics, a UK company providing expert services in antibody engineering.
- NeuroZone, an Italian service company for high content cell-based assays in the neuroscience/stem cell drug market.

Notwithstanding, Areta continues with an in-house R&D strategy (IN), conceiving alliances merely as a source of further innovation.

Other changes include the introduction of a Project Management activity to better support customer projects and ensure the respect of deadlines.

The role of the Business Development function has also been increased, in line with the company's growth in terms of clients and partners.

Activities related to construction of cell lines for biologists (located in Siena) have been ceased, along with the line batches release.

By analyzing the company's business model changes over the time, it becomes clear that the main distinguisher of Areta's positioning is its attention and commitment to quality and R&D. These activities are the main pillars for the company's growth and international expansion.

ACTIVITY LIST	FOCUS	LOCUS	MODUS		
			Brain intensity	Technology intensity	Labor intensity
R&D					
1-Product Development and Purification	10	Italy, Canada, UK	IN/JOINT	3	5	6
2-Manufacturing	9	Italy	IN	5	4	7
GMP					
GMP Construction of Cell Lines for Biologists	10	Italy	IN	4	10	2
GMP Production of Cell Banks for Cell Therapies	10	Italy	IN	6	6	6
Quality Control	8	Italy, Europe	IN/OUT	3	6	8
Quality and Regulatory System	8	Europe	JOINT	3	3	8
Fill & Finishing	8	Italy	IN/OUT	5	4	8
Line Batches Release	6	Italy	JOINT	7		
Business Development	8	Italy	IN	10	2	6
Project Management	7	Italy	IN	9	3	5

Figure 6.5   The Milestone Bridge: Areta (Current)
Source: Author's elaboration

MOLMED

MolMed S.p.A. (full name: Molecular Medicine) is a medical bio-technology company founded in 1996 as a joint venture between Boehringer Mannheim and the San Raffaele Biomedical Science Park. The company currently employs 82 people, and its primary focus is the development of novel and superior therapies to prevent cancer.

MolMed is located in Milan (Italy), within the San Raffaele Biomedical Science Park, which includes the renowned Research Hospital and Scientific Institute, along with several biotechnology companies and a private university.

After an initial period as a cell therapy service provider, in 2000 MolMed reorganized its internal structure and evolved into a bio-pharmaceutical company. In 2004, three major Italian private investors (Fininvest, Herule Finance—now H-Equity—and La Leonardo Finanziaria—now Delfin S.à.r.l.) entered as new shareholders, generating a capital increase of 20 million euros. In 2006 and 2007 the capital was further increased by 26 million euros. In 2008 Mol-Med went public on the Milan Stock Exchange with 56 million euro gross proceeds.

Company Core Technologies

MolMed is currently working on two different main technologies: NGR-h TNF and TK.

NGR-h TNF is a novel biological protein created for the treatment of solid tumors. NGR-h is supposed to be able to individuate specific body areas affected by cancer and, thanks to a targeted action, isolate cancers causing death of cells.

TK is a cell therapy enabling safe haploidentical haematopoietic stem cell transplantation (HSCT) for the treatment of hematological malignancies, and it is particularly indicated to treat leukemia. Mol-Med offers TK under the form of a sophisticated clinical service (both highly capital and labor intensive) that needs to be customized to each specific patient.

Both these technologies are facing Phase 3 clinical trial, and the company has just entered the registration process both in the US (FDA) and Europe (EPO).

TODAY: TWO CORE TECHNOLOGIES WITH TWO DIFFERENT BUSINESS MODELS

From 2000 onwards, MolMed has evolved into a biopharmaceutical development company, with a primary focus on novel cancer therapies. Today, MolMed is a mature company covering the whole activity value chain, from discovery to clinical activities. MolMed's strategy for growth is based on four key points:

- Focus on oncology indications that require new therapy options.
- Efficient improvement of clinical and pharmaceutical development, independently or with partners.
- In-house GMP-based manufacturing of cell and gene therapy products.
- Diversified the product portfolio to create value.

The two main technologies, NGR-h TNF and DK, are very different in nature: the first is a product, the latter is a service. Therefore, MolMed chose to implement two different business models (this is quite typical pattern for companies with diversified products). This way, MolMed is able to maximize the value of both technologies since they have different target market and characteristics.

NGR-H TNF: *VIRTUAL BIOTECH*

NGH-h TNF has up to seven therapeutic applications for different solid cancer types. In order to exploit this potential, MolMed decides to concentrate the majority of its human resources on research activities. The goal here is to find additional explanation for the mechanism of action, in order to accelerate the regulatory process. Apart from R&D and preclinical trials—that have been done in-house together with the San Raffaele Research Hospital—MolMed has always benefited from external partners (JOINT).

Part of Phase 1 and Phase 2 are carried out in collaboration with Eurogentec, a Belgium-based company. These activities are brain and technology intensive, and MolMed's researchers play the role of process activators, supervisors, and result testers.

Also Pilot Manufacturing activities are considered strategic. These activities have been partially externalized to gather additional know-how and competences. The MODUS decisions for Phase 3 (activities to be outsourced and selection of partners) has been completed based on the recommendations of four expert consultants (one for each sub-activity constitutive of Phase 3). Partners for manufacturing activities are located all over the world. Among others, MolMed chose a UK company (Avecia Biologics) with specific contract manufacturing skills and outsourced the activities related to analytical methods to three different US laboratories.

Thanks to this "virtual" collaborative network, MolMed is able to create the conditions for advancing the NGR-h TNF protein all along the pipeline. A legal firm in Milan has been engaged in order to go through the first steps of the approval process. Manufacturing and sales are not yet activated at this stage but the management is already working for identifying the best options in terms of LOCUS and MODUS.

ACTIVITY LIST	FOCUS	LOCUS		MODUS		
				Brain intensity	Technology intensity	Labor intensity
R&D/Preclinical	3	Italy	JOINT	8	7	6
Phase 1	3	Italy, Belgium	JOINT	7	7	3
Phase 2	3	Italy, Belgium	JOINT	7	7	3
Phase 3 + Pilot Manufacturing						
1. Manufacturing	7	UK	JOINT	2	7	7
2. Analytical methods	8	US	JOINT	8	6	6
3. Fill & Finishing	5	Italy	OUT	6	3	6
4. Toxicology + Clinical Trials + Testing	10	UK	OUT	8	8	8
Regulatory	2	Italy	JOINT	8	3	6
Business Development	3	Italy	IN	9	3	8
Registration	6	TBD	TBD	6	1	
Manufacturing	4	TBD	TBD	5	8	8
Sales	5	Italy, Japan	JOINT	2	3	5

Figure 6.6   *The Milestone Bridge:* MolMed—NGR-h TNF (Current)

Source: Authors' elaboration

TK: BUSINESS MODEL FOR HIGH-TECH SERVICE PROVIDERS

TK is a personalized therapy that makes possible marrow transplants to patients who do not have a fully compatible donor. The therapy involves the genetic modification of a donor's marrow cells plus accurate control and safety tests. The modified cells are then sent back to the clinic or hospital of origin and transplanted into the patient. In this case, the whole technology has been developed through MolMed's in-house GMP facility.

In order to take TK through Phase 1 and Phase 2, a specific reagent was needed. MolMed started a supply relationship with a Japanese company (Takara Bio). The supply relationship turned into a partnership since Takara started also to perform TK clinical trials in its own facility.

The cell modification/manufacturing process is high tech and, brain and labor intensive, since the procedures cannot be automated and require around 10 days for each patient/case.

Now the current FOCUS is on Phase 3. Although Phase 1 and Phase 2 are now formally completed, some effort is still required for the formalization and diffusion of the results within the clinical medicine environment; this activity would speed up Phase 3 trials because it would increase the acceptability of procedures.

MolMed engaged a legal firm in Milan in order to start to approach the regulatory process.

As the services will be ready to be fully commercialized, logistic activities will become relevant. The MODUS and LOCUS for such activities still need to be finalized, but it is anticipated that it will absorb also internal resources, although part of the services will be outsourced.

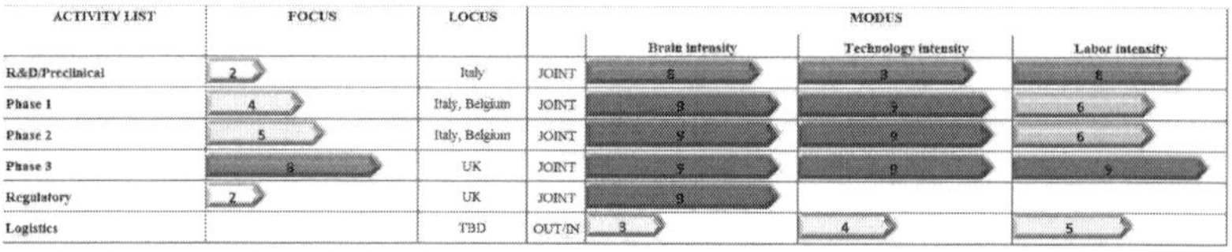

Figure 6.7   The Milestone Bridge: MolMed—TK (Current)
Source: Authors' elaboration

NICOX

Nicox S.A. is a French pharmaceutical company that was conceived in Italy (Milan)[2] in 1996, by an Italian-American team (Michele Garufi, Piero Del Soldato, and Elizabeth "Betsy" Robinson) with strong technical background and prior experience in the pharmaceutical industry. The company was built around its proprietary nitric oxide (NO)-donating research platform.

Nicox developed naproxcinod, a CINOD (Cyclooxygenase-Inhibiting Nitric Oxide-Donating) anti-inflammatory candidate for the relief of the signs and symptoms of osteoarthritis, from preclinical to regulatory submission. In line with its strategic re-positioning in the ophthalmic space, Nicox's research platform is now focused on ocular diseases where NO has been shown to play an important role.

Nicox was funded by a venture capital investors' consortium including Apax France, Sofinnova, Auriga, and HealthCap. The company went public in 1999 on the Nouveau Marché of the Paris Stock Exchange raising 33 million euros.

Nicox is headquartered in Sophia Antipolis (Nice, France). North American operations are based in Dallas (Texas, United States) and research capabilities are based in Bresso (Milan, Italy). Nicox employs currently around 40 people worldwide.

Main Product/Technology

Nitric oxide (NO) is an endogenous cell-signaling molecule of fundamental importance in physiology due to its chemical properties that make it an intra-cellular and intercellular chemical messenger. Over the years, Nicox has developed a world-leading position in the discovery, synthesis, and evaluation of NO-donating compounds for therapeutic use. The company has several molecules in the pipeline, and its lead compound is an anti-inflammatory drug (naproxcinod) that belongs to the CINOD (COX-inhibiting nitric oxide donator) class for the treatment of osteoarthritis.

THE SEED PHASE: THE MOVE FROM ITALY TO FRANCE

At the very beginning, the main idea behind Nicox was to create new drugs able to release nitric oxide into the tissues and bloodstream in a sustained and controlled manner. The initial plan was to combine two existing drugs, in particular the naproxen and nitric oxide, into a new molecule with the same structure of naproxen.

In order to start the business, the founders' team needed funding, but it was difficult to find venture capital in their home country at the end of the 1990s. So they started looking for financial partners abroad. Finally, after several months spent pitching to investors all over the world, some French investors (Sofinnova Partners) showed interest in the project. With 2.5 million dollars of initial funding, Nicox S.A. was created in 1998 in France. The company's headquarter was originally located in Paris and, immediately thereafter, moved to the technology park of Sophia Antipolis, close to Nice.

GOING PUBLIC: THE BUSINESS MODEL IN THE LATE NINETIES

During the 1990s, Nicox's main goal was to develop the NO-NSAIDs (nitric oxide-releasing nonsteroidal anti-inflammatory drugs), a novel class of drugs (HCT and NCX families) with broad therapeutic applications and superior therapeutic/risk ratio in comparison with existing therapies for inflammation, pain, thrombosis, urological disorders, and gastroenterological disorders.

The main activities characterizing this phase of Nicox business life were Basic Research, Preclinical, Phase 1 and Phase 2 development plus Patenting. The main FOCUS was on Research. The company's activities were mostly located in France. Dominant MODUS was through partnerships (JOINT), except for preclinical activities, which were performed internally.

HCT 1026 was the lead compound. It successfully passed Phase 1 clinical trials at the University of Nottingham (UK) in 1997 and received notice of allowance from the European Patent Office. Nicox filed a series of patent applications world-wide, providing broad proprietary coverage of its nitrocox- inhibitor drug candidates.

Due to the lack of its own research facility, basic research was initially conducted jointly with various universities in France. For the same reason, initial preclinical and clinical activities were also done in collaboration with third parties (JOINT).

In 1998 Nicox entered a licensing agreement with Astra AB, a Swedish multinational pharmaceutical company, which gained an exclusive worldwide license—with the exclusion of Japan—to develop and market NO-NSAIDS in the areas of pain and inflammation. Nicox retained the rights to develop and market selected NO-NSAIDS in other therapeutic areas. In 1999 Nicox advanced HCT-1026 into Phase 2 (human clinical trials) for different indications, through partnerships with the University of Aberdeen (UK), the Institut Propara in Montpellier, and Hospital St. Jacques in Nantes (France).

In March 1998 the company entered into an exclusive research collaboration agreement with Bayer AG for NO-acetylsalisylic acid derivatives—NCX-4016 was the lead compound.

These strategic agreements (and the underlying royalty opportunities) contributed to increase Nicox's value and allowed the company to go public in France in 1999.

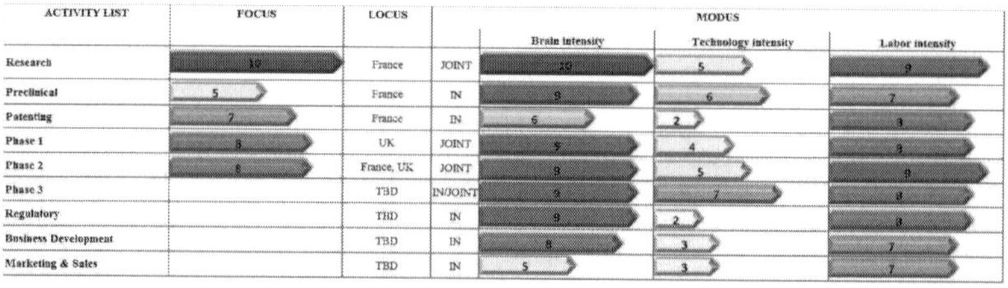

Figure 6.8   The Milestone Bridge: Nicox (1996–1999)
Source: Authors' elaboration

BUSINESS MODEL CHANGES IN THE PERIOD 2000–2009: LOCUS AND MODUS

The first decade of the new millennium was characterized by some important changes in the Nicox's business model, both in terms of LOCUS (expansion of the activity value chain to Italy and the US) and MODUS (growing internalization of activities). Also, the FOCUS progressively changed, shifting down from early clinical activities to Phase 3, Business Development and Marketing. But let's look at them one by one.

In 2001, all the research activities of the group were relocated to Italy (Bresso, north of Milan) where a fully owned subsidiary have been set up to run the pharmacology, chemistry, and pharmacokinetics laboratories. All preclinical and clinical trials were maintained in Sophia Antipolis (France). Thanks to the new subsidiary, Nicox was able to perform research in-house (IN), with a larger degree of autonomy from other institutions. The logic behind the decision to internalize research on Nitric oxide was to keep internally key strategic activities.

In 2003, the results of Phase 2 clinical trials of Naproxcinod (a NO-NSAID compound) did not fulfil the strategic criteria identified by Astra Zeneca, which decided to discontinue its partnership with Nicox. Nicox's share price dropped by 80%. As a consequence, the company was forced to implement some RIFs (reduction in force) and started the research of new partners for the development of compounds of the CINOD class. After a few months, a preliminary research agreement with Merck and a strategic agreement with Pfizer were established. Nicox share price went up again. In 2005, Naproxcinod entered the Phase 3 trial, which was completed in 2008.

In 2007, Nicox opened a subsidiary in the United States (Nicox Inc.) and in 2009 filed Naproxcinod for regulatory approval by both the FDA and the European Medicines Agency. Nicox Inc.'s main FOCUS was to prepare the commercialization of Naproxcinod in the Unites States. All of the commercial and the marketing activities were performed in-house (IN).

ACTIVITY LIST	FOCUS	LOCUS		MODUS		
				Brain intensity	Technology intensity	Labor intensity
Research	10	Italy	IN	10	10	3
Preclinical	3	France, Spain	JOINT	7	6	5
Phase 1	1	France	IN	6	4	6
Phase 2	9	US, France, Italy, Switzerland, Canada	IN/JOINT	4	7	8
Phase 3	8	Us, France	IN/JOINT	3	7	8
Regulatory	6	France	IN	3	2	8
Business Development	4	France, US	IN	4	3	8
Marketing & Sales	5	US	IN	5	3	7

Figure 6.9   The Milestone Bridge: Nicox (2000–2009)
Source: Authors' elaboration

2010: THE STRATEGY CHANGE

Regulatory submissions for Naproxcinod were made in the United States and in Europe at the end of 2009. In the United States, the FDA communicated in July 2010 that it did not approve the application submitted by Nicox. As a consequence, Nicox decided to withdraw its application and was forced to change its corporate strategy. The plan was to "pivot" from a biotech platform company—that develops and licenses news compounds to pharmaceutical companies—into a fully integrated biopharmaceutical company that markets its own products (FIPCO using the terminology we introduced in Chapter One). Contextually, Nicox modified its scientific specialization, focusing its research platform on ocular diseases. Another important organizational change was represented by the appointment of a new Executive Vice President and General Manager with an extensive knowledge of the ophthalmology market in the United States. The business objective was to establish its own commercial infrastructure for marketing ophthalmic products and solutions in the US and in the major European countries.

The first step to realize the new strategy was taken in March 2012, when Nicox acquired 11.8% of the shares of Altacor, a privately held ophthalmology company located in the United Kingdom (BUY-IN). Additionally, the company signed in June 2012 a world-wide in-licensing agreement with Rapid Pathogen Screening with the goal to market AdenoPlus—a test for the differential diagnosis of acute conjunctivitis—to eye care practitioners.

The company's pipeline today includes latanoprostene bunod, a novel drug-candidate based on Nicox's proprietary nitric oxide (NO)-donating research platform, developed in collaboration with a US company (Bausch + Lomb), for the treatment of glaucoma and ocular hypertension. Following positive Phase 2b results, Bausch + Lomb initiated a Phase 3 program for latanoprostene bunod in January 2013.

In March 2013, Nicox entered into an exclusive supply and distribution agreement for a range of eye care products with an undisclosed private European pharmaceutical company specializing in ophthalmics. This new range of products has been developed for a major therapeutic class with a differentiated formulation. Nicox expects to launch these products from late 2013 onwards.

The change of strategy has obviously impacted the business model. The FOCUS is now on Phase 3, Marketing and Sales (acquisition and partnerships, combined with its research background, allowed Nicox to skip the preclinical and early clinical phases). In terms of MODUS, the current business model is centred around internal research capabilities (IN) and industry partnerships (the role of partnership has been revaluated to reduce the time to market) (JOINT). In terms of LOCUS, the US is getting a growing relevance, while the

Italian research subsidiary remains focused in the ophthalmic field to identify new lead compounds for various ocular disorders.

ACTIVITY LIST	FOCUS	LOCUS		MODUS		
				Brain intensity	Technology intensity	Labor intensity
Research	7	Italy	IN	10	10	2
Preclinical	4	France, Spain	JOINT	7	6	5
Phase 1	2	France	IN	6	4	6
Phase 2	2	France	IN	9	7	9
Phase 3	7	US, France	IN/JOINT	9	7	9
Regulatory	8	France	IN	5	2	4
Business Development	10	US, Europe	IN/JOINT	8	3	7
Marketing & Sales	5	US, Europe	IN/JOINT	5	3	7

Figure 6.10   The Milestone Bridge: Nicox (Current)
Source: Author's elaboration

QUIPU

Quipu is a spin-off company of the Italian National Research Council (CNR) and the University of Pisa. The company's IP is based on patent technology from the Italian National Research Council. The mission of Quipu is to provide products and services in the high-tech diagnostic and preventive medicine field. Specially, the core businesses are systems and techniques for assessing early markers of cardiovascular risk by image/signal processing.

The company is located in the Research Area of Pisa (Tuscany, Italy), and the team is composed of 4 people, supported by 3 scientific advisors.

Main Product/Technology

Quipu's main product is the Cardiovascular (CV) Suite, a family of software products for non-invasive assessment of early markers of cardiovascular risk. The CV Suite is used in conjunction with ultrasound equipment that can measure the morphology and function of peripheral vessels (brachial artery by assessing the endothelial function) and central arteries (carotid artery by assessing its thickness and elasticity).

THE START-UP PHASE

Quipu began its activity in late 2010 as three young Italian researchers with a strong entrepreneurial attitude (Elisabetta Bianchini, Francesco

Faita, and Vincenzo Gemignani) decided to start a new venture to exploit a prototype technology developed at the University of Pisa and CRN.

Following *The Milestone Bridge* approach, they identified the milestones and the list of activities required to bring the first prototype software to the market.

The first milestone was to "build" the software product and get the scientific validation of its efficacy. The Cardiovascular Suite is a highly innovative product and its validation needs the collaboration and support of specialists and doctors particularly prone to innovation and research. Its diffusion requires a sort of "cultural maturation"—i.e., to be adopted by opinion leaders confirming its efficacy and to be covered by scientific literature. During the initial year, Quipu decided to concentrate its main efforts on software development and validation of the methodology through epidemiological studies. Both activities are highly brain and technology intensive.

In parallel, Quipu was working to get the medical certification for Europe and the US (FDA) to be authorized to sell the software for diagnostic purpose.

R&D, preclinical, and clinical phases had already been completed (at University of Pisa and CNR) before starting the company.

Figure 6.11   The Milestone Bridge: Quipu (2010–2012)
Source: Authors' elaboration

TURNING RESEARCH INTO COMMERCIALIZATION

After having completed the methodology validation and software certification phase in March 2013 (just a few months beyond the targeted deadline), Quipu is currently focused on putting its Cardiovascular Suite to the market. Quipu addresses a niche market of world-wide research centers, hospitals, and firms with a strong orientation towards innovation. The product's target users are doctors who need a tool to get accurate and early diagnosis of the risk of cardiovascular diseases. The main competitors are two SMEs, one based in Australia and one in the US, which have similar solutions. The most important differentiators for the Cardiovascular Suite are usability and low cost.

Currently the main FOCUS of Quipu is on Marketing/Evangelization, Business Development/Sales, and Post-Sales activities.

In order to support the sales activities, Quipu has increased its presence on the Web. Promotion campaigns, and participation in events and scientific conferences are the leading tools for increasing product awareness and supporting its adoption.

In particular, there are two main business development actions the company is trying to develop. On the one hand, it is evaluating partnerships with ultrasound equipment producers, in order to explore new potential markets and product applications. On the other hand, Quipu is looking for extending its sales network to the US, through a sales agreement with a local hardware producer.

Sales activity is a mostly labor intensive activity, while post-sales support is not anticipated to require large numbers (though quite skilled employees will be needed).

The nature of the product calls for a diversification strategy aimed at developing new products and identifying new applications for diagnostic. Therefore the FOCUS on applied R&D activities remains high because it represents the lifeblood for further growth.

Quipu is also completing the process of corporate quality certification, which has been outsourced to an Italian consulting firm.

Overall, Quipu has been able to make real progress in just three years (a validated product on the market, the first revenue, etc.) by completing the targeted milestones and respecting the identified deadlines. The lesson learned from Quipu is that it is possible to succeed in your business in a very short period of time and without much external capital's help. All you need is to identify realistic milestones and deadlines and properly structure your activities, i.e., stay focused and select the most appropriate MODUS and LOCUS.

ACTIVITY LIST	FOCUS	LOCUS		MODUS		
				Brain intensity	Technology intensity	Labor intensity
R&D	3	Italy	IN	10	10	9
Preclinical/Clinical	1	Italy, UK, US, France	JOINT	10	6	5
Validation/Epidemiological Studies	2	Worldwide	OUT	10	4	6
Software Development Production	2	Italy	IN	5	7	9
Certification/Approval	1	Italy	OUT	6	7	8
Quality Certification	2	Italy	OUT	1	1	5
Marketing/Evangelization	9	Italy, Europe	JOINT	8	2	8
Business Development and Sales	9	Italy, Europe	JOINT	3	3	7
Post-Sales Support	4	TBD	TBD	6	7	4

Figure 6.12   The Milestone Bridge: Quipu (Current)

Source: Authors' elaboration

OXIGENE

OXiGENE is an international biopharmaceutical company developing a heterogeneous portfolio of innovative small molecule therapeutics designed to complement and enhance the effectiveness of existing cancer therapies.

The company is based in South San Francisco with a presence in Sweden (Stockholm and Lund). OXiGENE, Inc. oversees clinical trials, regulatory affairs, and product management in the US, while OXiGENE Europe AB (closed at the end of December 2003) coordinated investor relations activities and managed European clinical trials and regulatory affairs.

OXiGENE is listed on the NASDAQ Global Markets exchange. Until 2010, it had also been listed on the Stockholm Stock Exchange.

Although it has global reach, OXiGENE has currently only 22 employees, 13 of whom are engaged in research and development and monitoring of clinical trials.

The company strategy is to be a global "virtual firm," exploiting innovative technologies through a world-wide network of partners.

Main Product

Vascular Disrupting Agents, or VDAs, represent a new type of potential cancer therapy that works by collapsing the blood vessels inside of a tumor and "starving" the tumor from the inside. ZYBRESTAT (combretastatin-A4 phosphate / CA4P) is OXiGENE's lead VDA product candidate and is currently being evaluated in multiple clinical trials as a treatment for solid tumors. ZYBRESTAT exerts its anti-tumor effects through the well-validated therapeutic mechanism of tumor blood supply deprivation.

THE INITIAL PHASE: A MULTINATIONAL STARTUP FOCUSED ON RESEARCH AND EARLY CLINICAL ACTIVITIES

In 1972, Ronald Pero (Ph.D. in Biological Sciences from the University of Rhode Island and Post-doctorate at North Carolina State University) started his research in the US on the ability of cells to repair DNA.

In 1988, 16 years later, he founded OXiGENE in the US in order to develop his patents within DNA repair technology, both clinically and commercially. The company was financed by an American venture capital firm and, after five years, it was listed on the NASDAQ exchange.

In 1990 the Swedish Cancer Foundation financed a study on biological markers at the University of Lund. Living and working in Sweden,

Pero continued to run the company in the United States and opened a Swedish subsidiary in 1994, as OXiGENE went public on the Stockholm Stock Exchange (raising 10 million dollars).

Since its inception, OXiGENE positioned itself as a value-added layer between universities/research institutions and large pharmaceutical firms, picking up ideas from academia and developing through Phase 1 and Phase 2. In order to keep a flexible structure, most of the company's preclinical testing and clinical trials are subcontracted to universities and contract research organizations in the United States and Europe. This business model choice (MODUS) has enabled the company to file patents for important compounds since the beginning of the company's life while maintaining a lean infrastructure.

ACTIVITY LIST	FOCUS	LOCUS	MODUS		
			Brain intensity	Technology intensity	Labor intensity
Research	10	US, Sweden	IN/JOINT 10	9	8
Preclinical	6	Worldwide	OUT 6	6	5
Patenting	10	US, Sweden	OUT 1	2	8
Phase 1	2	Worldwide	OUT/JOINT 6	3	4
Phase 2	7	Worldwide	OUT/JOINT 5	3	4
Phase 3	6	Europe, US	OUT/JOINT 3	2	3
Business Development	4	US, Sweden	IN	5	
Marketing and Sales	TBD	TBD	TBD	TBD	TBD

Figure 6.13   The Milestone Bridge: OXiGENE (1988–1999)
Source: Authors' elaboration

EXPLOITING THE BUSINESS MODEL STRUCTURE

Being a "virtual firm" allowed OXiGENE to maintain a flexible cost structure, low burn rate, and a solid financial position. There were no plans for turning OXiGENE into a large pharmaceutical company. According to the top management vision, research firms like OXiGENE represent key partners for large pharmaceutical companies.

Therefore the company confirmed the initial business model structure, just adapting it to factor the progressive growing of the company (and its product pipeline) into maturity. More specifically, on the MODUS side, the main decisions were as follows:

- Continuing and enhancing R&D of their core technologies (IN).
- Identifying and acquiring additional relevant technologies (BUY-IN).
- Working with clinical research organizations (CROs) and universities for preclinical and early clinical development (OUT/JOINT).
- Partnering with large pharmaceutical companies for late clinical development and marketing/sales (OUT/JOINT).

The main business model change of this period refers to Patenting activities. Given the key importance of patents for the company, a patent office was set up in-house (IN). This way the company internalized the knowledge required for preparing and filing patents.

During these years, more than 75% of personnel was engaged in research activities with the task of coordinating and controlling the work performed by external partners.

In terms of LOCUS, business development activities continued to expand the international network of partners, both upstream (research and early clinical) and downstream (late clinical). At the time, OXiGENE contracted out research services from 16 universities/institutes (one in Canada, five in Europe, and ten in the US), with approximately over a hundred persons involved, although not on a full-time basis. Two key partners were the Wallenberg Laboratory at the University of Lund and the medical center at the Boston University. OXiGENE contributed to research projects and got options to buy the technologic outcomes.

ACTIVITY LIST	FOCUS	LOCUS		MODUS		
				Brain intensity	Technology intensity	Labor intensity
Research	10	US, Sweden	IN/JOINT	10	9	9
Preclinical	6	Europe, US	OUT	6	6	5
Patenting	10	US, Sweden	IN	8	2	9
Phase 1	7	Europe, US	OUT/JOINT	6	3	4
Phase 2	7	Europe, US	OUT/JOINT	5	3	4
Phase 3	6	Europe, US	OUT/JOINT	3	2	3
Business Development	10	US, Sweden	IN	10	5	10
Marketing and Sales		TBD	TBD	TBD	TBD	TBD

Figure 6.14   The Milestone Bridge: OXiGENE (2000–2010)
Source: Authors' elaboration

TODAY: A GLOBAL MISSION-BASED STRATEGY

OXiGENE's current FOCUS is to sell licenses to large pharmaceutical companies and cooperate with them in developing and marketing the products.

Rather than expand the in-house research and development activities, OXiGENE continues to rely on relationships and uses its own internal resources to initiate and control the collaborative agreements. Currently, it has agreements with a large number of institutions in the United States and abroad, such as:

- Baylor University, Waco, Texas
- UT Southwestern, Texas

- University of Florida
- University of Oxford, Oxford, United Kingdom
- University College London, London, United Kingdom
- National Cancer Institute (NCI), United States
- Institute for Cancer Research UK.

The MODUS decision centered on partnership (JOINT) is therefore enhanced. Some examples of collaborative agreements can help to understand the OXiGENE business model. OXiGENE has secured an exclusive, world-wide technology license from Arizona State University for commercial development, use, and sale of products or services covered by certain patent rights to particular molecules (including, among others, OXi4503, one of OXiGENE's main products). In line with the company's strategy, this agreement grants OXiGENE the right to sublicense the technologies. The same counts for anther exclusive license from Baylor University, according to which OXiGENE is entitled to file, prosecute, and maintain patent applications on licensed products. The license from Bristol-Myers Squibb (BMS) grants OXiGENE the right to develop, use, and sell products or services covered by certain patent rights to particular molecules (including, among others, ZYBRESTAT). OXiGENE has also the right to grant sublicenses. OXiGENE bears the costs of preparing, filing, prosecuting, and maintaining all patent applications under this license, while BMS is entitled to low-single-digit royalty payments for all commercial sales plus any remuneration OXiGENE receives for sale of ZYBRESTAT.

The ambition of OXiGENE is to keep the focus in the area of cancer and ophthalmology, while maintaining a large technologies portfolio in order to diversify risks. The MODUS choice of leveraging partnership with third parties allows the company to keep a flexible and low-burning cost structure. In addition, multi-location remains a key factor for success. Having points of presence in the most important research clusters—such as the Silicon Valley and Medical Valley—allows the company to access critical technologies and stay on the cutting edge of innovation in its areas of specialization.

ACTIVITY LIST	FOCUS	LOCUS		MODUS		
				Brain intensity	Technology Intensity	Labor intensity
Research	5	US, Sweden	IN/JOINT	10	8	3
Preclinical	5	Europe, US	OUT/JOINT	6	6	5
Patenting	10	US, Sweden	IN	6	2	9
Phase 1	5	Europe, US	OUT/JOINT	6	3	4
Phase 2	5	Europe, US	OUT/JOINT	5	3	4
Phase 3	7	Europe, US	OUT/JOINT	3	2	3
Business Development	10	US, Sweden	IN	10	5	10
Marketing and Sales	8	Europe, US	OUT	3	3	3

Figure 6.15   The Milestone Bridge: OXiGENE (Current)

Source: Authors' elaboration

NEUROSILICON

Neurosilicon is a life science company advancing healthcare-related research through enabling rapid, non-invasive, targeted excitation of excitable cells. Neurosilicon was founded in Canada in March of 2005 and is a spin-off of the University of Calgary. The company is privately held and has been boot-strapped with the support of some angel investors and grant funds. The founding team is composed of six Ph.D. life science researchers and engineers with experience in technology commercialization. The company currently works with partners in North America and Europe.

Neurosilicon's strategy is to enter the market through positioning the technology as an academic life science research tool and thereafter target a broader commercialization into the larger industrial market. This allows the company to leverage the founders' experience, expertise, and reputation in academic research and the relatively lower barrier to entry into the academic research market.

The Core Technology

The company's core technology is the Photoconductive Stimulation Device (PSD) that enables neuroscience researchers and pharmaceutical technicians to depolarize dissociated neurons non-invasively and in a highly targeted manner. PSD is based on the application of a well-known physical phenomenon called photoconduction. Photoconductive stimulation is a technique that allows the rapid, non-invasive depolarization of excitable cells, such as neurons. It can be used to induce action potentials in neurons grown in culture, reproducing a user defined activity pattern. Cells are grown on silicon wafers in industry-standard 24 well plates, and then mounted in a reusable dish for live observation under a microscope.

THE BEGINNING

The company's intellectual property portfolio covered a broad area of developmental and application processes. The initial goal for Neurosilicon was to apply its core technology towards the development of neuro-centered medical devices suitable for transplantation. Specifically, they aimed at creating a new class of transplantable medical devices that would serve to reintegrate degenerated and/or damaged neuronal tissue and thus restore lost nervous system functions.

The business model in the first years was focused on R&D and Product Development. These activities are extremely brain and technology intensive. Access to academic laboratories and other resources served to minimize initial capital expenditures. Additionally, the research highly benefited from contributions from several universities and institutions all over the world. Therefore, in terms of LOCUS, Neurosilicon is an international network, with Calgary as a fulcrum.

In parallel to research and product development, growing attention has been dedicated to the development and refinement of the early production line for PSD.

For Neurosilicon, the challenge moving forward—quite typical for most of the academic spin-offs and startup companies with a prevalent scientific and technical background (Onetti et al., 2009)—was how to successfully commercialize the technology and its application. Thus, an initial strategy was developed by the company to continue research and development of future therapeutic applications for its technology, while developing research applications/products for immediate commercialization in the area of cell research.

ACTIVITY LIST	FOCUS	LOCUS		MODUS		
				Brain intensity	Technology intensity	Labor intensity
R&D	6	Canada, US	IN/JOINT	9	8	7
Product Development	7	Canada	IN	5	8	5
(Pilot) Manufacturing	5	Canada	IN	7	6	5
Marketing		TBD	TBD	TBD	TBD	TBD
Sales		TBD	TBD	TBD	TBD	TBD
Business Development		TBD	TBD	TBD	TBD	TBD
Post-sales		TBD	TBD	TBD	TBD	TBD

Figure 6.16　The Milestone Bridge: Neurosilicon (2005–2010)
Source: Authors' elaboration

MODELING THE SALES INFRASTRUCTURE

Completed the development of the Photoconductive Stimulation Device (PSD), the next identified milestone for Neurosilicon was to collect some market validation (i.e., early-adopter traction and sales revenue) required to target a large financing round. Neurosilicon's strategic decision was to pursue the academic research market first. A direct entry into the larger industrial market would have required a bigger Financial Prerequisite. At this stage—without a solid track record of results—going for a large financing round would have been challenging.

Consistently, the main FOCUS of the current Neurosilicon's business model is on Marketing and Sales activities. Specifically, Neurosilicon is working to set up the marketing and sales infrastructure that would enable and support the commercialization of PSD into the life science academic research market.

In terms of MODUS, Neurosilicon has opted for an external sales structure (OUT): the plan is to recruit researchers (typically MS/Ph.D.-level scientists) in key regions both in the US and Canada to serve as the local company's sale representatives. Outside sales representatives are supported through virtual connectivity tools and ongoing training/coaching. This model is characterized by high intensity for brain, technology, and labor. By "virtualizing" it, Neurosilicon was able to provide a quite widespread sales presence while keeping fixed sales expenses low.

In parallel to the virtual sales team, Neurosilicon has been developing strategic relationships with reseller partners both in the United States and Europe. This Business Development effort is aimed at marketing the PSD with complementary technologies and leveraging the partners' distribution channels.

On the Marketing side, the main efforts have been addressed to increase Neurosilicon's product visibility in the life science academic research arena by leveraging the name recognition of the founders in the area of neuroscience. So, the marketing actions have been focused mainly on peer-reviewed academic publications that highlighted the application of the PSD technology. Furthermore, some traditional approaches such as attending scientific meetings and conferences have been adopted to reach potential leads and increase Neurosilicon's overall company visibility. Additionally, digital and print materials describing the product's value proposition and capabilities (ease of use and rapid implementation, low costs) were also prepared.

In parallel, Neurosilicon is to a greater extent focusing on Manufacturing activities. The manufacturing processes needed to be structured to be able either to cope with a modest demand for the product in the initial period and to be ready to scale-up. Therefore it has been decided to maintain manufacturing in-house during the first phase. This way Neurosilicon can get optimization feedback from early sales and beta testing of the product that could be used for streamlining the production process. For the future—as the product will be commercialized on the industrial market—manufacturing outsourcing will be considered.

The combined virtual sales team/reseller partnership business model could serve to position the company for growth and an increased share of their target market. At this point, a larger funding round will be possible and provide Neurosilicon with the financial prerequisite for successfully approaching the larger industrial market.

ACTIVITY LIST	FOCUS	LOCUS		MODUS		
				Brain intensity	Technology intensity	Labor intensity
R&D	4	Canada, US	IN/JOINT	9	8	7
Product Development	5	Canada	IN	9	8	5
(Pilot) Manufacturing	7	Canada	IN	7	8	8
Marketing	8	Canada	IN	6	2	2
Sales	8	Canada, US	OUT	7	8	8
Business Development	6	US, Germany	OUT	4	4	4
Post-sales	2	Canada	IN	6	3	4

Figure 6.17 The Milestone Bridge: Neurosilicon (Current)

Source: Authors' elaboration

NOTES

1. From Andry Dunn's blog post: "The Risk Not Taken." Published in 2013 (https://medium.com/i-m-h-o/40cf0a8919cb).
2. Actually, the idea was conceived in Elisabeth Robinson's home kitchen . . . the perfect Italian answer to the Silicon Valley garage innovation.

REFERENCE

Onetti, Alberto, Charles S. Versaggi, and Bruce F. Mackler. 2009. "Italian Biotech Revamps Old-World Mindset. Casting Off Traditional Business Customs Expected to Push the Industry Forward." *Genetic Engineering & Biotechnology News* 29, no. 14.

7 Conclusion

"Most men would rather deny a hard truth than face it."
—*George R. R. Martin*[1]

We set out to explain the key factors to consider when launching and guiding a company through the early stages of therapeutic development in the biotech industry. Along the way through the broad range of topics covered, we have tried to give a realistic overview of the challenges and risks involved.

The difficulties in transforming basic science into promising drugs are many and different in nature. For most, the best chance of finding a promising drug is to move on swiftly from less promising leads. Thus, the attrition rate for projects is, and should always be, very high. Most small companies will ultimately run out of leads before finding success. Even when the science works, the strategy can be wrong, and getting both right in order to be able to profit from therapeutic innovation, is difficult. Finally, assuming the strategy is right, a properly designed business model is required for successful execution.

Recent surveys in venture capital investments suggest that investors have become wary of investing in biotechnology and life science companies, and there is little sign of this situation improving quickly. It is therefore clear that only the best companies, with truly innovative science and promising leads, driven by equally promising strategies and business models, will survive and prosper, and even these will need some luck.

Our aim in this book has been to encourage entrepreneurs to develop their own business model that will help them to find mindful and rational ways of leading their business to success. Another aim has been to help them avoid the more common mistakes we have seen individually and collectively as consultants and advisors in the industry. We conclude here with some final advice, drawn from prior chapters and building on these, to inform the way you approach your business plan and ultimately your leadership and networks.

KNOWLEDGE PILLS

Strategy is a long-term commitment.

- It is the directional plan of action a company takes to grow and develop its business.
- Adjustments are possible, although expensive.
- In certain extreme cases (quite recurrent for startups) a radical change ("pivoting") is required to avoid further loss of time and money.

The business model is the comprehensive set of decisions that jointly defines how to execute the strategy. It shapes the company's business activities by:

- FOCUSing on what business activities demand priority, resources, and attention.
- Determining the best geographical LOCUS for conducting these activities.
- Identifying the MODUS in which these different activities are executed to achieve critical milestones during a company's growth and development.

The business model may change over time.

- Day by day, companies makes decisions that may affect FOCUS, LOCUS, and MODUS.
- Each decision, separately considered, is not necessarily a radical change; they are often just a fine-tuning of prior decisions.
- But the sum of all these decisions may radically change the way the company works and its business model.

The FOCUS changes as the company evolves.

- Life science firms typically change FOCUS as their research moves from early to later phases.
- Some companies do not (i.e., "satellite" companies, CROs).

Not just FOCUS, but also LOCUS and MODUS.

- Companies can locate activities in different places.
- This can open up new business opportunities or develop new partnerships.
- Companies can initiate new alliances.
- Partnerships can change the way the company works.

The more parameters are modified, the more radical the business model change is.

- In some cases, business model changes are so radical they drive strategy change.

The Milestone Bridge:

- Provides a comprehensive overview of your operations.
- Enables the company to effectively connect business activities to the achievement of successive milestones that signal value creation for the company.
- Helps to visualize the company's business model (VALUE ARCHITECTURE);

HOW CAN *THE MILESTONE BRIDGE* TOOL HELP YOU?

Plan and manage your evolution; do not just be driven by events.

- How do you see your company in 3 years? What actions are required to reach your destination?
- Plan in advance and don't just react to where the science or the money is.
- Drive (and don't be surprised about) the company's evolution.

Check the company's evolution path and learn from your past.

- Are we today what we wanted to become?
- What drove our evolution? The analysis of the past can help plan for future actions.

Communicate what your company does.

- Keep it simple,[2] although life science and high tech companies are not easy to pitch.
- Think and talk business, not just science.

NOTES

1. From *A Game of Thrones* by George R. R. Martin.
2. I.e., K.I.S.S. (Keep It Simple Stupid), quoting Charles Versaggi.

Bibliography

Amit, Raphael, and Paul J. H. Schoemaker. 1993. "Strategic Assets and Organizational Rent." *Strategic Management Journal,* 14(1), 33–46.

Beyond Borders: Global Biotechnology Report. 2010. EYGM Limited.

Blank, Steve. 2013. "Why the Lean Start-Up Changes Everything." *Harvard Business Review,* 91(5), 63–72.

Burns, Lawton R. 2002. *The Health Care Value Chain.* San Francisco, CA: Jossey-Bass.

Chesbrough, Henry. 2010. "Business Model Innovation: Opportunities and Barriers." *Long Range Planning,* 43, 354–363.

Christensen, Clayton, Gerome H. Grossman, and Jason Hwang. 2008. *The Innovator's Prescription: A Disruptive Solution for Health Care.* New York: McGraw Hill.

Cotta Ramusino, Enrico, and Alberto Onetti. 2013. *Strategia d'impresa,* 4th edition. Milan, IT: Il Sole 24 Ore.

Daley, Lane, Vikas Mehrotra, and Ranjini Sivakumar. 1997. "Corporate Focus and Value Creation. Evidence from Spinoffs," *Journal of Financial Economics,* 257–281.

Drucker, Peter F. 1968. *The Age of Discontinuity.* New York, NY: Harper & Row.

Dunning, John H. 1988. *Explaining International Production.* London: Allen & Unwin.

Feeny, David F., and Leslie P. Willcocks. 1998. "Core IS Capabilities for Exploiting Information Technology." *Sloan Management Review,* 39(3), 10.

Foster, Richard N., and Sarah Kaplan. 2001. *Creative Destruction: Why Companies That Are Built to Last Underperform the Market—and How to Successfully Transform Them.* New York NY: Random House.

Friedman, Yali. 2008. *Building Biotechnology.* ThinkBiotech LLC, 3rd edition.

Glick, Leslie J. 2008. "Biotechnology Business Models Work: Evidence from the Pharmaceutical Marketplace." *Journal of Commercial Biotechnology,* 14(2), 106–17.

Golinelli, Gaetano M. 2010. *Viable Systems Approach (VSA). Governing Business Dynamics.* Padova: Cedam.

Hordes, Mark, Anthony Clancy, and Julie Baddaley. 1995. "A Primer for Global Start-ups." *Academy of Management Executive,* 9(2), 7–11.

Isaacson, Walter. 2011. *Steve Jobs.* New York, NY: Simon & Schuster.

Jones, Marian V. 1999. "The Internationalization of Small High-Technology Firms." *Journal of International Marketing,* 7(4), 15–41.

Jones, Marian, and Nicole E. Coviello. 2005. "Internationalization: Conceptualizing an Entrepreneurial Process of Behavior in Time." *Journal of International Business Studies,* 36, 284–303.

Kolchinsky, Peter. 2004. *The Entrepreneur's Guide to a Biotech Startup.* www.evel exa.com/resources/egbs4_kolchinsky.pdf.

Kruger, Kurt. 2005. "The Medical Device Sector." In *The Business of Healthcare Innovation,* edited by Lawton R. Burns. New York: Cambridge University Press.

Lewis, Clive S. 1942. *The Screwtape Letters.* England: Geoffrey Bles.

McDougall, Patricia P., Scott Shane, and Benjamin M. Oviatt. 1994. "Explaining the Formation of International New Ventures." *Journal of Business Venturing,* 9(6), 469–487.

McKenna, Regis. 1986. *The Regis Touch: New Marketing Strategies for Uncertain Times.* New York, NY: Basic Books.

Moore, Geoffrey A. 2001. *Crossing the Chasm: Marketing and Selling Disruptive Products to Mainstream Customers.* New York, NY: Harper Business Essentials.

Onetti, Alberto, Marco Talaia, Vincenza Odorici, Manuela Presutti, and Sameer Verma. 2010. "The Role of Serial Entrepreneurs in the Internationalization of Global Start-Ups. A Business Case." *Journal of Strategic Management Education,* 6(1): 79–94 (ISSN 1649–3877).

Onetti Alberto, Antonella Zucchella, Marian V. Jones, and Patricia McDougall-Covin. 2012. "Internationalization, Innovation and Entrepreneurship: Business Models for New Technology-based Firms." *Journal of Management and Governance,* Special Issue: "Entrepreneurship and Strategic Management in Life Sciences. Business Models for High-Tech Companies." First online 2010 (doi:10.1007/s10997–010–9154–1). Print version: August 2012, (16)3, 337–368.

———. 2012. "Guest Editor's Introduction to the Special Issue: Entrepreneurship and Strategic Management in New Technology Based Companies." *Journal of Management and Governance,* Special Issue: "Entrepreneurship and Strategic Management in Life Sciences. Business Models for High-Tech Companies." First online 2010 (doi:10.1007/s10997–010–9153–2). Print version: August 2012, (16)3: 333–336.

Oviatt, Benjamin M., and Patricia P. McDougall. 1994. "Toward a Theory of International New Ventures." *Journal of International Business Studies.* 25(1), 45–64.

———. 1997. "Challenges for International Process Theory: The Case of International New Ventures." *Management International Review,* 37(2), 85–89.

Oviatt, Benjamin M., and Patricia P. McDougall-Covin. 2005. "Defining International Entrepreneurship and Modeling the Speed of Internationalization." *Entrepreneurship Theory and Practice,* 29(5), 537–554.

Pisano, Gary P. 2006. Science Business: The Promise, the Reality, and the Future of Biotech. Boston: Harvard Business School Press.

Porter, Michael E. 1980. *Competitive Strategy: Techniques for Analyzing Industries and Competitors.* Free Press, New York NY.

———. 1985. *Competitive Advantage: Creating and Sustaining Superior Performance.* New York NY: Free Press.

———. 1996. "What is Strategy." *Harvard Business Review,* 74(6), 61–78.

———. 2000. "Location, Competition, and Economic Development: Local Clusters in a Global Economy." *Economic Development Quarterly,* 14(1), 15–34).

Prahalad, Coimbatore K., and Gary Hamel. 1990. "The Core Competence of the Corporation." *Harvard Business Review,* 68(3), 79–91.

Preece, Stephen B., Grant Miles, and Mark C. Baetz. 1998. "Explaining the International Intensity and Global Diversity of Early Stage Technology Based Firms." *Journal of Business Venturing,* 14(3), 259–281.

Presutti, Manuela, Alberto Onetti, and Vincenza Odorici. 2008. "Serial Entrepreneurship and Born-Global New Ventures. A Case Study." *International Journal of Entrepreneurship Education,* 6, 255–278.

Rialp, Alex, Josep Rialp, and Gary A. Knight. 2005. "The Phenomenon of International New Ventures, Global Start Ups and Born Globals: What Do We Know

After a Decade (1993–2002) of Exhaustive Scientific Inquiry?" *International Business Review,* 14, 147–166;

Ries, Alf, and Jack Trout. 1981. *Positioning—The Battle for Your Mind.* New York, NY: MGraw-Hill.

Ries, Eric. 2011. *The Lean Startup: How Today's Entrepreneurs Use Continuous Innovation to Create Radically Successful Business.* New York, NY: Crown Business.

Rifkin, Leremy. 2000. *The Age of Access.* New York, NY: Putnum Books.

Sammut, Stephen M. 2005. "Biotechnology Business and Revenue Models: The Dynamic of Technological Evolution and Capital Market Ingenuity." In *The Business of Healthcare Innovation,* edited by Lawton R. Burns. New York: Cambridge University Press.

Shimasaki, Craig. 2009. *The Business of Bioscience.* BioSource Consulting Inter-Genetics Inc.

Simon, Francoise, and Philip Kotler. 2009. *Building Global BioBrands: Taking Biotechnology to Market.* New York, NY: Simon and Schuster Inc.

Sundelin, Anderson. 2009. "What is a Value Proposition." *The Business Model Database.* http://tbmdb.blogspot.com.

Toffler, Alvin. 1970. *Future Shock.* New York, NY: Bantom Books.

———. 1980. *The Third Wave.* New York, NY: Bantam Books.

Treacy, Michael, and Fred Wiersema. 1995.*The Discipline of Market Leaders.* Reading, MA: Addison Wesley.

Watson, David. 2005. *Business Models.* Petersfield, Hampshire: Harriman House, Ltd.

Wernerfelt, Birger. 1984. "A Resource-Based View of the Firm." *Strategic Management Journal,* 5(2), 171–180.

Appendices

Appendix A
Business Model

In competitive, complex, and risky environments such as high tech and science-based industries, the business model concept is becoming more and more popular. Despite the growing importance of this concept, our literature review establishes the absence of a generally accepted definition of what a *business model* is. This is why we want to provide you a little guide for a better understanding of the existent literature on the topic.

We will use a brief extract of an article we published in the *Journal of Management and Governance* in 2010 (Onetti et al., 2010a) together with our esteemed colleagues. This paper has a solid research base, and we are comfortable in suggesting you use it as benchmark for reviewing business model literature to date.[1]

The literature on business models is really fragmented and heterogeneous. Early studies in the strategic management field, for example Van de Ven and Walker (1984), draw attention to the role of strategic design as an overall framework for business modeling and to its importance for the survival and success of new ventures. However, this literature stream did not attract many contributions for over a decade until the phenomenon of Internet companies indicated that new designs and business models had become a matter of some importance.

Since that time, two main strands of literature have become identifiable. The earlier one emerged in the mid 1990s and generally focused on e-business contexts. A later, but more generic, stream appears to have emerged at the beginning of the new millennium. This later stream of research assumes a more comprehensive approach and is aimed at identifying business tools that are not necessarily restricted to high-tech companies.

A.1 THE E-BUSINESS STREAM

Growing interest in the business model concept therefore seems to have coincided with the advent of *e-business* in the mid 1990s, as many new young ventures began developing Internet-based offers (Mahadevan, 2000). Rapid technological change in this new business era (Kelly, 1998; Tapscott,

1997) heralded dramatic changes to competitive approaches in many industries. Viscio and Pasternack (1996) argued that traditional business models were unable to adapt to the Internet era. Some scholars have introduced and used the business model concept in an attempt to explain the challenges that high-tech companies face in the new Web-business era.

Consequently, the definitions they propose are strongly e-business oriented and tend to refer mainly to Web-based companies. Typical of the e-business literature stream are categorizations and taxonomies of companies operating in the Web- or e-commerce sphere. Authors described alternative business models rather than introducing a structured and generally accepted definition of what they mean by the term business model. In the following we highlight the most relevant publications ascribable to the e-business literature stream.

- Timmers (1998) defined the business model of a company as composed by the product, service, and information flows; potential benefits; and sources of revenue. Timmers also introduced a taxonomy of 11 business models for Internet companies, categorizing them on the basis of two criteria: functional integration and degree of innovation. Timmers' business model definition may be considered the first "structured" definition of the business model (Alt and Zimmermann, 2001).
- Tapscott, Lowry, and Ticoll (2000) described a business model for "b-Webs" as "a distinct system of supplies, distributors, commerce services providers and customers that use the Internet for their primary business communication and transactions."
- Rappa (2001) proposed a taxonomy of business models for "digital enterprises," distinguishing between nine basic categories.
- Collico Savio (2001) indentified the business model as "the method of doing business by which a company can generate revenue and then sustain itself" and proposed a possible taxonomy of business models.
- Petrovic, Kittl, and Teksen (2001) proposed a methodology for developing e-business models. According to them an e-business model is comprised of seven sub models: the value model, resource model, production model; customer relations model (comprising three other subcomponents: distribution model, marketing model, and service model), revenue model, capital model, and market model.

A.2   THE GENERIC STREAM

Since the beginning of the new millennium, scholars have been studying the business model topic by introducing reference models and ontologies. From basic definitions and taxonomies, scholars have been moving to more articulated definitions and identifying building blocks and components. Moreover, from its initial focus on Internet-based business, the business model concept became more universally applicable to other types of firms. The strengths of this literature stream lie in efforts to understand business by dissecting strategy into a system of inter-related decisions, relationships, and organizational boundaries. A primary weakness of this literature stream is its failure, to date, to accommodate location decisions and internationalization. In the following bullet points, we highlight the most relevant publications from the generic stream of the business model literature.

- Hamel (2000) defined the business model starting from four main building blocks (i.e., customer logic, strategy, resources, and network). Mahadevan (2000) provided a definition of business model that includes the value stream, the revenue stream, and the logistical stream.
- Afuah and Tucci (2001) described the business model as "a model designed to make money for their owners in the long term" composed by 10 blocks (i.e., profit site, customer value, scope, price, revenue sources, connected activities, implementation, capabilities, sustainability, and cost structure).
- Weill and Vitale (2001) described a business model as "the roles and relationship among a firm's consumers, customers, allies and suppliers that identifies the major flow of product, information, and money, and the major benefits to participants."
- Influenced by the Balanced Scorecard approach (Kaplan and Norton, 1992), Osterwalder (2004) proposed a framework based on four pillars (product, customer interface, infrastructure management, and financial aspects) and nine building blocks (value proposition, target customer, distribution channel, relationship, value configuration, capability, partnership, cost structure, and revenue model).
- Yip (2004) posited that a business model defines the value proposition, the nature of inputs and outputs, the scope (vertical, horizontal, and geographical), the target customers, and the structure.
- Shafer, Smith, and Linder (2005) analyzed 12 definitions of the business model and built an affinity diagram (Pyzdek, 2003) to categorize the various business model components used in the literature. Shafer and colleagues identified four categories (strategic choices, creating value, capturing value, and value network). Zott and Amit (2008) completed their definition by proposing a quantitative research approach to establish the effects of product market strategy and business model choices on firm performance.
- Richardson (2008) categorized the business model as an integrative framework for strategy execution based on three blocks: the value proposition (the offering, the target customer, the basic strategy), the value creation and delivery system (resources and capabilities, organization, position in the value network) and the value capture (revenue sources and the economics of the business).

In parallel, the business model topic has also been addressed by practitioners. Among the others we refer to the following:

- Linder and Cantrell (2001) proposed a definition of the business model articulated in seven components (pricing model, revenue model, channel model, commerce process model, Internet-enabled commerce relationship, organizational form, and value proposition).
- Chesbrough (2003, 2006) described the business model as "a cognitive map across domains," able to help managers in identifying a target market, articulating the value proposition, building the value chain and the costs/margins structure, describing the position of the firm in the value network, and formulating the competitive strategy.
- Mitchell and Coles (2004a, 2004b) described a business model as "the combination of who, what, when, where, why, and how much an organization uses to provide its goods and services and develop resources to continue its efforts."

A.3 BUSINESS MODEL LITERATURE BACKGROUND: COMPARATIVE ANALYSIS METHODOLOGY

From the literature review it is apparent that while many authors offer definitions of the term business model, definitions are fairly heterogeneous, and none appears to be generally accepted.

This definitional ambiguity suggests a need to conceptualize the business model more formally, and to distinguish it from the business strategy, supporting processes and metrics, thus separating and de-layering it from the multi-layer business decision process (Osterwalder, Pigneur, and Tucci, 2005).

We then described the state of extant knowledge on business models, identifying and categorizing the main *business model components* proposed by the literature. We next analyze and critique extant knowledge on business models and relate the results and criticisms from analysis to challenges facing new technology based firms as drawn from the international entrepreneurship/internationalization literature.

Our goal is to address this definitional ambiguity and contribute to fill this gap, suggesting a more comprehensive conceptualization that synthesizes earlier work in this area and incorporates international entrepreneurship/internationalization literature elements. We performed an in-depth literature review based on 70 definitions published from 1996 to 2009[2] whose output is summarized in Table A.1.

From our analysis we identified main areas of improvement for *defining the business model* and offer five *recommendations*:

1. There is a need for a clear separation between the business model and the strategy concepts.

Table A.1 Categorization of Business Model Definitions

	Mission/ Objectives	Strategy	Focus	Modus	Locus	Financials
Horowitz 1996		×	×	×		
Slywdzky 1996		×	×	×		×
Timmers 1998	×	×		×		×
Donath 1999		×	×	×		
Markides 1999	×			×		×
Mayo & Brown 1999	×	×		×		
Gordijn et al. 2000 Gordijn & Akkermans 2001, 2003	×	×	×	×		×
Hamel 2000	×	×	×	×		
Mahadevan 2000		×	×			×
Stewart & Zhao 2000	×		×	×		×
Afuah & Tuod 2001	×	×	×	×		×
At & Zimmermann 2001	×	×	×	×		×
Amit & Zott 2001 Zott & Amit 2008	×		×	×		
Applegate 2001	×	×	×	×		×
Collico Savio 2001	×		×			×
De et al. 2001		×		×		×
Hawkins 2001	×	×				×
Linder & Cartrell 2001	×	×	×	×		×
Petrovic et al. 2001 Auer & Follack 2002		×	×	×		×
Rappa 2001	×		×			×
Well & Vitale 2001				×		×
Betz 2002			×			×
Chesbrough & Rosenbloom 2002 Chesbrough 2003, 2006		×	×	×		×
Dubosson-Torbay et al. 2002	×	×		×		×
Hoque 2002	×	×	×	×		
Magretta 2002			×	×		
Osterwalder & Pigneur 2002	×	×		×		×
Rayport & Jaworski 2002		×	×	×		×
Van Der Vorst et al. 2002		×	×	×		
Christensen & Methlie 2003	×	×		×		×
Hedman & Kalling 2003	×	×	×	×		
Hoppe & Bretner 2003	×		×	×		×
Mitchel & Coles 2003, 2004		×	×	×	×	×
Pateli & Giagis 2003	×	×	×	×		×
Osterwalder 2004 Osterwalder et al. 2005	×	×	×	×		×
Yip 2004		×	×	×		
Morris et al. 2005	×	×	×	×		×
Shafer et al. 2005	×	×	×	×		×
Schweizer 2005	×		×	×		×
Voelpel et al. 2005	×	×	×	×		×
Watson 2005		×		×		×
Peters & Young 2006	×					×

Source: Onetti et al., 2010a

2. A separation between the business model concept and the financial implications is also required.
3. Business model definitions have to include location decisions that are more and more relevant in the extant competitive scenario.
4. Business model definitions have to integrate and synthesize the earlier work in this area that seems to identify, as building blocks, activities (value chain) and network.
5. Business model conceptualizations must be reasonably simple and generalizable so that they can be applicable to firms of all sorts and sizes (managerial implication).

The goal of this book is to introduce a definitional framework for the business model (*The Milestone Bridge*) that is intended to address the recommmendations we described above and incorporate the main elements we extracted from the international entrepreneurship/internationalization literature. More specifically we used "FOCUS, "MODUS," and "LOCUS" as analytical building blocks of the business model concept. Accordingly, we define the business model as the way a company structures its own activities in determining the FOCUS, LOCUS, and MODUS of its business.

Table A.2   Learning Blocks—Appendix A

Business Model	E-Business	Taxonomy
Business Strategy	Financials	Business Model Components

NOTES

1. Please refer to the quoted article for the complete bibliography. The main works quoted in this Appendix are listed in the references below.
2. To avoid duplications we grouped authors that proposed the same definitions in different contributions, and we excluded 13 articles that refer only to third-party taxonomies and definitions. This reduced the number of relevant definitions to 48. The citations for each of the 48 definitions are presented in the left-hand column of Table A.1.

REFERENCES

Afuah, Allan, and Christopher L. Tucci. 2001. *Internet Business Models & Strategies. Text & Cases.*Desoto, TX: McGraw-Hill International Edition.
Alt, Rainer, and Hans-Dieter Zimmermann. 2001. "Introduction to Special Section—Business Models." *Electronic Markets* 11, no. 1: 1019–6781.
Chesbrough, Henry W. 2003. *Open innovation: The New Imperative for Creating and Profiting from Technology.* Boston: Harvard Business School Press.
———. 2006. *Open Business Models. How to Thrive in the New Innovation Landscape.* Boston: Harvard Business School Press.
Collico Savio, Daniel. 2001. "Internet Business Models." Accessed November 14, 2013, from http://userpage.fu-berlin.de/~jmueller/its/conf/dub01/papers/collico.pdf

Hamel, Gary. 2000. *Leading the Revolution.* Boston, MA: Harvard Business School Press.

Kaplan, Robert S., and David P. Norton. 1996. "Using the Balanced Scorecard as a Strategic Management System." *Harvard Business Review* 74, no. 1: 75–85.

Kelly, Kevin. 1998. *New Rules for a New Economy: 10 Radical Strategies for a Connected World.* New York: Penguin Books.

Linder, Janenne, and Susan Cantrell. 2001. "Changing Business Models: Surveying the Landscape." Report, Accenture—Institute for Strategic Change, May 24.

Mahadevan, B. 2000. Business Models for Internet Based e-Commerce. An Anatomy. *California Management Review* 42, no. 4: 55–69.

Mitchell, Donald W., and Carol Bruckner Coles. 2004a. "Business Model Innovation Breakthrough Moves." *Journal of Business Strategy* 25, no. 1: 16–26.

———. 2004b. "Establishing a Continuing Business Model Innovation Process." *Journal of Business Strategy* 25, no. 3: 39–49.

Onetti Alberto, Antonella Zucchella, Marian V. Jones, and Patricia McDougall-Covin. 2010a. "Internationalization, Innovation and Entrepreneurship: Business Models for New Technology-based Firms." *Journal of Management and Governance* 16, no. 3 (SI): 337–368.

Osterwalder, Alexander. 2004. "The Business Model Ontology: A Proposition in a Design Science Approach." Working paper, University of Lausanne, Ecole des Hautes Etudes Commerciales (HEC 173).

Osterwalder, Alexander, Yves Pigneur, and Christopher L. Tucci. 2005. "Clarifying Business Models: Origins, Present, and Future of the Concept." *Communications of AIS, the Association for Information Systems* 15: 1–40.

Petrovic, Otto, Christian Kittl, and Ryan D. Teksen. 2001. "Developing Business Models for e-Business." Paper presented at the International Conference on Electronic Commerce, Vienna, Austria, October 31–November 4.

Pyzdek, Thomas. 2003. *The Six Sigma Handbook.* New York: McGraw-Hill.

Rappa, Michael. 2001. "Business Models on the Web." Digitalenterprise.com. Accessed July 20, 2009, from www.digitalenterprise.org: http://digitalenterprise.org/models/models.html.

Richardson, James. 2008. "The Business Model: An Integrative Framework for Strategy Execution." *Strategic Change* 17, no. 5–6: 133–144.

Shafer, Scott M., Jeff H. Smith, and Jane C. Linder. 2005. "The Power of Business Models." *Business Horizons* 48, no. 3: 199–207.

Tapscott, Don T. 1997. "Strategy in the New Economy." *Strategy & Leadership* 25, no. 6: 8–14.

Tapscott, Don, Alex Lowy, and David Ticoll. 2000. *Digital Capital—Harnessing the Power of Business Webs.* Boston: Harvard Business Press.

Timmers, Paul. 1998. "Business Models for Electronic Markets." *Electronic Markets* 8, no. 2: 3–8.

Van de Ven, Andrew H., and Gordon Walker. 1984. "The Dynamics of Interorganizational Coordination." *Administrative Science Quarterly* 29, no. 4: 598–621.

Viscio, Albert J., and Bruce A. Pasternack. 1996. "Toward a New Business Model." Strategy-business.com. Accessed July 20, 2009, from www.strategy-business.com/press/16635507/14974

Weill, Peter, and Michael R. Vitale. 2001. *Place to Space: Migrating to e-Business Models.* Boston: Harvard Business School Press.

Yip, George S. 2004. "Using Strategy to Change Your Business Model." *Business Strategy Review* 15, no. 2: 17–24.

Zott, Christoph, and Raphael Amit. 2008. "The Fit between Product Market Strategy and Business Model: Implications for Firm Performance." *Strategic Management Journal* 29: 1–26.

Appendix B
Biotechnology

Today few leaders in the *biotechnology and life sciences industry* can feel secure or confident that their company has what it takes to succeed in an increasingly turbulent environment. The day-to-day work is focused on managing projects and people and being concerned about costs, fund raising, producing results, and so on.

In this scenario, it is a must to spend some time looking at the overall strategic picture. Being aware of where you and your company are in the broader competitive landscape is a pivotal skill for any manager or entrepreneur, particularly in a field as fast paced as biotechnology (O'Neil and Hopkins, 2012). In the next pages we help you get a deeper understanding of this industry, with a specific focus on life sciences.

B.1 BIOTECHNOLOGY AS A META-INDUSTRY

Biotechnology represents a quite heterogeneous landscape. Literature and business praxis define the life sciences aggregate in different ways and identify it by using different terms. Biotechnology and life sciences are often used as synonyms, whereas others consider biotechnology as the broader industry and life sciences as a subset of it.[1] Sometimes medical devices, biomedical devices as well as diagnostic devices, are considered part of the industry. In some cases nanotechnologies are also included.

Before starting to provide definitions and categories, it is important to state that nowadays it is almost impossible to draw a line in the sand between different industries. This is true not only for life sciences and biotechnology. Clearly identifying the boundaries of a business is becoming a hard task for every industry, including the more traditional and mature ones. Technological innovation more and more crosses and breaches the boundaries between the traditional industries, creating wide areas of intersection and overlap between businesses. In Chapter 1 we introduced the term *meta-industry* for singling out the melt-down process that is currently affecting traditional industries. How much electronics and informatics do you buy in a car? How much are digital graphics penetrating the movie industry?

It is apparent that nowadays making distinctions between industries and markets is increasingly difficult, almost impossible. Therefore the traditional approaches based on industry and market no longer work and need to be replaced by *technology platform oriented approaches*. New technologies are cross-platform and apply to different industries and markets. They are increasingly pervasive and transversal.

This requires a focus shift for the analysis: from the industry to the company. When you analyze a company, it is of little help to tell to which industry it belongs. What really matters is the strategy and business model the company has chosen, i.e., its ultimate goal as well as the activities it decides to focus on and the way it decides to run each of them. In this case it is the company that decides where (i.e., the industry and market), and how to play (i.e., the business model). The activity mix the firm has chosen ultimately defines its competitive positioning , which is often at the intersection of different industries and markets. Therefore, we may assert that business model decisions not only reflect the industry in which the company operates (the "strategy follows industry" approach à la Theodore Levitt [Levitt, 1965]), but, most importantly, they drive the creation of new industries (*business model brings to industry creation*).

Biotechnology is not an exception. It is a meta-industry since biotechnologies are cross-platform, transversal, and pervasive and supply new knowledge to various industries. More than any other technology, biotechnology companies live in the intersection of multiple sectors and businesses. Therefore business model decisions play a key role for their competitive and strategic positioning.

B.1.1   Biotechnology: Definition and History

A good starting point in defining the term *biotechnology* is certainly the definition given by the Organization for Economic Co-operation and Development (OECD) in 1982. According to OECD, biotechnology is "the application of science and technology to living organisms, as well as parts, products and models thereof, to alter living or non-living materials for the production of knowledge, goods and services."

The European Federation of Biotechnology[2] also defines biotechnology as the "integration of natural sciences as well as organisms, cells, their parts or molecular analogues in industrial processes for the production of goods and services." However, the most complete definition is probably the one provided by the Convention on Biological Diversity:[3] "Biotechnology means any technological application that uses biological systems, living organisms, or derivatives thereof, to make or modify products or processes for specific use." Biotechnology includes technologies that make use of living organisms (bacteria, animal cells from both simple and complex organisms) or their derivatives (such as enzymes) to develop products for healthcare, improve the characteristics of plants and animals, or develop micro-organisms for specific uses.

Therefore, the biotechnology industry includes all firms that are involved in research, development, and commercialization of those products and platform technologies that come under the domain of these knowledge bases.

Biotechnology is a young industry, since it is only 35 years old. It started with a handful of pioneering companies in the seventies and was initially largely confined to the Boston and San Francisco areas. Since then, biotech has grown into a truly global sector, with an established European presence and is an emerging trend in most of the developing countries (Ernst and Young, 2012).

During 2001 and 2002, the industry experienced the first significant backlash in its history. The market downturn slowed down the global expansion of the biotechnology industry. Even though the decline impacted the industry negatively, biotech companies have not suffered the same drastic reduction in venture capital funding as other high-tech industries.[4]

The global financial crisis initiated in 2008 is having implications for the biotechnology industry because of the capital-intensive nature of the companies (Ernst and Young, 2012). In this capital-constrained environment, investors and companies have responded with creative approaches to make R&D more efficient and sustainable. They have tweaked the existing drug development paradigm (e.g., fail fast approaches) and/or made reductions in operating costs and overhead. This will likely accelerate the emergence of new business models, such as "risk sharing" deals to share development costs with outside investors.

B.1.2   Biotechnology as a Science-Based Business

For a better understanding of what biotechnology stands for, we first need to define which technologies can be characterized as science-based. In fact, the categorization of a specific technology as science-based is not universally accepted.

Meyer-Krahmer and Schmoch (1998) define *"science-based technology"* as a field with frequent references to scientific publications, hence with a major interest is the observation of science. In general, compared to others companies, a science-based business entails unique challenges that require different kinds of organizational and institutional arrangements and different management approaches.

Gary Pisano (2006), more precisely, points out the distinctive qualities of science-based business. Many firms use scientific knowledge to create innovative products and solutions. But the use of science in and of itself does not characterize a science-based business. The author defines science-based companies as companies that attempt to both create science and capture value from it. That is, the science-based business actively participates in the process of advancing and creating science and, in this sense, biotechnology falls within this category (Pisano, 2006).

As we have discussed before, biotechnology is an interdisciplinary field built on the interaction between different areas, such as biology and engineering. It draws upon a wide array of scientific fields, such as micro-biology, biochemistry, molecular biology, cell biology, immunology, protein engineering, and the full range of bioprocess technologies.[5] Over the past decades, a hallmark of such *knowledge-intensive* industries was hiring a relatively high percentage of people with advanced education, training, and experience. Results from a longitudinal analysis of more than 300 US bio-technology firms, conducted by Luo, Koput, and Powell (2009), show that about one-third of the employees held a Ph.D. or M.D. degree.

Furthermore, in accordance with Niosi (2003), biotechnology is a science-based activity since it is highly *research-intensive*. And research is not only performed internally in the R&D department of the firms, but also in partnerships with universities, research centers, and other companies. From 1999 to date, the pharmaceutical industry has noticeably increased the amount of R&D partnerships, due to the high costs of the clinical trials and also the high risk profile of the R&D activities. R&D in biotechnol-ogy is based on the development of science, in universities and in public laboratories, with which these firms join in dense collaborations. In fact, as a science-based technology, biotechnology is especially dependent on the cooperation and interaction with academic institutions, government, and industry since academic knowledge needs to be transferred to the industry at an early stage (Giesecke, 2000).

B.1.3   Biotech Industry Segmentation

Multidisciplinarity is one of the salient features of the biotechnology industry. For example, the use of living organisms for the production of organic prod-ucts such as beer and milk is a biotechnological application. It is also possible to apply biotechnology in the recycling and treating of waste and the clean-up of contaminated sites, as well as the manufacturing of biological weapons.

The most important applications are in the medical-pharmaceutical and agricultural/food fields. However, other branches—such as industrial application and environmental protection—are becoming more and more relevant.

Many industry reports categorize the main branches of biotechnology as follows:

- *Green biotechnology* applies to agricultural and veterinary processes. For example, through green micro-propagation technologies it is pos-sible to select and domesticate plants. Other technologies allow for the design of transgenic plants able to grow in very specific environments, characterized by the presence (or absence) of chemical elements. Com-pared to traditional industrial agriculture, green biotechnology aims at creating solutions that are more environmentally friendly.
- *Blue biotechnology* refers to marine and aquatic applications of biotechnology.

- *Red biotechnology* applies to the healthcare and life sciences-related processes, specifically in areas such as pharmacogenomics,[6] drug production, genetic testing,[7] and gene therapy.[8] While the traditional pharmaceutical industry has been based on chemically synthesized small molecule drugs, the biotech sector works differently. Biopharmaceuticals are complex macromolecules created through the genetic manipulation of living organisms using gene cloning, recombinant DNA, or cell fusion technologies. These result in different types of products such as recombinant proteins, recombinant antigen vaccines and vaccines generated from genetic material such as DNA, therapeutic monoclonal antibodies, and oligonucleotides.[9] Thanks to biotechnology, it is also possible to manufacture existing medicines in a relatively easier and cheaper way.
- *White* or *Grey biotechnology* applies to industrial processes (i.e., industrial biotechnology). Modern biotech methods are used for the production and processing of chemicals, materials, and fuel as well as environmental bioremediation (e.g., waste disposal and treatment of polluted water as well as identification of toxic substances in the land, air, and water). An example is the use of enzymes as industrial catalysts to either produce valuable chemicals or destroy hazardous/polluting chemicals (Wikipedia, 2013). Compared to traditional industrial processes, the adoption of white biotechnology implies the use of fewer resources (DaSilva, 2005).
- *Bioinformatics* is an interdisciplinary area that deals with biological data/problems/challenges by using computational techniques. It allows companies to effectively examine and manage biological data. The field can also be referred to as computational biology, defined as, "conceptualizing biology in terms of molecules and then applying informatics techniques to understand and organize the information associated with these molecules, on a large scale" (Gerstein, 2007). Bioinformatics plays an extremely important role for both the biotechnology and pharmaceutical sector, specifically in areas such as functional genomics, structural genomics, and proteomics.

B.1.4   Biotech Industry in the World

The biotechnology industry predominantly consists of companies that use at least one biotechnological technique to produce goods and services or to perform biotechnology R&D. These companies have been historically differentiated from the mainstream pharmaceutical industry, which includes traditional pharmaceutical companies and bases its approach to drug development more on chemistry than on genetics. Over time, this distinction has become more and more subtle, and the business models of companies operating in the industry have continued to evolve. Nowadays, as we discussed in Chapter 1, biotech firms can often afford to move their drugs further along the clinical phases, maintaining more control on the revenue, and adopt strategies of multiple alliances to outsource the regulatory, marketing, and distribution activities that the big pharmaceutical companies are usually better equipped to handle.

The OECD Biotechnology Statistics Database shows that currently[10] Europe has the largest number of biotechnology firms (6,500+ firms). The United States counts approximately the same number of companies as Europe, but it currently leads the world in the area of biotechnology because its patent law and legislation—such as the Bayh-Dole Act (1980)—have provided favorable incentives to mitigate the high risks associated with this business (Biotechnology Industry Organization, 2012). In their research, Zucker, Darby, and Brewer (1999) show that the American biotechnology industry was essentially nonexistent in 1975 and has grown to 700 active firms in only 15 years.[11] In their study, the authors suggest the existence of a tight connection between the intellectual capital created by frontier research and the creation of firms in the industry, claiming that the presence of intellectual capital was the main driver for the growth of the industry itself.

Compared to Europe, the US biotech industry has the largest and most successful companies, benefits from a greater availability of venture capital, invests three times more on R&D, and generates twice as much revenue in total (OECD, 2007). The US's leading position is also due to a greater entrepreneurial culture, a greater mobility for research scientists, and the US's strength in information technologies, which are critical for life sciences research. Moreover, the development of the US biotech industry has largely been financed in the initial stages by venture capital firms, whereas the European venture capital market is still fragmented and not sufficiently structured to support the biopharmaceutical sector (European Commission, 2009). As reported by OECD, about two-thirds of the 2012 total venture capital in the US is invested in life sciences, compared to 20% in the European Union.

Biotech companies range in size from small startups to multi-billion-dollar firms, but most of them are still not yet cash-flow positive and are burning investors' capital on research and development. In Europe, biotech companies are typically research-intensive SMEs that generate very limited revenue (European Commission, 2009).

B.2   THE BIOPHARMACEUTICAL SEGMENT

The pharmaceutical industry experienced a structural break in terms of performance in the mid-1980s after the introduction of the first successful biotechnology drugs (such as human insulin, launched in 1982). The emergence of biotechnology has not led to the destruction of the existing pharmaceutical companies (Rothaermel, 2001). Rather, the traditional pharmaceutical industry has turned into the biopharmaceutical industry, a combination of traditional pharmaceutical firms, like Merck or Pfizer, and new biotechnology firms, such as Biogen or Immunex. Sharp (1999) identifies three main historical phases in the relationship between established firms and biotechnology companies. The initial phase involved the formation of the biotechnology industry and was mainly characterized by uncertainty and skepticism in that most established companies distanced themselves from the new-born industry. These companies also invested in sufficient scientific expertise to keep abreast of developments and monitor the industry. At a second stage, the established pharmaceutical companies recognized the valuable market potential of biotechnology and began to invest into it, either through acquisitions/alliances of biotechnology firms or the development of in-house competences. The last, most recent, phase involves the commercialization of biotechnology products: the large pharmaceutical companies took the products developed by biotechnology companies and evolved them into large-scale marketed products (Sharp, 1999).

Biopharmaceutical clusters typically arise in close proximity to academic medical centers, universities, and non-profit research institutions with strong biomedical R&D bases, where there are many opportunities for collaboration and public/private partnerships (Casper and Karamanos, 2003; Cooke, 2001). As mentioned earlier, the interconnection among these key figures is critical. No wonder biotechnology is the industry with the highest absolute number of *strategic alliances* (Hagedoorn, 1993). Biotech research is a field where the growth of strategic alliances has been really remarkable from inception, with an annual average growth rate of 25% (Audretsch and Feldman, 2003). For example, biopharmaceutical companies are increasingly forming partnerships with the public sector, in particular universities and academic medical centers, to identify breakthroughs in basic research that may translate into clinical development opportunities. In the vertical alliance chain, typical of this sector, many young biotechnology firms act as intermediaries: they enter upstream partnerships with public sector research institutions and universities and—later on—build downstream commercialization alliances with incumbent firms (Stuart, Ozdemir, and Ding, 2007). A possible explanation is that the development of biotech requires complementary and heterogeneous assets that often reside in different types of organizations. Established large companies usually have more experience in large-scale production, marketing, and distribution and, most of all, they have the resources required to bring products to the market. On the other hand, new biotech startups are very specialized and better able to deal with innovative compounds and technologies.[12]

Therefore, strategic alliances between large and small firms are often formed to bring these complementary competencies together and are pervasive in the biotechnology industry. In fact, they do not only allow firms to leverage their competitive assets, but also to benefit from larger-scale economies and productivity for both the companies involved, especially in terms of product development and go-to-market (Audretsch and Feldman, 2003). Stuart et al. (2007) emphasize that the enormously costly process for commercializing biotechnologies distinguishes biotechnologies from many other university-originated technologies. Early-stage biotechnology firms cannot raise sufficient capital to directly market their products, and hence depend on downstream alliances. The substantial financial and capability-based requirements for commercializing biomedical technologies dictates that early stage companies partner with established organizations.

In line with this concept, Rothaermel (2001) describes the new *biopharmaceutical industry* as the result of extensive interfirm cooperation between established pharmaceutical firms and new biotech firms. According to the author, that happens because pharmaceutical firms face severe difficulties in adapting to radical technological change, whereas new biotechnology firms lack the necessary competences and scale to commercialize the outputs of their drug discovery and development research, and also the capital to fund them. Therefore they succeed in accessing mutually complementary value chain activities through extensive interfirm cooperation.

B.2.1 Main Players in the Value Creation Process

What stands out about the biopharmaceutical industry is that it takes many partners to create economic value. To go from new ideas to new innovative treatments calls for a wide range of collaborations, from university scientists to physicians (Battelle, 2010). The biotechnology industry depends heavily on public science, defined as knowledge that originates from universities, research institutions, and government laboratories (McMillan, Narin, and Deeds, 2000). The World Intellectual Property Organization (WIPO) suggests that in the biotechnology sector, basic and applied research are often deeply inter-connected, unlike many other sectors, in which there is a clear distinction between the basic research performed in universities and the public sector R&D institutions and the applied research and development undertaken by private enterprises.[13] The history of the biotechnology industry can be viewed as a series of licensing and collaborative relationships, from universities to biotech firms and, ultimately, to large pharmaceutical companies.

Universities, as well as research institutes, are the source of basic scientific knowledge and new breakthroughs and represent an input to innovation, playing a key role in the process of patenting innovations. In particular, the approval of the Bayh-Dole Act in 1980 has created a uniform patent policy among the many federal agencies that fund research, enabling universities to retain title to inventions made under federally funded research programs. In recent times, however, universities have assumed a more active role in the commercialization of scientific ideas through patenting and the establishment of technology licensing as part of their academic life. Many universities grant licenses to biotechnology companies, usually through various economic provisions, like licensing fees, milestone payments, and royalty schemes (Edwards, Murray, and Yu, 2003). The importance of academic research to the successful commercialization of scientific discoveries is confirmed by Di Gregorio and Shane (2003). Jensen and Thursby (2001) confirm that active, self-interested participation of university professors is an essential condition for successful commercial licensing of university inventions.

The traditional pharmaceutical companies, often referred to as *Big Pharma,* encompass some of the world's largest and most profitable firms,[14] whose main focus is to identify promising discoveries and then take these to the market. The Big Pharma firms have the critical resources necessary for the commercialization process, for example internal laboratories and experience in managing the FDA approval procedures, but also the ability to screen and understand potential commercial breakthroughs, often made in research-intensive companies like biotech firms or universities and research institutes (Haanes and Fjeldstad, 2000). During the start-up phase of biotech industry development, US biotech companies were particularly interested in forming strategic alliances with domestic pharmaceutical companies, since they needed strong partners with established distribution networks to conquer the US market (Forrest and Martin, 1992).

As Hara (2004) points out, historically, large pharmaceutical houses have been understandably proud of their own research discovery capabilities, which they housed internally, and tried to manufacture their own products and develop huge sales and distribution forces. Recently, however, a number of venture-backed companies have emerged as potentially significant horizontal players that are transforming the way pharmaceuticals are discovered, developed, and brought to market. Large, vertically integrated pharmaceutical companies[15] have become more horizontal in order to try to minimize costs, especially since they have been multiplying over the past few years. Big Pharma companies are better at drug refinement than at drug discovery, and they are superior at bringing a drug through the intricate phases of testing, manufacturing, and marketing. Whereas most of the resources allocated by large, established firms are devoted to downstream activities, upstart biotechnology firms and universities generally dedicate their resources to the upstream segments of the value chain (Stuart et al., 2007), as shown in Figure B.1.

Rader (2005) defines biopharmaceutical companies as the firms "primarily involved in the research, development, manufacturing and/or marketing of biotechnology-based pharmaceuticals products or surrogates, including gene and protein sequences" (Rader, 2005). Most biopharmaceutical firms, however, do not have historical experience in manufacturing, sales, and marketing and often engage in collaborations with Big Pharma to manage these phases together.

The boundaries between these last two groups are blurred: the pharmaceutical industry is undergoing a transformation, becoming more research-driven through adoption of biotechnologies for research and strategic alliances with biotech companies. Basically, biopharmaceutical companies have the same characteristics of Big Pharma (fully integrated, from discovery to sales and marketing), with the exception of focusing much more on biopharmaceuticals drugs rather than chemistry-based drugs. However, all these entities are strongly interdependent and interconnected by extensive cooperative arrangements (Arora and Gambardella, 1990; Powell, 1996).

Figure B.1 The Value Chain of the Biopharmaceutical Industry

Source: Authors' elaboration from https://web.duke.edu/soc142/team2/images/mychain2.jpg

B.2.2 The Product Development Process

Within the last 10–15 years, the biopharmaceutical sector has become one of the most research-intensive sectors and a key part of the knowledge-based economy. The WIPO reports that, also compared to other major industries—such as the chemical industry—that rely on *research and development (R&D)*, biotech companies generally invest a significantly higher proportion of their revenues in R&D, often between 40% and 50%.[16]

Economic analyses of the R&D process in pharmaceuticals indicate that it is high-risk, even for large, established firms. The main reasons for that are the following:

- Drug development is extremely capital intensive, costing an estimated $300 to $600 million dollars and taking 12 to 15 years to get from preclinical to market (IRS, 2013).
- Most of the new drug candidates fail to reach the market.
- The process of bringing a new compound to the market takes a long time.
- The ability of revenue generation of marketed products is highly skewed.
- The biopharmaceutical approval process is rigorous and complex, since biotechnology companies must comply with the standards of the Food & Drug Administration (FDA) that regulates the introduction of new drugs or the U.S. Department of Agriculture (USDA) and the Environmental Protection Agency (EPA) that both impose safety/performance standards on the development of pesticides, herbicides, and genetically altered crops.

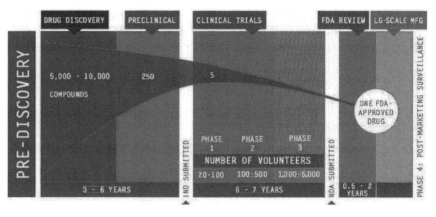

Figure B.2 Timeframe of the Biotechnology Drug Discovery and Development Process
Source: www.innovation.org/drug_discovery/objects/images/chart_print.gif

The *discovering and developing process* of new therapeutics consists of different phases:

- Discovery and early research.
- Preclinical testing.
- Clinical trials (phases 1, 2, and 3).
- Phase 4, post-approval and marketing testing.

The timeframe for biotechnology drug discovery and development process is described in Figure B.2. Below we will walk you through the different steps required to bring a new compound to the market.

Early Discovery and Preclinical Development

Preclinical testing analyzes the bioactivity, safety, and efficacy of the formulated drug product. These testing activities are critical to the drug's eventual success and, as such, are scrutinized by many regulatory entities. The preclinical stage of drug development requires the application of rigorous scientific standards and expertise to effectively advance drug candidates from the laboratory to clinical trials. During this phase, plans for clinical trials and an Investigative New Drug (IND) application are prepared.

Clinical Trials

Clinical trials are aimed at proving the safety and efficacy of the new drug candidate in humans. Clinical activity is articulated in four subsequent phases.

Phase 1: Clinical Development—Human Pharmacology

Thirty days after the IND application has been filed, the biopharmaceutical company may begin a small-scale *Phase 1* clinical trial unless the FDA places the study on hold. Phase 1 studies are used to evaluate pharmacokinetic parameters and tolerance, generally in healthy volunteers. These studies include initial single-dose studies, dose escalation, and short-term repeated-dose studies.

Phase 2: Clinical Development—Therapeutic Exploratory

Phase 2 clinical studies are small-scale trials to evaluate a drug's preliminary efficacy and side-effect profile in a small group of patients (typically ranging from 100 to 250). The participants studied in this phase are usually patients who suffer diseases that the experimental medicine is intended to treat. They are usually identified by physicians in multiple sites (research centers, clinics, and hospitals) all over the world. Additional safety and clinical pharmacology studies are also included in this category.

Phase 3: Clinical Development—Therapeutic Confirmatory

Phase 3 studies are large-scale clinical trials for safety and efficacy in large patient populations. These trials generally provide the primary basis for the benefit-risk assessment for the new medicine and much of the core information about the drug that is analyzed to be included in the future label of the medicine.

While Phase 3 studies are in progress, preparations are made for submitting the Biologics License Application (BLA) or the New Drug Application (NDA). NDAs are reviewed by the Center for Drug Evaluation and Research (CDER). This application, which includes reams of data from all stages of testing, is a requirement for FDA approval to market the new medicine.

Sometimes, when side effects come to light, the FDA may require additional studies (*Phase 4*) to evaluate long-term effects.

Phase 4: Post-Approval Marketing Testing

The final post-marketing phase of drug testing is becoming more and more important to explore the safety in larger number of patients after longer-term treatment (IRS, 2013). In fact, through such trials, researchers collect additional information about long-term risks, benefits, and optimal use. These trials often involve thousands of subjects and may continue for several years.

Finally, once the new drug receives the FDA approval, it has to be manufactured and sold.

The development times are similar between the US and Europe and also have not changed much over the past decades. Not only is the time required by new drug development very long, but attrition rates are also really high. According to Pharmaceutical Research and Manufacturers of America (PhRMA), for every 10,000 compounds synthesized, only one will be approved by the FDA (Alexander and Salazar, 2009). Failure can result from toxicity, manufacturing difficulties, inadequate efficacy, economic and competitive factors, and various other problems.

A successful drug can be very profitable. If companies do manage to make a safe and effective treatment for a major disease[17] (such as lung cancer or a burdensome disease such as senile dementia) and get the drug onto the market, the rewards can be enormous (the so-called "*blockbuster drugs*").[18]

B.2.3   Key Performance Indicators

Profitability and revenue growth is not easy to achieve in general, and—for technology-based companies—it is an even greater challenge. For technology-based businesses, such as biopharmaceuticals, the *value chain* is particularly complex and difficult to develop and manage.

In a competitive market, characterized by rapid change and uncertainty, many interconnected factors influence the success of a firm.

First of all, a fluid *venture capital* environment is important since biotech firms tend to cluster in regions where venture capital is abundant (Niosi, 2003). Deeds, DeCarolis, and Coombs (1998, 1999) point out that, for high technology firms, rapid development of new products is key for success. In fact, it allows firms to gain cash flow, external visibility, reputation, and market share. New product development capabilities are therefore a function of a firm's scientific, technology and managerial skills (Deeds et al., 1998, 1999).

Several cross-industry studies have shown how *patents* are crucial for biotech companies since, as in any research-based industry, the protection of research results is a key determinant for the firms' growth. Regulatory and patent issues can still hamper and distort trade flows. For example, the World Trade Organization Agreement on Trade Related Aspects of Intellectual Property (TRIPs) establishes certain minimum protections for intellectual property. Also, it is necessary to consider that the biotechnology industry has relatively low imitation costs and patents are a fundamental condition for future exclusive products (Niosi, 2003). In addition, *collaborations* are viewed as increasingly important to make significant progress, improve productivity, and increase efficiency for biotech firms. Many companies expand R&D collaboration vertically with grants, licensing, and acquisitions, as well as horizontally with private/public partnerships and pre-competitive collaborations. Many theories put the accent on external factors to explain growth in biotechnology firms, considering strategic alliances to be the major determinant, since firms must keep contact with the sources of constantly evolving knowledge to succeed (Gambardella, 1995; Niosi, 1995; Powell, Koput, and Smith-Doerr, 1996). Therefore, both internal activities and strategies, such as the product area and protection of intellectual property through patents, as well as external factors, such as venture capital financing and strategic alliances, have an impact on rapid growth in the biopharmaceutical sector.

The whole range of factors influencing the success of the biopharmaceutical firms can be illustrated by the following figure.

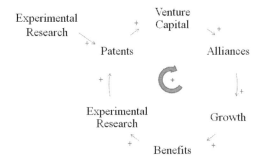

Figure B.3 Factors Influencing the Success of Biopharmaceutical Firms
Source: Authors' elaboration

Biotech firms basically need to effectively get products into the market-place and get shareholders a return on investment. This includes advancing existing projects in clinical trials, expanding R&D infrastructures, and negotiating collaborations that retain maximum downstream value possibly acquiring other technologies or companies.

Table B.1 Learning Blocks—Appendix B

Meta-Industry	Technology Platform	Science-Based
Knowledge Intensive	Research Intensive	Green/Blue Biotechnology
Red Biotechnology	White/Gray Biotechnology	Bioinformatics
Biopharmaceutical	Big Pharma	Preclinical
Clinical Phase 1	Clinical Phase 2	Clinical Phase 3
Phase 4		Blockbuster Drugs

NOTES

1. You can also find authors who support the opposite view, i.e., biotechnology is part of the broader life sciences industry.
2. The European Federation of Biotechnology (E.F.B.) is a European non-profit federation that brings together national associations, universities, scientific institutes, biotech companies, and individual researchers in the field of bio-technology for the purpose of promoting biotechnologies in Europe and the world at large.
3. The Convention on Biological Diversity is an international treaty that was adopted in 1992 to safeguard biodiversity, the long-term use of its elements, and the fair sharing of advantages deriving from the exploitation of genetic resources.

4. In Europe, biotech firms garnered 26 percent of the venture capital investments in all industries, which was the joint highest proportion, along with computer software (Ernst and Young, 2012).
5. Bioprocess Technology is the sub-discipline within biotechnology that combines living matter, in the form of organisms or enzymes, with nutrients under specific optimal conditions to make a desired product. It is responsible for translating discoveries of life sciences into practical and industrial products, processes, and techniques that can serve the needs of society (Enfors and Häggström, 2000).
6. Pharmacogenomics is the study of how the genetic inheritance of an individual affects the body's response to drugs. Its main objective is to design and manufacture drugs adaptable to the individual's genetic makeup (e.g., better vaccines, development of tailor-made medicines, more precise methodologies for the identification of the proper drug dosages, and improvements in the drug discovery and approval process).
7. Genetic testing regards direct study of the DNA molecule. The most common uses are: carrier screening, confirmational diagnosis of symptomatic individuals, forensic/identity testing, newborn and prenatal diagnostic screening, presymptomatic testing for estimating the risk of developing adult-onset cancers, and predicting adult-onset disorders.
8. Gene therapy is used for the cure or treatment of genetic and familiar diseases such as cancer and AIDS. There are two ways to conduct a gene therapy treatment: ex vivo (cells from the patient's blood or bone marrow are first removed and grown in the laboratory before being returned to the patient by injection into a vein) and in vivo (cells are not removed from the patient and vectors are used to deliver the desired gene to cells directly in the patient's body).
9. They are represented by short sequences of DNA or RNA (such as antisense molecules) that stop the production of disease-causing proteins by inhibiting the function of the cognate gene.
10. Data presented here refer to 2011 (www.oecd.org/innovation/inno/keybio technologyindicators.htm). Various sources provide significantly different data since different methodologies and definitions are used.
11. The study refers to the period 1976–1989.
12. It is useful to refer to the large body of literature on the "attacker's advantage" and the "resistance" to innovate by incumbent companies (Foster, 1986; Beinhocker, 1999; Snull, 1999; Englehardt and Simmons, 2002).
13. www.wipo.int/patent-law/en/developments/biotechnology.html
14. In 2013 Johnson and Johnson, Pfizer, GlaxoSmithKline, Merck, Sanofi Aventis and Novartis are in the top ten list of World's largest Big Pharma.
15. What we have defined as Fully Integrated Pharmaceutical Company (FIPCO) in Chapter 1.
16. www.wipo.int/sme/en/documents/patents_biotech.htm.
17. Data (O'Neil and Hopkins, 2012) reveal that there are several million people world-wide affected by diseases that are not treated with adequate intensity. Due to the high costs related to R&D, pharmaceutical companies typically concentrate their pipeline investments in drugs that promise huge returns. This is the cause of the still too limited attention to illnesses such as tropical disease that, although represent a large diffusion at a global level, are not widespread in developed countries. On the other hand, diseases affecting the prosperous, developed world, where patients and governments are willing and have funds to pay for treatments, feature much more prominently in drug development projects.
18. More than 120 drugs earned more than $1 billion in revenues in 2009 (O'Neil and Hopkins, 2012).

REFERENCES

Alexander, John C., and Daniel E. Salazar. 2009. "Modern Drug Discovery and Development." In *Clinical and Translational Science: Principles of Human Research,* edited by D. Robertson and G. H. Williams, 361–377. Burlington: Elsevier.

Arora, Ashish, and Alfonso Gambardella. 1990. "Complementarity and External Linkages: The Strategies of the Large Firms in Biotechnology." *The Journal of Industrial Economics:* 361–379.

Audretsch, David, and Maryann Feldman. 2003. "Small-firm strategic Research Partnerships: The Case of Biotechnology." *Technology Analysis & Strategic Management* 15, no. 2: 273–288.

Battelle. 2010. *2011 Global R&D Funding Forecast.* Columbus: Battelle.

Beinhocker Eric. D. 1999. "Robust Adaptive Strategies." *Sloan Management Review* 40, no. 3: 83–94.

Biotechnology Industry Organization. 2012. "Bioscience Economic Development." Report, May, www.bio.org/sites/default/files/State-Leg-Best-Practices_0.pdf.

Casper, Steven, and Anastasios Karamanos. 2003. "Commercializing Science in Europe: The Cambridge Biotechnology Cluster." *European Planning Studies* 11, no. 7: 805–822.

Cooke, Philip. 2001. "Biotechnology Clusters in the UK: Lessons from Localisation in the Commercialisation of Science." *Small Business Economics* 17, no. 1–2: 43–59.

DaSilva, Edgar J. 2005. "The Colours of Biotechnology: Science, Development and Humankind." *Editorial Journal of Biotechnology* 7, no. 3.

Deeds, David L., Donna Marie DeCarolis, and Joseph E. Coombs. 1998. "Firm-Specific Resources and Wealth Creation in High-Technology Ventures: Evidence from Newly Public Biotechnology Firms." *Entrepreneurship Theory and Practice* 22, no. 3: 55.

———. 1999. "The Impact of Firm-Specific Capabilities on the Amount of Capital Raised in an Initial Public Offering: An Empirical Investigation of the Biotechnology Industry." *Strategic Management Journal* 20: 953–968.

Di Gregorio, Dante, and Scott Shane. 2003. "Why Do Some Universities Generate More Start-Ups Than Others?" *Research Policy* 32, no. 2: 209–227.

Edwards, Mark G., Fiona Murray, and Robert Yu. 2003. "Value Creation and Sharing Among Universities, Biotechnology and Pharma." *Nature Biotechnology* 21, no. 6: 618–624.

Enfors, Sven-Olof, and Lena Häggström. 2000. *Bioprocess Technology: Fundamentals and Applications.* Stockholm: Royal Institute of Technology.

Englehardt, Charles S., and Peter R. Simmons. 2002. "Creating an Organizational Space for Learning." *The Learning Organization. An International Journal* 9, no. 1: 39–47.

Ernst, and Young. 2012. "Beyond Borders: The Global Biotechnology Industry Reports." Report, www.ey.com/Publication/vwLUAssets/Beyond_borders_2012/$FILE/Beyond_borders_2012.pdf.

European Commission. 2009. "The Financing of Biopharmaceutical Product Development in Europe." Report, October. (http://ec.europa.eu/enterprise/sectors/biotechnology/files/docs/financing_biopharma_product_dev_en.pdf).

Forrest, Janet E., and Michael J. C. Martin. 1992. "Strategic Alliances Between Large and Small Research Intensive Organizations: Experiences in the Biotechnology Industry." *R&D Management* 22, no. 1: 41–54.

Foster, Richard. 1986. *Innovation: The Attackers Advantage.* New York: Summit Books.

Gambardella, Alfonso. 1995. *Science and Innovation: The US Pharmaceutical Industry During the 1980s*. Cambridge: Cambridge University Press.

Gerstein, Mark. 2007. "Bioinformatics Introduction." Accessed November 15, 2013, from http://bioinfo.mbb.yale.edu/mbb452a/intro/intro.pdf

Giesecke, Susanne. 2000. "The Contrasting Roles of Government in the Development of Biotechnology Industry in the US and Germany." *Research Policy* 29, no. 2: 205–223.

Haanes, Knut, and Øystein Fjeldstad. 2000. "Linking Intangible Resources and Competition." *European Management Journal* 18, no. 1: 52–62.

Hagedoorn, John. 1993. "Understanding the Rationale of Strategic Technology Partnering: Interorganizational Modes of Cooperation and Sectorial Differences." *Strategic Management Journal* 14, no. 5: 371–385.

Hara, Takuji. 2004. "Innovation in the Pharmaceutical Industry: The Process of Drug Discovery and Development. "*Administrative Science Quarterly* 49, no. 2: 312–314.

Internal Revenue Service (IRS). 2013. "Biotech Industry Overview." Last modified March 4 (www.irs.gov/Businesses/Biotech-Industry-Overview-1).

Jensen, Richard, and Marie Thursby. 2001. "Proofs and Prototypes for Sale: The Licensing of University Inventions." *American Economic Review*: 240–259.

Levitt, Theodore (1965) "Exploit the Product Life Cycle." *Harvard Business Review* 43, November–December: 81–94.

Luo, Xiaowei Rose, Kenneth W. Koput, and Walter W. Powell. 2009. "Intellectual Capital or Signal? The Effects of Scientists on Alliance Formation in Knowledge-Intensive Industries." *Research Policy* 38, no. 8: 1313–1325.

McMillan, G. Steven, Francis Narin, and David L. Deeds. 2000. "An Analysis of the Critical Role of Public Science in Innovation: The Case of Biotechnology." *Research Policy* 29, no. 1: 1–8.

Meyer-Krahmer, Frieder, and Ulrich Schmoch. 1998. "Science-Based Technologies: University–Industry Interactions in Four Fields." *Research Policy* 27, no. 8: 835–851.

Niosi, Jorge. 2003. "Alliances are Not Enough Explaining Rapid Growth in Biotechnology Firms." *Research Policy* 32, no. 5: 737–750.

OECD. 1982. "Biotechnology. International trends and perspectives." Accessed November 15, 2013, from www.oecd.org/sti/biotech/2097562.pdf

O'Neil, Michael, and Michael Hopkins. 2012. "The Bioscience Sector: Challenges and Opportunities." In *A Biotech Manager's Handbook,* edited by M. Murray and M. Hopkins, 1–19. Cambridge: Woodhead Publishing.

Onetti, Alberto, and Antonella Zucchella. 2008. *Imprenditorialità, internazionalizzazione e innovazione. Il business model delle imprese biotech*. Roma: Carocci.

Pharmaceutical Research and Manufacturers of America (PhRMA). 2010. "Driving State Economic Growth in the 21st Century: Advancing the Biopharmaceutical Sector." Report, November, www.phrma.org/sites/default/files/pdf/phrmafinal_report_11_15_2010_.pdf.

Pisano, Gary. 2006. "Can Science be a Business?" *Harvard Business Review* 84, no. 10: 114.

Powell, Walter W. 1996. Inter-Organizational Collaboration in the Biotechnology Industry. *Journal of Institutional and Theoretical Economics* 152, no. 1: 197–215.

Powell, Walter W., Kenneth W. Koput, and Laurel Smith-Doerr. 1996. "Interorganizational Collaboration and the Locus of Innovation: Networks of Learning in Biotechnology." *Administrative Science Quarterly* 41, no. 1: 116–145.

Rader, Ronald A. 2005. "What is a Biopharmaceutical." Report, Biopharma, www.biopharma.com/bioexec_pt2.pdf.

Rothaermel, Frank T. 2001. "Complementary Assets, Strategic Alliances, and the Incumbent's Advantage: An Empirical Study of Industry and Firm Effects in the Biopharmaceutical Industry." *Research Policy* 30, no. 8: 1235–1251.

Sharp, Margaret. 1999. "The Science of Nations: European Multinationals and American Biotechnology." *International Journal of Biotechnology* 1, no. 1: 132–162.

Snull Donald N. 1999. "Why Good Companies Go Bad." *Harvard Business Review* 77, no. 4: 42–52.

Stuart, Toby E., Salih Zeki Ozdemir, and Waverly W. Ding. 2007. "Vertical alliance Networks: The Case of University–Biotechnology–Pharmaceutical Alliance Chains." *Research Policy* 36, no. 4: 477–498.

Wikipedia. 2013. "Biotechnology." Last modified September 12. (http://en.wikipedia. org/wiki/Biotechnology).

Zucker, Lynne G., Michael R. Darby, and Marilynn B. Brewer. 1999. "Intellectual Capital and the Birth of US Biotechnology Enterprises." Working paper, National Bureau of Economic Research (No. w4653).

Appendix C
Entrepreneurship

Entrepreneurship is a process whereby firms and individuals in firms (*entrepreneurs*) explore and exploit opportunities (March, 1991), leveraging their ability to manage uncertainty in a proactive way. The current business environment is characterized by growing complexity, triggered by hyper-competition (D'Aveni and Gunther, 1994) and globalization (Knight, 2000). Moreover, the financial crisis of 2008 and the consequent recession left an indelible mark on the economic system, since it spread to all Western countries at an impressive speed, soon involving all economic agents: countries/governments, (central) banks, households, and firms. Within this framework, entrepreneurs have a central role in economic improvement and growth; this because of their ability to identify new business opportunities and exploit them through the creation of innovative business ventures. In fact, as theorized by several scholars, "new business creation has a significant impact on economic growth, innovation, and job creation."[1] Particularly for a start-up company, the best way to achieve a high growth rate and scale up is to disrupt an existing market or to create a new one (Rachleff, 2013). It is the way to grow rapidly with a limited investment of resources if compared with more conventional businesses.

However, creating a new firm is not so simple, as it takes different abilities, knowledge, and skills, as well as a lot of passion. Therefore, it is interesting to investigate the entrepreneurial process of opportunity identification and analyze the individuals who decide to pursue it.

Thus, we decided to conduct an in-depth literature review of the research field on entrepreneurship. At first we will introduce entrepreneurship and describe the main types of entrepreneurs, together with a comprehensive analysis of the main approaches to entrepreneurial opportunity identification. Secondly, we will provide a literature background about corporate (i.e., firm-level) entrepreneurship (which we also defined as entrepreneurship) and innovation.

C.1   DIFFERENT CATEGORIES OF ENTREPRENEURS

Entrepreneurship has been studied since the seventies (Cooper, 2003). Although most of the initial research has been prevalently theoretical,[2] it is possible to identify several studies (Aldrich and Fiol, 1994; Aldrich and Kenworthy, 1999; Aldrich and Ruef, 2006; Alvarez and Barney, 2005; Alvarez and Barney, 2007; Alvarez and Parker, 2009; Baker and Nelson, 2005; Casson, 1982; Eckhardt and Ciuchta, 2008; Gartner, 1985; Gloria-Palermo, 1999; McMullen and Shepherd, 2006; Sarasvathy, 2001; Sarasvathy et al., 2003; Shane, 2003; Shane and Eckhardt, 2003; Shane and Venkataraman, 2000; Venkataraman, 1997) with a common defining research question: where do business opportunities come from?

Therefore, it is possible to define *entrepreneurship* as a process whereby firms—and individuals in firms (entrepreneurs)—explore and exploit opportunities (March, 1991), leveraging their ability to manage uncertainty in a proactive way.

The *individual entrepreneur* is characterized by the ability to detect and to execute business opportunities, which he/she exploits through new ventures. He/she participates in funding the startup, carries out the role of arbitrator, or "sells the idea" of the business project.

The *corporate entrepreneur* must also be considered. The chief executive of large firms no longer deals with managing assets and coordinating and controlling its activities. This role also involves anticipating, articulating, and managing change. In the current economic environment, corporate entrepreneurs reinvent the firm on a daily basis: they must create new enterprises (the so called spin-offs) and develop novel business opportunities.

There is also a particular category of entrepreneurs, who "habitually" detect new business opportunities and start-up new businesses (Iacobucci and Rosa, 2005). Ronstadt (1982) was the first to define *habitual entrepreneurs* as individuals that start several businesses before launching a successful one. This typology of individuals is usually compared to *novice entrepreneurs,* who are at their first venture (Birley and Westhead, 1993; Wright, Robbie, and Ennew, 1997). Hall (1995) argues that two different types of habitual entrepreneurs exist. He made a distinction between serial and portfolio entrepreneurs. *Serial entrepreneurs* are entrepreneurs who start several independent ventures but actually run only one business at a time. Previous businesses may have been sold, closed, or run by third parties without a direct involvement. *Portfolio entrepreneurs* are entrepreneurs who start more companies at the same time. Hall also made a distinction between *voluntary serial owners* (i.e., those who terminated their previous business experience before initiating a new venture) and *involuntary serial owners* (i.e., in case of an involuntary cessation of the business). Extending Hall's insightful definitions, Westhead and Wright (1998) define serial entrepreneurs as those individuals who have sold/closed their original independent business but, at a later date, have established, purchased, and/or inherited another independent business. Portfolio entrepreneurs, on the other hand, are defined as individuals who own two or more independent businesses at the same time, i.e., they retain their original business and establish, purchase, and/or inherit another business. Finally, novice entrepreneurs are defined as those individuals who currently own one independent business and have no prior business ownership experience as a founder, purchaser, or inheritor of a business.

This classification is based on the assumption, common to every process of categorization, that these classes have important performance implications (Westhead and Wright, 1998). Accordingly, current studies show that:

- The creation of an effective network[3] (McGrath and MacMillan, 2000),
- Easier access to financial resources, and
- The possibility to hire skilled labor (Hellman and Puri, 2002) are the main observable features that differentiate habitual from novice entrepreneurs (Iacobucci and Rosa, 2005).

Thus, many researchers consider entrepreneurship not as a one-time action (Westhead and Wright, 1998) but a continuum of different activities performed by habitual entrepreneurs that lead to the creation of new businesses. In this vision, the success and failure of a firm does not represent the success and failure of the entrepreneur him/herself (Sarasvathy, Menon, and Kuechle, 2013), since new ventures always represent a successful instrument of learning (Westhead, Ucbasaran, Wright, and Binks, 2005), independently of their actual performance (Presutti, Onetti, and Odorici, 2008).

Thus, in order to survive and prosper, individuals and organizations need to continually identify new opportunities beyond existing competences (Hamel and Prahalad, 1989; McGrath et al., 1996). This is particularly true in dynamic environments, where windows of opportunity rapidly open and close (Nordman and Mélen, 2008).

As stated above, the identification of opportunities has been recognized as one of the most important abilities of successful entrepreneurs (Ardichvili, Cardozo, and Ray, 2003), and consequently has become a key topic in the studies of entrepreneurship. Gaglio and Katz (2001) state that "understanding the opportunity identification process represents one of the core intellectual questions for the domain of entrepreneurship." The research of Alvarez and Busenitz (2001) on entrepreneurship and resource-based theory has extended its boundaries to include identification of opportunities as a resource that, through the process of exploitation, can lead to competitive advantage (Shepherd and DeTienne, 2005). A recent definition of the International Entrepreneurship literature[4] also emphasized the opportunity-centered aspect of internationalization: "International entrepreneurship is the discovery, enactment, evaluation, and exploitation of opportunities—across national borders—to create future goods and services" (Oviatt and McDougall, 2005). According to this definition, entrepreneurial firms must be successful in how quickly, efficiently, and holistically they sense and deal with opportunities abroad (Crick and Spence, 2005; Dimitratos and Jones, 2005). Consistently, many authors (Shane and Venkataraman, 2000) have focused their research on the motivations, methods, and circumstances underlying the ability to identify opportunities, which only certain individuals seem to possess.

C.2   OPPORTUNITY IDENTIFICATION

A large part of the entrepreneurship research (Stevenson and Sahlman, 1989) focuses on the concept of *opportunity identification*. We can distinguish between three main approaches, which originate from very different fields of study. The *functional perspective* focuses on the entrepreneur's interaction with the economic environment (Casson, 1982; Hebert and Link, 1989) where entrepreneurship is mostly considered as an economic function.[5]

The *personality perspective* assumes that the predisposition of certain individuals to perform entrepreneurial actions and activities depends on their unique personality traits (Greenberger and Sexton, 1988). Although this perspective sheds light on the subjective factors that influence entrepreneurial behaviors, it has received much criticism for being too static (Gartner, 1988; Shaver, 1995).

In this sense, the *behavioral perspective* assumes a more dynamic and comprehensive viewpoint, focusing also on what entrepreneurs do, rather than only on who they are (Gartner, 1988).

C.2.1   The Functional Perspective

Economic theory represents the foundation on which early entrepreneurship theories have been based on. Here, entrepreneurial action is analyzed as an economic function (Casson, 1982), which essentially encompasses the activities and behavioral characteristic of the entrepreneur. This "functional approach" focuses on the economic system (Coase, 1937), and the entrepreneurial phenomena are considered as the result of the entrepreneur's interaction with the economic environment (Casson, 1982; Knight, 1921).

According to a neoclassical view of entrepreneurship, opportunities are considered as independent variables, available to everyone, not only entrepreneurs (Shane, 2000). Entrepreneurship is driven by incentives and by the willingness to pay for relevant information (Casson, 1998), given the heterogeneous distribution of knowledge in the economic environment (Hayek, 1945). In their attempt to study how economic actors identify opportunities, Amit, Glosten, and Muller (1993) and Bull and Willard (1993) describe a situation where different costs and different incentives and rewards are the main drivers of entrepreneurial decisions (Casson, 1995). The following paragraphs contextualize the main cost- and incentive-based theories (transaction costs, agency, and extrinsic motivations) within the entrepreneurship stream in general and the opportunity identification field in particular.

The Transaction Costs Theory

The traditional transaction cost theory of economics (Williamson, 1975, 1985) is based on two main hypotheses: information dispersion and uncertainty in the outcomes of economic activities. Given the random distribution of information in the economic environment (Hayek, 1945), individuals perceive that different opportunities are pursuable at different costs and with different returns. Thus, the mainstream opinion here is that opportunities are selected based on their respective *transaction costs*.

In recent years, researches have gone further and linked the transaction cost theory to the concept of entrepreneurial discovery. Drawing from early considerations on entrepreneurial phenomena in economics (Casson, 1982; Knight, 1921; Mises, 1949), Foss et al. (2006) assimilate entrepreneurship to a "judgment" of possible outcomes under uncertain conditions. Thus, such judgment is influenced by transaction costs. Entrepreneurs are expected to actively look for new solutions to reduce transaction costs and, consequently, increase the potential value of the opportunity (Foss and Foss, 2005; Foss et al., 2006). At the same time, Foss et al. (2006) agree that entrepreneurship is not only about reducing transaction costs, but is also about proactively searching for new value-creating opportunities (Conner, 1991; Foss et al., 2006; Kim and Mahoney, 2006).

Through the identification of new business opportunities, entrepreneurs are able to equilibrate markets that have been destabilized by unexpected events and thus characterized by higher transaction costs (Barzel, 1997; Foss et al., 2006; Hayek, 1945). In this sense, Foss et al. (2006) see transaction costs as factors that "shape" the process of entrepreneurial discovery.

The Agency Theory

The neoclassical view of economics considers entrepreneurs as individuals with bounded rationality (Williamson, 1975, 1985), while entrepreneurial behavior depends on appropriate *incentive systems*.

According to the agency theory, firm characteristics are dependent on the congruence in agents' and principals' incentives (Holstrom and Tirole, 1989; Jensen and Meckling, 1976). The fundamentals of this approach are then similar to the transaction cost theory, whereas costs are replaced by incentives as a driver for entrepreneurial behaviors. As previously explained, entrepreneurs in economic theories turn informational advantages into opportunities when information is randomly distributed across agents (Hayek, 1945). Therefore, given a certain level of uncertainty, information asymmetry, and conflicting objectives, appropriate incentive structures can encourage or limit the identification of entrepreneurial opportunities.[6]

Moving from entrepreneurs to firms, the problem with opportunity identification is that a company may not have the appropriate incentive system or cannot bear the costs to change it. Jones and Butler (1992) prove that, in order to boost entrepreneurial capabilities at the firm level, companies should solve internal agency problems, such as aligning interests between principals and agents through appropriate incentive structures. In addition, because of higher agency costs related to a greater organizational complexity, returns of entrepreneurial activities appear to be lower (Jones and Butler, 1992).

Extrinsic Motivation

According to economics literature, extrinsic motivation, i.e., *financial rewards*, play a key role in determining entrepreneurship (Baumol, 1996; Kuratko, Hornsby, and Naffziger, 1997; Langan-Fox and Roth, 1995). High potential financial returns increase individuals' propensity and motivation for finding opportunities (Campbell, 1992; Schumpeter, 1961; Venkataraman, 1997). In addition, the level of financial reward has been found to be closely related to the number of generated opportunities in general (Shepherd and DeTienne, 2005) and to innovation and creativity in particular (Abbey and Dickson, 1983; Woodman, Sawyer, and Griffin, 1993).

C.2.2   The Personality Perspective

More recently, the literature on opportunity identification has shifted its research focus from the "functional approach" to the "*personality approach*": an individual's unique personality is assumed as the key driving force for the entrepreneurial activity. The goal of the personality perspective research field is to identify the specific individual traits that delineate the profile of successful entrepreneurs (McClelland, 1961; Timmons and Spinelli, 1994). In particular, two factors are strongly related to the ability to identify new business opportunities: entrepreneurial alertness (Kirzner, 1978) and prior knowledge and experience (Shane, 2000; Venkataraman, 1997).

The personality perspective is greatly based on psychological theories. Many authors distinguish entrepreneurs from other individuals by looking for particular cognitive traits, such as risk propensity, need for achievement, and self-confidence (Begley and Boyd, 1988; Brockhaus, 1980; Forlani and Mullins, 2000; McClelland, 1961; Shaver and Scott, 1991). However, since empirical studies on the topic have not produced persuasive results (Brockhaus and Horowitz, 1986; Low and MacMillan, 1988), researchers have gradually shifted the focus from cognitive traits to cognitive processes and mechanisms that entrepreneurs use for collecting, selecting, and processing information required to identify opportunities in the external environment (Baron, 1998; Nicholls-Nixon, Cooper, and Woo, 2000; Shane and Venkataraman, 2000).

The paragraphs below illustrate the relationship between opportunity identification and the main two personality factors: entrepreneurial alertness and prior knowledge and experience.

Entrepreneurial Alertness

Kirzner (1973) is the first to explain the identification of entrepreneurial opportunities with the concept of "*entrepreneurial alertness*," i.e., a unique attitude to sense environmental variations and recognize related opportunities (Kirzner, 1973). In line with that, Ray and Cardozo (1996) sustain that opportunity identification is preceded by—and positively related to—"entrepreneurial awareness," defined as a superior "alertness to information." The similar idea of "entrepreneurial preparedness"[7] was introduced by Ray and Cardozo (1996), who defined it as "a propensity to notice and be sensitive to information about objects, incidents, and patterns of behavior in the environment, with special sensitivity to maker and user problems, unmet needs and interests, and novel entrepreneurial combinations of resources," shaped by the entrepreneur's specific set of skills and capabilities (Harvey and Evans, 1995). However, other researchers have failed to demonstrate the positive link between alertness and opportunity identification (Buzenitz, 1996).

Prior Knowledge and Experience

An individual's prior knowledge and experience is related to opportunity value recognition, learning, and application to new profitable ends (Cohen and Levinthal, 1990). Therefore it is considered a key driver in the opportunity identification process (Venkataraman, 1997). In line with the view of entrepreneurship as an outcome of information asymmetries amongst economic agents (Hayek, 1945) research demonstrates that individuals are more likely to detect information and identify opportunities related to their existing knowledge base (Fiet, 1996; Shane, 2000; Venkataraman, 1997; Von Hippel, 1994), whereas the value of new information often calls for integration with prior knowledge in order to be identified and exploited (Shane and Venkataraman, 2000). If we observe the phenomenon from a learning perspective, the way individuals exploit new information to identify unexplored and more valuable opportunities is highly related to the Cohen and Levinthal's *absorptive capacity* construct (1990). The identification of only certain opportunities is then due to the specific knowledge base individuals have previously accrued, which creates "knowledge corridors" that influence the learning process (Hayek, 1945; Ronstadt, 1988).

Prior knowledge may be the outcome of work experience (Cooper, Gimeno-Gascon, and Woo 1994; Evans and Leighton, 2002), as well as education (Gimeno et al., 1997). Past experience broadens the set of opportunities and the number of opportunity sources entrepreneurs have access to (Cyert and March, 1963; Fiet, Piskounov, and Gustavsson, 2000; Shane, 2003). Prior knowledge deriving from education smoothes the process of new knowledge accumulation and absorption, and thus increases the number of available opportunities (Gimeno et al., 1997).

Prior knowledge may also be increased through *ground learning* (Huber, 1991). In particular, opportunity identification has been proven to be related to prior knowledge of markets, such as knowledge about competitors, products, and existing and emerging technologies (Schumpeter, 1934; Von Hippel, 1988), that can improve the way to exploit innovation (Shane, 2000). On the same position, Sigrist (1999) asserts that the integration between knowledge related to the entrepreneur's domain (e.g., pharmaceutical, IT, chemicals, etc.) and different knowledge previously accumulated leads to a more effective opportunity detection process.

C.2.3 The Behavioral Perspective

Until recently, the majority of entrepreneurship studies on opportunity identification concentrated on the unique characteristics of the entrepreneur's personality (McClelland, 1961; Timmons, 1999). Although it may represent a valid point of view, Deakins and Freel (1998) criticized this approach because it underestimates the role learning plays in the acquisition of certain abilities. In addition, Lee and Venkataraman (2006) point out the importance of the position in social networks as a key variable for understanding the opportunity identification process. Early research also supports that the focus of entrepreneurship theory must be on individual's behaviors (which are also influenced by personality) rather than merely on their personality traits—i.e., what entrepreneurs do rather than who they are (Gartner, 1988). As a consequence, networking represents a key factor of the entrepreneur's behavior towards opportunity identification.

Networking and Opportunity Identification

Many scholars suggest that the prime determinant of entrepreneurship is the entrepreneur's network position (Aldrich and Zimmer, 1986; Burt, 1992). In particular, Aldrich and Zimmer (1986) sustain that the social network of entrepreneurs[8] plays a pivotal role in the entrepreneurial process.

Many researches that study how social networks influence entrepreneurial decisions (Borch, 1994; Starr and MacMillan, 1990) are inspired by the seminal work of Jacobs (1961), who introduces the notion of social capital.

The "social capital theory" explains how interpersonal relationships in social networks provide access to information and know-how (Adler and Kwon, 2002; Burt, 1997; Lin, 2002; Nahapiet and Goshal, 1998). In particular, research on entrepreneurs' social networks analyzes the impact on innovation (Powell, Koput, and Smith Doerr, 1996), opportunity identification (Singh, Hills, and Lumpkin, 1999; Singh, 2000), and opportunity exploitation (Aldrich and Wiedenmayer, 1993).

In general, there are three key network-related aspects on which the entrepreneurship literature has focused: *network content*, network governance, and network structure (Hoang and Antoncic, 2003). The first relates to relationships that occur at both the interpersonal and inter-organizational levels; these relationships enable entrepreneurs to access different types of resources (Cromie, Birley, and Callaghan, 1993; Johannisson, 2000), collect information, and develop new potential entrepreneurial initiatives (Hoang and Young, 2000; Singh et al., 1999). *Network governance* analyzes the distinct governance systems—such as power, influence (Brass, 1984; Krackhardt, 1990; Thorelli, 1986), and also trust (Larson, 1992; Lorenzoni and

Lipparini, 1999)—that facilitate the resource exchange. Such mechanisms imply a more effective exploitation of inter-organizational networks, significant for gathering information that may enhance opportunity identification (Singh et al., 1999).

Finally, *network structure* describes the characteristics of ties—both direct and indirect—that connect individuals and/or firms. It may involve factors such as the embeddedness and density of networks (Granovetter, 1973; Hills, Lumpkin, and Singh, 1997), as well as the strength of the ties (Burt, 2000; Eisenhardt and Tabrizi, 1995; Henderson and Cockburn, 1994).

C.2.4 Opportunity Identification: Summary and Resulting Models

As discussed above and wrapped-up in Table C.1, entrepreneurial opportunity identification can be examined from three dominant theoretical perspectives (Stevenson and Sahlman, 1989): functional, personality, and behavioral.

Since the above described approaches are built on different and often conflicting assumptions, they explain the *opportunity identification* process through diverse and specific driving factors (Bhave, 1994; De Koning and Muzyka, 1999; Schwartz and Teach, 2000; Sigrist, 1999; Singh et al., 1999). Notwithstanding, they are not necessarily mutually exclusive. In fact, they provide complementary insights that may shed light about the process of opportunity discovery. Factors related to the economic environment as well as personality traits and behaviors of the entrepreneur may co-determine the process of opportunity identification.

Some more recent research tries to integrate the traditional approaches. Most of these models depict opportunity identification as a staged process (Bhave, 1994; Christensen et al., 1990). Ardichvili and colleagues (2003) see "entrepreneurial alertness" as a precondition for opportunity identification and identify the three central factors that determine it: personality traits, prior knowledge and experience, and social networks. A more creativity-based framework of opportunity identification is proposed by Hills, Shrader, and Lumpkin (1999) that focuses on the social study network context. They

Table.C.1 Opportunity Identification: Main Theoretical Perspectives

Opportunity Identification Approach	Theoretical Focus
Functional Perspective	Entrepreneur's interaction with the economic enviroment
Personality Perspective	Personality traits of the individual entrepreneur and their link to opportunity identification
Behavioral Perspective	Individual entrepreneur's activity

distinguish the opportunity discovery phase from the opportunity formation. Also Sigrist (1999) and Shane (2000) propose models of opportunity identification, analyzing, respectively, the cognitive processes involved in and the prior knowledge and experience necessary for successful opportunity recognition.

All the above mentioned research is aimed at analyzing the opportunity identification process from the entrepreneur's point of view. Opportunity identification can be significant not only for individual entrepreneurs, but also for organizations (Hamel and Prahalad, 1989; McGrath et al., 1996), and thus merits further investigation. That is the goal of the next section.

C.3 OPPORTUNITY IDENTIFICATION FOR ENTREPRENEURIAL FIRMS

After an exhaustive overview of entrepreneurship from an individual standpoint, this section sheds light on the relevant research that studies entrepreneurial phenomena within established organizations. This is what is referred as *corporate entrepreneurship* or *corporate intrapreneurship*. This firm-level approach is consistent with classical economics where individuals with entrepreneurial behaviors are assimilated into firms. Schumpeter (1942) moves the focus from the individual to the firm level by suggesting that organizations are able to invest more resources in innovative projects and/or activities than individuals. More recent literature also recognizes that entrepreneurial activities are not only relevant for startups or SMEs, but it may also take place within large firms (Ahuja and Lampert, 2001). Corporate entrepreneurship is in fact pivotal to the survival, renewal, and growth of established organizations (Ahuja and Lampert, 2001; Dess et al., 2003; Guth and Ginsberg, 1990; Kuratko et al., 1990; Lumpkin and Dess, 1996; Zahra and Covin, 1995; Zahra et al., 1999).

Thus, entrepreneurship can also be present in established firms that need to constantly identify new opportunities, beyond existing competencies, in order to survive and prosper (Hamel and Prahalad, 1989; McGrath et al., 1996). Therefore, opportunity identification represents one of the most powerful stimuli for corporate entrepreneurship: entrepreneurial activities, whether they are associated with an individual or a firm, originate from the identification of relevant opportunities.

Consequently, we provide an overview of the corporate entrepreneurial phenomenon and the most significant factors that enable firms to identify new business opportunities.

C.3.1 Drivers for Corporate Entrepreneurship

Research on corporate entrepreneurship calls attention to the multi-dimensional nature of entrepreneurship. In order to explain the processes and mechanisms that firms use when they behave entrepreneurially, scholars refer to entrepreneurial posture (Covin and Slevin, 1991), entrepreneurial style (Naman and Slevin, 1993), entrepreneurial orientation (Lumpkin and Dess, 1996), entrepreneurial management (Stevenson and Jarillo, 1990), and entrepreneurial strategy-making (Dess, Lumpkin, and Covin, 1997). More specifically, the terms *entrepreneurial orientation* have been mostly used to describe an entrepreneurial firm's strategic orientation, i.e., the decision-making styles, methods, and practices (Lumpkin and Dess, 1996). In general, researchers commonly view entrepreneurial orientation as the combination of three particular dimensions:[9] innovativeness, proactiveness, and risk-taking. Innovativeness is the tendency to engage in and support new ideas, experimentations, and creative processes, thus adapting new viewpoints and abandoning existing practices (Guth and Ginsberg, 1990; Lumpkin and Dess, 1996). Proactiveness refers to the anticipation of actions in the market that may lead to a first-mover advantage (Lumpkin and Dess, 1996; Miller, 1983). By adopting a forward-looking perspective, proactive organizations are usually the first to benefit from new emerging market opportunities. Lastly, risk-taking involves the willingness to invest significant resources to exploit or explore highly uncertain opportunities (Keh, Foo, and Lim, 2002; Miller, 1983; Morris, 1998).

Corporate entrepreneurship is impacted by many factors that can be categorized in two groups. The first group refers to the internal environment of the firm, i.e., the organizational features, while the second group relates to the external environment.

Internal/Organizational Factors

Among all the factors that may impact the corporate entrepreneurial behavior, a key role is played by the firm's internal environment. Main characteristics that are considered to nurture entrepreneurial activities are the following: communication openness (Kanter, 1984; Pinchot, 1985), control mechanisms (Sathe, 1985), organizational structure (Covin and Slevin, 1991; Naman and Slevin, 1993), and managerial support (Kuratko et al., 1993; Stevenson and Jarillo, 1990).

Open communication is defined as the way information and resources are shared within the company. Communication, classified by its amount and quality, has proven to be a pivotal element of the success of entrepreneurial initiative in large organizations (Peters and Waterman, 2004; Zahra, 1991). In addition, authors argue that the presence of *control mechanisms* affect corporate entrepreneurship in different ways. For example, Kuratko et al. (1993) emphasize the significance of control as an efficient way of promoting firm-level entrepreneurial attempts, while MacMillan et al. (1984) and Zahra (1991) report inhibiting effects due to a disproportionate use of formal control itself. A third aspect that has been associated with corporate entrepreneurship is the presence of a supportive *organizational structure* (Burgelman and Sayles, 1986; Covin and Slevin, 1991; Guth and Ginsberg,

1990; Hornsby et al., 1993; Zahra, 1991, 1993). Accordingly, flexible intra-organizational boundaries are considered significant for the promotion of firm-level entrepreneurial activity (Hornsby et al., 1993). Finally, *managerial support* refers to the willingness of the manager to support and promote entrepreneurial activities within the firm (Kuratko et al., 1993; MacMillian et al., 1984; Pearce, Kramer, and Robbins, 1997; Sathe, 1989; Stevenson and Jarillo, 1990; Sykes and Block, 1989). It can be realized through the promotion of innovative ideas and the allocation of the necessary resources. Without a strong commitment by the top management, intrapreneurship initiatives are not likely to be successful.

According to many authors, the above intra-organizational factors, both individually and in combination, are important driving factors of corporate entrepreneurial efforts and have also been associated with a firm's greater ability to innovate (Burgelman, 1983).

External/Environmental Factors

Although internal organizational factors have been widely studied as the most important determinants of corporate entrepreneurship, authors recognize that the external environment also influences entrepreneurial activity at both the individual and firm levels (Covin and Slevin, 1991; Khandwalla, 1987; Miller, 1983; Zahra, 1991, 1993). Specifically, some authors identify particular environmental characteristics that positively influence corporate entrepreneurship activities and their outcomes (munificent environments), while others have some adverse effects (hostile environments). *Environmental munificence* (Guth and Ginsberg, 1990; Khandwalla, 1987; Zahra, 1991, 1993) includes multiple dimensions: dynamism, technological opportunities, industry growth, and demand for new products (Zahra, 1993).

Dynamism relates to the perceived instability and constant change in the market. According to Zahra (1991), dynamism stimulates the involvement in entrepreneurial activities since it creates new opportunities in the market. In order to operate in such highly dynamic environments, firms need to pro-actively search and identify business opportunities (Covin and Covin, 1990) and pursue radical innovation (Utterback, 1974). *Technological change* also opens new windows of opportunities (Tushman and Anderson, 1986), which firms usually approach through adopting an entrepreneurial posture (Guth and Ginsberg, 1990; Khandwalla, 1987).

While market growth may create a similar positive effect on entrepreneurial activities, the perceived market recession may push companies to pursue corporate renewal initiatives. Finally, the *demand for new products* is proven to be a demand-driven stimulus to corporate entrepreneurship (Zahra, 1993).

While some authors consider environmental munificence to persuade organizations in assuming an entrepreneurial posture (Guth and Ginsberg, 1990; Khandwalla, 1987; Zahra, 1991), others have demonstrated that the lack of munificence—i.e., *environmental hostility*—may generate threats that encourage firms to adopt entrepreneurial behaviors (Covin and Slevin, 1991; Hitt et al., 1997; Lumpkin and Dess, 2001; Miller and Friesen, 1983).

Indeed, hostile environments are essentially characterized by adverse conditions, such as unfavorable changes and extremely intense rivalry (Miller, 1993; Morris, 1998; Zahra, 1993). However, the literature suggests that hostile environments can also intensify firm-level entrepreneurial activity (Zahra, 1993) because of the threats they create for the firm (Zahra, 1991). In fact, organizations dealing with critical environmental changes are likely to explore new ways of managing such adverse effects through adoption of entrepreneurial behaviors (Miller, 1983; Morris, 1998; Zahra, 1991, 1993). Correspondingly, the research finds a positive correlation between environmental hostility and a strong entrepreneurial posture (Covin and Slevin, 1991).

C.4 ENTREPRENEURSHIP AND INNOVATION

As already mentioned at the beginning of this Appendix, entrepreneurs are responsible for the economic development through the introduction of innovative ideas, in terms of products, processes, markets, and organization. In order to reach this goal, an entrepreneur must be able to successfully implement these innovations, which means satisfying (new) customers and thus contributing to economic growth and employment.

Innovativeness is then one of the key characteristic that identifies entrepreneurial firms, along with risk-taking and proactiveness. In the next pages, we provide you with some literature background on the topic, which provides different definitions and classifications of *innovation*.

C.4.1 The Sources of Innovation

There is an extensive debate on the sources of innovation. The traditional approaches—the *technology push* (Dosi, 1982; Pavitt and Salomon, 1971; Rosenberg, 1982; Schumpeter 1939), which identifies research and development activity as the innovation engine (Figure C.1), and the *market/demand pull* (Gilpin, 1975; Lambin, 1997; Millier, 1999; Myers and Marquis, 1969; Schmookler, 1966; Utterback, 1974), which assumes the innovation process to be based on market requirements (Figure C.2), seem barely able to explain the innovative behavior of firms and their genesis in the current competitive framework.

Recent studies (Leonard and Rayport 1997; Tidd, Bessant, and Pavitt, 1997) have pointed out the limits of the traditional approaches underlining all the complex mutual relations and the multiplicity of incentives that lead to innovation: from this perspective, the *"innovation push–customer pull"* model introduced by Berthon, Hulbert, and Pitt (1999) probably represents the best approach to describe the genesis of innovation, signaling the need

TECHNOLOGY PUSH APPROACH

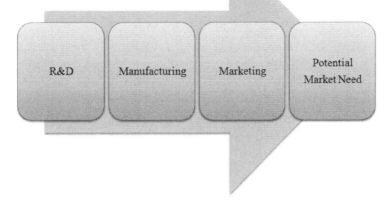

Figure C.1 The Technology Push Approach to Innovation
Source: Authors' elaboration

MARKET PULL APPROACH

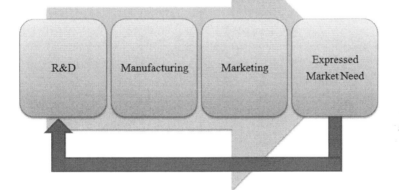

Figure C.2 The Market/Demand Pull Approach to Innovation
Source: Authors' elaboration

to combine both technological efforts and customer orientation in order to achieve a competitive advantage.

The innovation potential resides in the capacity to leverage relations with customers and suppliers as well (Doz, Santos, and Williamson, 2001). The importance of the customer as co-producer or concurrent producer of innovation has been pointed out by several studies (Miller, 1995). The role of suppliers in the development of innovation has been recently singled out. Actually, innovation conditions—mainly the technology-driven ones—often proceed from suppliers. Suppliers increasingly put the firm in the position to develop a new value proposition. Product innovation is—from this perspective—the result of the new strategic elaboration of an innovation developed somewhere else, often in sectors that are far away and very different from those of application. The term "supplier-enabled" (Onetti and Lodi, 2004) highlights, in a synthetic way, the suppliers' contribution to the innovation process.

C.4.2　Types of Innovation

Booz et al. (1982) define innovation based on the novelty of a product/service that can be achieved through

- the creation of a new product/service line;
- upgrades of products/services;
- new market positioning or
- cost reductions on existing product/services.

As represented in Table C.2, several authors have provided different definitions of innovation: radical vs. incremental innovation, sustaining vs.

Table.C.2　Types of Innovation

Categories of Innovation	Areas of Application	Major	Dimensions Involved	Author
Radical/ Incremental/ Breakthrough	Product/ Technology	Customers	Intensity of innovation with respect to the existing dominant design	Ettie et al., 1984; Dewar and Dutton, 1986; Gaynor, 2002
Sustaining/ Disruptive	Market/Value Proposition	Competitors and customers	Novelty in the technology and value for the customers	Christensen, 1997
Architectural/ Modular	Process	Competitors	Composition of the product (not its components)	Henderson and Clark, 1990
Continuous/ Discontinuous	Standards of the market	Producers and customers	Path of innovation	Miller and Morris, 1999

disruptive innovation, architectural vs. modular innovation, and continuous vs. discontinuous innovation.

Although such classifications have not been universally accepted in the literature, they are useful for a comprehensive understanding of the innovation process inside organizations.

The most utilized classification is based on novelty of results. Here you have *radical innovation* and *incremental innovation*. Radical innovation produces new technologies that allow market introduction of new products/services and/or processes that are so superior that existing products are rendered noncompetitive. They have a high degree of novelty and customers are usually not able to compare these innovative products/services with the products/services currently available on the market. Such innovation requires know-how[10] and know-why[11] knowledge along with the ability to identify signals from the market, pursue new opportunities, and realize real technological progress. A radical innovation may have a strong impact on the organization: it requires changes in the market approach, new organizational routines, and sometimes new strategies and business models. On the other hand, incremental innovation leverages existing knowledge and resources and produces modest technological changes. It results in improvements of existing services, products, or processes. This type of innovation enhances the capabilities of established organizations, while radical innovation forces them to adopt new problem-solving approaches (Burns and Stalker, 1966; Ettlie, et al., 1984; Hage, 1980; Tushman and Anderson, 1986).

Radical innovation often establishes a new dominant design and, hence, a new core design concept that requires a new architecture. Incremental innovation fine-tunes an established design, introducing relatively minor changes to the existing product/service concept. Incremental innovation often reinforces the dominance of established firms since it leverages and exploits the existing core competencies (Abernathy and Clark, 1985; Dewar and Dutton, 1986; Ettlie et al., 1984; Nelson and Winter, 1982; Tushman and Anderson, 1986). Radical innovation, in contrast, is based on a different set of engineering and scientific principles and often may open up new markets (Dewar and Dutton, 1986; Ettlie et al., 1984).[12] Radical innovation often creates great difficulties for incumbent firms (Tushman and Anderson, 1986) because it contributes to the deterioration of the usefulness of existing capabilities and may be the trigger for the successful entry of new competitors (the so called "attacker's advantage" [Foster, 2001]) or even the redefinition of the industry/market structure (also known as "first mover's advantage" [Lieberman and Montgomery, 1988]).

A *disruptive innovation* is able to create a new market by applying a different set of values, which eventually (and unexpectedly) overtakes (goes on to disrupt) an existing market, displacing an earlier technology. It usually enters the market at a slow pace, because it attracts niche customers—the so called "pioneers"—who can better understand and manage the new product/service thanks to their technical competences. Moreover, the introduction phase (Levitt, 1965) of the disruptive innovative in the market is quite expensive (Christensen, 1997; Christensen and Raynor, 2003).

On the other side, a *sustaining innovation* does not create new markets but rather only evolves existing ones, providing them with better value (introduces an improvement in the quality of the product/process/service and/or in its performance). It can be both a radical or an incremental innovation, and rarely constitutes a challenge for established firms. The distinction between radical/incremental and disruptive/sustaining innovation is strong: while the former refers to a firm's technology, the latter assumes the customers' perspective, i.e., the value/benefit they retrieve from the innovation.

Shifting the focus to the innovation process, it is possible to distinguish between architectural and modular innovation (Henderson and Clark, 1990). This classification is based on the distinction between the product's components and the ways they are integrated into the overall product architecture[13] (Henderson and Clark, 1990). An *architectural innovation* concerns a novel combination of pre-existing knowledge base: it produces an alteration in the product architecture without innovating its components (Clark, 1985). It doesn't change the value proposition nor the knowledge bases. The output is a better organization of the components of a product/service, which ends up in the reinforcement of the core concept. A *modular innovation* is the result of changes in the modules/components of the product or service while maintaining the overall architecture. Typically, architectural innovation and modular innovation may lead, respectively, to radical change and to incremental improvements of a product or service.

Continuous and discontinuous innovation are assessed based on the standards of a market: *continuous innovation* (also defined as "evolutionary") complies with standards, while *discontinuous innovation* (also known as "transformational" or "revolutionary") displaces them by following a path not immediately comprehensible to competitors and clients. Continuous innovation is incremental, and takes place within existing infrastructures: it builds on existing knowledge in existing markets without challenging underlying strategies or assumptions (Miller and Morris, 1999). It introduces new models with almost no learning curve for consumers. Discontinuous innovation, instead, implies the creation of new knowledge in one or more dimensions of a product or service. It usually refers to radical innovations that require new experience, understanding and learning to be able to be used properly by customers. While continuous innovation is focused on existing needs, discontinuous innovation is aiming at addressing needs of customers that are not yet exploited and often rarely articulated. The process is driven not by technology itself, but by how technology is used.

Table C.3   Learning Blocks—Appendix C

Entrepreneurship	Habitual Entrepreneur	Novice Entrepreneur
Portfolio Entrepreneur	Serial Entrepreneur	Opportunity Identification
Extrinsic Motivation	Entrepreneurial Alertness	Absorptive Capacity
Social Network	Personality Perspective	Behavioral Perspective
Functional Perspective	Personality Perspective	Behavioral Perspective
Corporate Entrepreneurship	Intrapreneurship	Open Communication
Environmental Munificence	Innovation	Technology-Push
Market/Demand Pull	Innovation Push-Customer Pull	Incremental/Radical Innovation
Sustaining/Disruptive Innovation	Architectural/Modular Innovation	Continuous/Discontinuous Innovation

NOTES

1. See, among others: van Praag and Versloot (2007); Reynolds et al. (2001).
2. Entrepreneurship was considered as an overall framework by which to observe other theories (Alvarez and Barney, 2008).
3. This is useful to quickly and better identify and exploit opportunities.
4. For more details on International Entrepreneurship, refer to Appendix D, paragraph D.2.
5. However, some recent studies concentrate on the definition of entrepreneur as an individual characterized by specific "entrepreneurial traits."
6. For example, due to information asymmetry, principal–agent conflicts, and misaligned incentives, individuals may have an incentive to discover or create particular opportunities but not others.
7. More specifically, the same authors identified two main elements comprising the level of preparedness with which individuals approach the entrepreneurial process: tangible and intangible personal attributes and business skills (Harvey and Evans, 1995).
8. Social networks are essentially defined by a set of actors (individuals or organizations) and a set of linkages between actors (Brass, 1992).
9. These dimensions find their roots in the earlier works of Miller and Friesen (1983) and Khandwalla (1987).
10. *Know-how knowledge* refers to skills or the capability to do something (OECD, 1996).
11. *Know-why knowledge* refers to scientific knowledge of the principles and laws of nature. This kind of knowledge underlies that technological development and product and process advances in most industries (OECD, 1996).
12. In this case, innovation is also referred as "*breakthrough.*"
13. Product architecture refers to the way functional elements of a product or system are assigned to its constituent sections or subsystems, and of the way they interact.

REFERENCES

Abbey, Augustus, and John W. Dickson. 1983. "R&D Work Climate and Innovation in Semiconductors." *Academy of Management Journal* 26, no. 2: 362–368.

Abernathy, William J., and Kim B. Clark. 1985. "Innovation: Mapping the winds of creative destruction." *Research Policy* 14, no. 1: 3–22.

Adler, Paul S., and Seok-Woo Kwon. 2002. "Social Capital: Prospects for a New Concept." *Academy of Management Review* 27, no. 1: 17–40.

Ahuja, Gautam, and Morris C. Lampert. 2001. "Entrepreneurship in the Large Corporation: A Longitudinal Study of How Established Firms Create Breakthrough Inventions." *Strategic Management Journal* 22, no. 6–7: 521–543.

Aldrich, Howard E., and C. Marlene Fiol. 1994 "Fools Rush In? The Institutional Context of Industry Creation." *Academy of Management Review* 19, no. 4: 645–670.

Aldrich, Howard E., and Amy Kenworthy. 1999. "The Accidental Entrepreneur: Campbellian Antinomies and Organizational Foundings." In *Variations in Organization Science: In Honor of Donald T. Campbell,* edited by J. A. C. Baum and B. McKelvey, 19–33. Thousand Oaks: Sage.

Aldrich, Howard, and Martin Ruef. 2006. *Organizations Evolving,* 2nd ed. Thousand Oaks: Sage.

Aldrich, Howard E., and Gabriele Wiedenmayer. 1993. "From Traits to Rates: An Ecological Perspective on Organizational Foundings." In *Advances in Entrepreneurship, Firm Emergence, and Growth,* edited by J. A. Katz and R. H. Brockhaus, Sr., 145–195. Greenwich, CT: JAI Press.

Aldrich, Howard, and Catherine Zimmer. 1986. "Entrepreneurship Through Social Networks." In *The Art and Science of Entrepreneurship,* edited by D. Sexton and R. Smilor, 3–23. New York: Ballinger.

Alvarez, Sharon A., and Jay B. Barney. 2005. "How Do Entrepreneurs Organize Firms Under Conditions Of Uncertainty?" *Journal of Management* 31, no. 5: 776–793.

———. 2007 "Discovery and Creation: Alternative Theories of Entrepreneurial Action." *Strategic Entrepreneurship Journal* 1, no. 1–2: 11–26.

———. 2008. "Opportunities, Organizations, and Entrepreneurship." *Strategic Entrepreneurship Journal* 2, no. 4: 265–267.

Alvarez, Sharon A., and Lowell W. Busenitz. 2001. "The Entrepreneurship of Resource-Based Theory." *Journal of Management* 27, no. 6: 755–775.

Alvarez, Sharon A., and Simon Parker. 2009. "New Firm Organization and the Emergence of Control Rights: A Bayesian Approach." *Academy of Management Review* 34, no. 2: 209–227.

Amit, Raphael, Lawrence Glosten, and Eitan Muller. 1993. "Challenges to Theory Development in Entrepreneurship Research." *Journal of Management Studies* 30, no. 5: 815–834.

Ardichvili, Alexander, Richard Cardozo, and Sourav Ray. 2003. "A Theory Of Entrepreneurial Opportunity Identification And Development." *Journal of Business Venturing* 18, no. 1: 105–123.

Baker, Ted, and Reed E. Nelson. 2005. "Creating Something from Nothing: Resource Construction Through Entrepreneurial Bricolage." *Administrative Science Quarterly* 50, no. 3: 329–366.

Baron, Robert A. 1998. "Cognitive Mechanisms in Entrepreneurship: Why and When Entrepreneurs Think Differently Than Other People." *Journal of Business Venturing* 13, no. 4: 275–294.

Barzel, Yoram. 1997. *Economic Analysis of Property Rights,* 2nd ed. Cambridge: Cambridge University Press.

Baumol, William J. 1996. "Entrepreneurship: Productive, Unproductive, and Destructive." *Journal of Business Venturing* 11, no. 1: 3–22.

Begley, Thomas M., and David P. Boyd. 1988. "Psychological Characteristics Associated with Performance in Entrepreneurial Firms and Smaller Businesses." *Journal of Business Venturing* 2, no. 1: 79–93.

Berthon, Pierre, James M. Hulbert, and Leyland F. Pitt. 1999. "To Serve or Create? Strategic Orientations Toward Customers and Innovation." *California Management Review* 42, no. 1: 37–58.

Bhave, Mahesh P. 1994. "A Process Model of Entrepreneurial Venture Creation." *Journal of Business Venturing* 9, no. 3: 223–242.

Birley, Sue, and Paul Westhead. 1993. "A Comparison of New Businesses Established by 'Novice' and 'Habitual' Founders in Great Britain." *International Small Business Journal* 12, no. 1: 38–60.

———. 1994. "A Taxonomy of Business Start-Up Reasons and Their Impact on Firm Growth and Size." *Journal of Business Venturing* 9, no. 1: 7–31.

Booz, Allen &Hamilton.1982. *New Product Management for the 1980's.* New York: Booz Allen & Hamilton.

Borch, Odd Jarl. 1994. "The Process of Relational Contracting: Developing Trust-Based Strategic Alliances Among Small Business Enterprises." In *Advances in Strategic Management,* vol. 10B, edited by P. Shrivastava, A. Huff, and J. Dutton, 113–135. Oxford: JAY Press.

Brass, Daniel J. 1984. "Being in the Right Place: A Structural Analysis of Individual Influence in an Organization." *Administrative Science Quarterly* 29, no. 4: 518–539.

———. 1992. "Power in Organizations: A Social Network Perspective." *Research in Politics and Society* 4, no. 1: 295–323.

Brockhaus, Robert H. 1980. "Risk Taking Propensity of Entrepreneurs." *Academy of Management Journal* 23, no. 3: 509–520.

Brockhaus, Robert H., and P. S. Horwitz. 1986. "The Psychology of the Entrepreneur". In *The Art and Science of Entrepreneurship,* edited by D. Sexton and R. W. Smilor, 25–48. Cambridge: Ballinger.

Bull, Ivan, and Gary E. Willard. 1993. "Towards a Theory of Entrepreneurship." *Journal of Business Venturing* 8, no. 3: 183–195.

Burgelman, Robert A. 1983. "A Process Model of Internal Corporate Venturing in the Diversified Major Firm." *Administrative Science Quarterly:* 28, no. 2: 223–244.

Burgelman, Robert A., and Leonard R. Sayles. 1986. *Inside Corporate Innovation: Strategy, Structure and Managerial Skills .* New York: The Free Press.

Burns, Tom, and George Stalker. 1996. *The Management of Innovation.* London: Tavistock.

Burt, Ronald S. 1992. *Structural Holes: The Social Structure of Competition.* Cambridge: Harvard University Press.

———. 1997. "The Contingent Value of Social Capital." *Administrative Science Quarterly* 42, no. 2: 339–365.

———. 2000. "The Network Entrepreneur." In *Entrepreneurship: The Social Science View,* edited by R. Swedberg, 281–307. Oxford: Oxford University Press.

Busenitz, Lowell W. 1996. "Research on Entrepreneurial Alertness." *Journal of Small Business Management* 34, no. 4: 35–44.

Campbell, Charles A. 1992. "A Decision Theory Model for Entrepreneurial Acts." *Entrepreneurship Theory and Practice* 17: 21–21.

Casson, Mark. 1982. *The Entrepreneur: An Economic Theory.* 2nd ed. Oxford: Edward Elgar.

———. 1995. *Entrepreneurship and Business Culture.* Cheltenham: Edward Elgar.

———. 1998. "Institutional Economics and Business History: A Way Forward?" In *Institutions and the Evolution of Modern Business,* edited by M. Casson and M. B. Rose, 151–71. London: Frank Cass.

Christensen, Clayton M. 1997. *The Innovator's Dilemma: When New Technologies Cause Great Firms To Fail.* Cambridge: Harvard Business Press.

154 *Business Modeling for Life Science and Biotech*

Christensen, Clayton M., and Michael E. Raynor. 2003. *The Innovators Solution: Creating and Sustaining Successful Growth*. Cambridge: Harvard Business Press.

Clark, Kim B. 1985. "The Interaction of Design Hierarchies and Market Concepts in Technological Evolution." *Research Policy* 14, no. 5: 235–251.

Coase, Ronald H. 1937. "The Nature of the Firm. "*Economica* 4, no. 16: 386–405.

Cohen, Wesley M., and Daniel A. Levinthal. 1990. "Absorptive Capacity: A New Perspective on Learning and Innovation." *Administrative Science Quarterly* 35, no. 1: 128–152.

Conner, Kathleen R. 1991. "A Historical Comparison of Resource-based Theory and Five Schools of Thought within Industrial Organization Economics: Do We Have a New Theory of the Firm?" *Journal of Management* 17, no. 1: 121–154.

Cooper, Arnold. 2003. "Entrepreneurship: The Past, the Present, the Future." In *Handbook of Entrepreneurship Research,* vol. 1, edited by Z. J. Acs and D. B. Audretsch. Boston: Kluwer Academic Publishers.

Cooper, Arnold C., F. Javier Gimeno-Gascon, and Carolyn Y. Woo. 1994. "Initial Human and Financial Capital as Predictors of New Venture Performance." *Journal of Business Venturing* 9, no. 5: 371–395.

Covin, Jeffrey. G., and Teresa J. Covin. 1990. "Competitive Aggressiveness, Environmental Context, and Small Firm Performance." *Entrepreneurship, Theory and Practice* 14, no. 4: 35–50.

Covin, Jeffrey. G., and Dennis P. Slevin. 1991. "A Conceptual Model of Entrepreneurship as Firm Behaviour." *Entrepreneurship, Theory and Practice* 16, no. 1: 7–25.

Crick, Dave, and Martine Spence. 2005. "The Internationalisation of 'High Performing' UK High-Tech SMEs: A Study of Planned and Unplanned Strategies." *International Business Review* 14, no. 2: 167–185.

Cromie, Stanley, Sue Birley, and Ian Callaghan. 1993. "Community Brokers: Their Role in the Formation and Development of Business Ventures." *Entrepreneurship & Regional Development* 5, no. 3: 247–264.

Cyert, Richard M., and James March. 1963. *A Behavioral Theory of the Firm*. Englewood Cliffs: Prentice-Hall.

D'Aveni, Richard. 1994. *Hypercompetition: Managing the Dynamics of Strategic Management*. New York: The Free Press.

Deakins, David, and Mark Freel. 1998. "Entrepreneurial Learning and the Growth Process in SMEs." *The Learning Organization* 5, no. 3: 144–155.

De Koning, Alice, and Daniel Muzyka. 1999. "Conceptualizing Opportunity Recognition as a Socio-Cognitive Process." Working paper, Centre for Advanced Studies in Leadership, Stockholm.

Dess, Gregory G., R. Duane Ireland, Shaker A. Zahra, Steven W. Floyd, Jay J. Janney, and Peter J. Lane. 2003. "Emerging Issues in Corporate Entrepreneurship." *Journal of Management* 29, no. 3: 351–378.

Dess, Gregory G., George T. Lumpkin, and Jeffrey G. Covin. 1997. "Entrepreneurial Strategy Making and Firm Performance: Tests of Contingency and Configurational Models." *Strategic Management Journal* 18, no. 9: 677–695.

Dewar, Robert D., and Jane E. Dutton. 1986. "The Adoption of Radical and Incremental Innovations: An Empirical Analysis." *Management Science* 32, no. 11: 1422–1433.

Dimitratos, Pavlos, and Marian V. Jones. 2005. "Future Directions for International Entrepreneurship Research." *International Business Review* 14, no. 2: 119–128.

Dosi Giovanni. 1982. "Technological Paradigms and Technological Trajectories," *Research Policy* 11: 147–162.

Doz, Yves, Jose Santos, and Peter J. Williamson. 2001. *From Global to Metanational: How Companies Win in the Knowledge Economy*. Cambridge: Harvard Business Press.

Eckhardt, Jonathan T., and Michael P. Ciuchta. 2008. "Selected Variation: The Population-Level Implications of Multistage Selection in Entrepreneurship." *Strategic Entrepreneurship Journal* 2, no. 3: 209–224.

Eisenhardt, Kathleen M., and Behnam N. Tabrizi. 1995. "Accelerating Adaptive Processes: Product Innovation in the Global Computer Industry." *Administrative Science Quarterly* 45, no. 1: 84–110.

Ettlie, John E., William P. Bridges, and Robert D. O'keefe. 1984. "Organization Strategy and Structural Differences for Radical Versus Incremental Innovation." *Management Science* 30, no. 6: 682–695.

Evans, David S., and Linda S. Leighton. 2002. "Some Empirical Aspects of Entrepreneurship." *Entrepreneurship: Critical Perspectives on Business and Management* 1: 146.

Fiet, James O. 1996. "The Informational Basis of Entrepreneurial Discovery." *Small Business Economics* 8, no. 6: 419–430.

Fiet, James O., Alexandre Piskounov, and Veronica Gustavsson. 2000. "How to Decide How to Search For Entrepreneurial Discoveries." *Frontiers of Entrepreneurship Research*. Wellesley: Babson College.

Forlani, David, and John W. Mullins. 2000. "Perceived Risks and Choices in Entrepreneurs' New Venture Decisions." *Journal of Business Venturing* 15, no. 4: 305–322.

Foss, Kristen and Nicolai Foss. 2005. "Resources and Transaction Costs: How Property Rights Economics Furthers the Resource-based View.", *Strategic Management Journal* , Vol. 26, 541–555.

Foss, Kristen, Nicolai Foss, Peter G. Klein, and Sandra Klein. 2006. "The Entrepreneurial Organization of Heterogeneous Capital." Accessed November 18, 2013, from www. Mises.org: www.mises.org/journals/scholar/foss-foss-klein-klein2.pdf

Foster, Richard N. 1986. *Innovation: The Attacker's Advantage*. New York: Summit Books,

Gaglio, Connie Marie, and Jerome A. Katz. 2001. "The Psychological Basis of Opportunity Identification: Entrepreneurial Alertness." *Small Business Economics* 16, no. 2: 95–111.

Gartner, William B. 1985. "A Conceptual Framework for Describing the Phenomenon of New Venture Creation." *Academy of Management Review* 10, no. 4: 696–706.

———. 1988. "Who is an Entrepreneur? Is the Wrong Question." *American Journal of Small Business* 12, no. 4: 11– 32.

Gaynor, Gerard H. 2002. *Innovation by Design: What It Takes to Keep Your Company on the Cutting Edge*. New York: Amacom.

Gilpin Robert. 1975. *Technology, Economic Growth and International Competitiveness*. Washington DC: Government Printing Office.

Gimeno, Javier, Timothy B. Folta, Arnold C. Cooper, and Carolyn Y. Woo. 1997. "Survival of the Fittest? Entrepreneurial Human Capital and the Persistence of Underperforming Firms." *Administrative Science Quarterly* 42, no. 4: 750–783.

Gloria-Palermo, Sandye. 1999. "Discovery versus Creation: Implications of the Austrian View of the Market Process." In *Institutions and the Evolution of Capitalism: Implications of Evolutionary Economics*, edited by J. Groenewegen and J. Vromen. Cheltenham: Edward Elgar.

Granovetter, Mark S. 1973. "The Strength of Weak Ties." *American Journal of Sociology* 78, no. 6: 1360–1380.

Greenberger, David B., and Donald L. Sexton. 1988. "An Interactive Model of New Venture Initiation." *Journal of Small Business Management* 26, no. 3: 1–7.

Guth, William D. and Ari Ginsberg. 1990. "Guest Editors Introduction: Corporate Entrepreneurship." *Strategic Management Journal* 11: 5–15.

Hage, Jerald. 1980. *Theories of Organizations: Form, Process, and Transformation.* New York: Wiley.

Hall, Peter. 1995. "Habitual Owners of Small Businesses." In *Small Firms: Partnerships for Growth,* edited by F. Chittenden, M. Robertson, and I. Marshall, 217–217. London: Paul Chapman Publishing.

Hamel, Gary, and C. K. Prahalad. 1989. "To Revitalize Corporate Performance, We Need a Whole New Model of Strategy." *Harvard Business Review:* 63–76.

Harvey, Michael, and Rodney Evans. 1995. "Strategic Windows in the Entrepreneurial Process." *Journal of Business Venturing* 10, no. 5: 331–347.

Hayek, Friedrich August. 1945. "The Use of Knowledge in Society." *American Economic Review* 35, no. 4: 519–530.

Hébert, Robert F., and Albert N. Link. 1989. "In Search of the Meaning of Entrepreneurship." *Small Business Economics* 1, no. 1: 39–49.

Hellmann, Thomas, and Manju Puri. 2000. "Venture Capital and the Professionalization of Start-Up Firms: Empirical Evidence." *The Journal of Finance* 57, no. 1: 169–197.

Henderson, Rebecca M., and Kim B. Clark. 1990. "Architectural Innovation: The Reconfiguration of Existing Product Technologies and the Failure of Established Firms." *Administrative Science Quarterly* 35, no. 1: 9–30.

Henderson, Rebecca, and Iain Cockburn. 1994. "Measuring Competence? Exploring Firm Effects in Pharmaceutical Research." *Strategic Management Journal* 15, no. S1: 63–84.

Hill, Rosenberg, Nathan. 1982. *Inside The Black Box: Technology and Economics.* Cambridge: Cambridge University Press.

Hills, Gerald E., G. Thomas Lumpkin, and Robert P. Singh. 1997. "Opportunity Recognition: Perceptions and Behaviors of Entrepreneurs." *Frontiers of Entrepreneurship Research* 17: 168–182. Wellesley: Babson College.

Hills, Gerald E., Rodney C. Shrader, and G. Tom Lumpkin. 1999. "Opportunity Recognition as a Creative Process." *Frontiers of Entrepreneurship Research* 19, no. 19: 216–227. Wellesley: Babson College.

Hoang, Ha, and Bostjan Antoncic. 2003. "Network-Based Research in Entrepreneurship: A Critical Review." *Journal of Business Venturing* 18, no. 2: 165–187.

Hoang, Ha, and N. Young. 2000. "Social Embeddedness and Entrepreneurial Opportunities Recognition; (More) Evidence Of Embeddedness." *Frontiers of Entrepreneurship Research.* Wellesley: Babson College.

Holmstrom, Bengt, and Jean Tirole. 1989. "The Theory of the Firm." *Handbook of Industrial Organization* 1: 61–133.

Hornsby, Jeffrey S., Douglas W. Naffziger, Donald F. Kuratko, and Ray V. Montagno. 1993. "An Interactive Model of the Corporate Entrepreneurship Process." *Entrepreneurship Theory and Practice* 17: 29–29.

Huber, George P. 1991. "Organizational Learning: The Contributing Processes and the Literatures." *Organization Science* 2, no. 1: 88–115.

Iacobucci, Donato, and Peter Rosa. 2005. "Growth, Diversification, and Business Group Formation in Entrepreneurial Firms." *Small Business Economics* 25, no. 1: 65–82.

Jacobs, Jane. 1961. *The Death and Life of Great American Cities.* New York: Random House.

Jensen, Michael C., and William H. Meckling. 1976. "Theory of the Firm: Managerial Behavior, Agency Costs and Ownership Structure." *Journal of Financial Economics* 3, no. 4: 305–360.

Johannisson, Bengt. 2000. "Networking and Entrepreneurial Growth." *Handbook of Entrepreneurship,* 368–386.

Jones, Gareth R., and John E. Butler. 1992. "Managing Internal Corporate Entrepreneurship: An Agency Theory Perspective." *Journal of Management* 18, no. 4: 733–749.

Kanter, Rosabeth Moss. 1984. "Managing Transition in Organization Culture: The Case of Participative Management at Honeywell." In *Managing Organizational Transitions,* edited by J. R. Kimberly and R. E. Quinn, 195–217. Homewood: Irwin.

Keh, Hean Tat, Maw Der Foo, and Boon Chong Lim. 2002. "Opportunity Evaluation Under Risky Conditions: The Cognitive Processes of Entrepreneurs." *Entrepreneurship Theory and Practice* 27, no. 2: 125–148.

Khandwalla, Pradip N. 1977. *The Design of Organizations,* vol. 260. New York: Harcourt Brace Jovanovich.

———. 1987. "Generators of Pioneering-Innovative Management: Some Indian Evidence." *Organization Studies* 8, no. 1: 39–59.

Kim, Jongwook, and Joseph Mahoney. 2006. "How Property Rights Theory Furthers the Resource-based View: Resources, Transaction Costs and Entrepreneurial Discovery." *International Journal of Strategic Change Management* 1, no. 1–2: 40–52.

Kirzner, Israel M. 1978. *Competition and Entrepreneurship.* Chicago: University of Chicago Press.

Knight, Frank H. 1921. "Risk, Uncertainty and Profit." New York: Hart, Schaffner and Marx.

Knight, Gary. 2000. "Entrepreneurship and Marketing Strategy: The SME Under Globalization." *Journal of International Marketing* 8, no. 2: 12–32.

Krackhardt, David. 1990. "Assessing the Political Landscape: Structure, Cognition, and Power in Organizations." *Administrative Science Quarterly* 35, no. 2: 342–369.

Kuratko, Donald F., Jeffrey S. Hornsby, and Douglas W. Naffziger. 1997. "An Examination of Owner's Goals in Sustaining Entrepreneurship." *Journal of Small Business Management* 35, no. 1: 24–33.

Kuratko, Donald F., Jeffrey S. Hornsby, Douglas W. Naffziger, and Ray V. Montagno. 1993. "Implementing Entrepreneurial Thinking in Established Organizations." *SAM Advanced Management Journal* 58: 28–28.

Kuratko, Donald, Ray V. Montagno, and Jeffrey Hornsby. 1990. "Developing an Intrapreneurial Assessment Instrument for an Effective Corporate Entrepreneurial Environment." *Strategic Management Journal* 11, SI (Summer): 49–58.

Lambin, Jean-Jacques. 1997. *Strategic Marketing Management.* Maidenhead: McGraw-Hill.

Langan-Fox, Janice, and Susanna Roth. 1995. "Achievement Motivation and Female Entrepreneurs." *Journal of Occupational and Organizational Psychology* 68, no. 3: 209–218.

Larson, Andrea. 1992. "Network Dyads in Entrepreneurial Settings: A Study of the Governance of Exchange Relationships." *Administrative Science Quarterly* 37, no. 1: 76–104.

Lee, Joo-Heon, and Sankaran Venkataraman. 2006. "Aspirations, Market Offerings, and the Pursuit of Entrepreneurial Opportunities." *Journal of Business Venturing* 21, no. 1: 107–123.

Leonard, Dorothy, and Jeffrey F. Rayport. 1997. "Spark Innovation Through Empathic Design." *Harvard Business Review* 75: 102–115.

Levitt, Theodore. 1965. " Exploit the Product Life Cycle." *Harvard Business Review* 43: 81–94.

Lieberman, Marvin B., and David B. Montgomery. 1988. "First-Mover Advantages." *Strategic Management Journal* 9, SI: 41–58.

Lin, Nan. 2002. *Social Capital: A Theory of Social Structure and Action,* vol. 19. Cambridge: Cambridge University press.

Low, Murray B., and Ian C. MacMillan. 1988. "Entrepreneurship: Past Research and Future Challenges." *Journal of Management* 14, no. 2: 139–161.

Lumpkin, Tom G., and Gregory G. Dess. 1996. "Clarifying the Entrepreneurial Construct and Linking It to Performance," *Academy of Management Review* 21, no 1: 135–172.

MacMillan, Ian C., Zenas Block, and P. N. Subba Narasimha. 1984. "Obstacles and Experiences in Corporate Ventures." Frontiers of Entrepreneurship Research. Wellesley: Babson College.

March, James G. 1991. "Exploration and Exploitation in Organizational Learning." *Organization Science* 2, no. 1: 71–87.

McClelland, David C. 1961. *The Achieving Society.* London: Collier Macmillan.

McGrath, Rita Gunther. 1996. "Options and the Entrepreneur: Towards a Strategic Theory of Entrepreneurial Wealth Creation." *Academy of Management Proceedings:* 101–105.

McGrath, Rita Gunther, and Ian C. MacMillan. 2000. *The Entrepreneurial Mindset: Strategies for Continuously Creating Opportunity in an Age of Uncertainty,* vol. 284. Cambridge: Harvard Business Press.

McGrath, Rita Gunther, Ming-Hone Tsai, Sankaran Venkataraman, and Ian C. MacMillan. 1996. "Innovation, Competitive Advantage and Rent: A Model and Test." *Management Science* 42, no. 3: 389–403.

McMullen, Jeffery S., and Dean A. Shepherd. 2006. "Entrepreneurial Action and the Role of Uncertainty in the Theory of The Entrepreneur." *Academy of Management Review* 31, no. 1: 132–152.

Miller, Daniel, 1995. *Acknowledging Consumption.* London: Routledge.

Miller, Danny. 1983. "The Correlates of Entrepreneurship in Three Types of Firms." *Management Science* 29, no. 7: 770–791.

Miller, Danny, and Peter H. Friesen. 1983. "Strategy-Making and Environment: The Third Link." *Strategic Management Journal* 4, no. 3: 221–235.

Miller, William L. 1995 "A Broader Mission for R&D." *Research-Technology Management* 38, no. 6: 24–36.

Miller, William L., and Langdom Morris. 1999. *4th Generation R&D: Managing Knowledge, Technology, and Innovation.* New York: John Wiley.

Millier, Paul. 1999. *Marketing the Unknown: Developing Market Strategies for Technical Innovation.* London: John Wiley and Sons.

Mises, Ludwig. 1949. *Human Action.* London: William Hodge.

Morris, Michael H. 1998. *Entrepreneurial Intensity: Sustainable Advantages for Individuals, Organizations, and Societies.* Westport: Greenwood Publishing Group.

Myers, Sumner, and Donald George Marquis. 1969. *Successful Industrial Innovations: A Study of Factors Underlying Innovation in Selected Firms.* Washington, DC: National Science Foundation.

Nahapiet, Janine, and Sumantra Ghoshal. 1998. "Social Capital, Intellectual Capital, and the Organizational Advantage." *Academy of Management Review* 23, no. 2: 242–266.

Naman, John L., and Dennis P. Slevin. 1993. "Entrepreneurship and the Concept of Fit: A Model and Empirical Tests." *Strategic Management Journal* 14, no. 2: 137–153.

Nelson, Richard R., and Sidney Winter. 1982. *An Evolutionary Theory of Economic Change.* Cambridge: Harvard University Press.

Nicholls-Nixon, Charlene L., Arnold C. Cooper, and Carolyn Y. Woo. 2000. "Strategic Experimentation: Understanding Change and Performance in New Ventures." *Journal of Business Venturing* 15, no. 5: 493–521.

Nordman, Emilia Rovira, and Sara Melén. 2008. "The Impact of Different Kinds of Knowledge for the Internationalization Process of Born Globals in the Biotech Business." *Journal of World Business* 43, no. 2: 171–185.

OECD. 1996. "The Knowledge-Based Economy." Report, Paris, www.oecd.org/science/sci-tech/1913021.pdf.

Onetti, Alberto, and Fabio Lodi. 2004. "L'innovazione 'supplier-enabled.' Il caso Parah." Working paper, Facoltà di Economia, Università dell'Insubria (no. 19).

Oviatt, Benjamin M., and Patricia P. McDougall. 2005. "Defining International Entrepreneurship and Modeling the Speed of Internationalization." *Entrepreneurship Theory and Practice* 29, no. 5: 537–554.

Pavitt, Keith, and Wald Salomon. 1971. "The Conditions for Success in Technological Innovation." Report, OECD, Paris.

Pearce II, John A., Tracy Robertson Kramer, and D. Keith Robbins. 1997. "Effects of Managers' Entrepreneurial Behavior on Subordinates." *Journal of Business Venturing* 12, no. 2: 147–160.

Peters, Thomas J., and Robert H. Waterman. 2004. *In Search of Excellence: Lessons From America's Best-Run Companies*. New York: HarperCollins.

Pinchot, Gifford. 1985. *Intrepreneuring*. New York: Harper and Row.

Powell, Walter W., Kenneth W. Koput, and Laurel Smith-Doerr. 1996. "Interorganizational Collaboration and the Locus of Innovation: Networks of Learning in Biotechnology." *Administrative Science Quarterly* 41, no.1: 116–145.

Presutti, Manuela, Alberto Onetti, and Vincenza Odorici. 2008. "Serial Entrepreneurship and Born-Global New-Ventures. A Case Study." *International Review of Entrepreneurship (IRE)* (formerly *International Journal of Entrepreneurship Education [IJEE]*) 6, no. 4: 255–278.

Rachleff Andy. 2013. "What 'Disrupt' Really Means." TechCrunch, February 13, http://techcrunch.com/2013/02/16/the-truth-about-disruption/.

Ray, Sourav, and Richard Cardozo. 1996. "Sensitivity and Creativity in Entrepreneurial Opportunity Recognition: A Framework for Empirical Investigation." Presented at the Sixth Global Entrepreneurship Research Conference, Imperial College, London.

Ronstadt, Robert. 1982. "Does Entrepreneurial Career Path Really Matter." *Frontiers of Entrepreneurship Research*. Wellesley: Babson College.

———. 1989. "The Corridor Principle." *Journal of Business Venturing* 3, no. 1: 31–40.

Rosenberg, Nathan. 1982. *Inside the Black Box: Technology and Economics*. Cambridge University Press.

Sarasvathy, Saras D. 2001. "Causation and Effectuation: Toward a Theoretical Shift From Economic Inevitability to Entrepreneurial Contingency." *Academy of Management Review* 26, no. 2: 243–263.

Sarasvathy, Saras D., Nicholas Dew, S. Ramakrishna Velamuri, and Sankaran Venkataraman. 2003. "Three Views of Entrepreneurial Opportunity." In *Handbook of Entrepreneurship Research: An Interdisciplinary Survey and Introduction*, vol. I, edited by Z. J. Acs and D. B. Audretsch, 141–160. Dordrecht: Kluwer.

Sarasvathy, Saras D., Anil R. Menon, and Graciela Kuechle. 2013. "Failing Firms and Successful Entrepreneurs: Serial Entrepreneurship as a Temporal Portfolio." *Small Business Economics* 40, no. 2: 417–434.

Sathe, Vijay. 1985. "Managing an Entrepreneurial Dilemma: Nurturing Entrepreneurship and Control in Large Corporations." *Frontiers of Entrepreneurship Research*. Wellesley: Babson College.

———. 1989. "Fostering Entrepreneurship in the Large, Diversified Firm." *Organizational Dynamics* 18, no. 1: 20–32.

Schmookler, Jacob. 1966. *Invention and Economic Growth*, vol. 26. Cambridge: Harvard University Press.

Schumpeter, Joseph Alois. 1934. *The Theory of Economic Development*. Oxford: Oxford University Press.

———. 1939. *Business Cycles*. New York: McGraw-Hill.

———. 1942. *Capitalism, Socialism, and Democracy* . New York: Harper and Brothers.

———. 1961. *The Theory of Economic Development: An Inquiry into Profits, Capital, Credit, Interest and the Business Cycle.* New York: Oxford Press.

Schwartz, Robert G., and Richard D. Teach. 2000. "A Model of Opportunity Recognition and Exploitation: An Empirical Study of Incubator Firms." *Journal of Research in Marketing and Entrepreneurship* 2, no. 2: 93–107.

Shane, Scott. 2000. "Prior Knowledge and the Discovery of Entrepreneurial Opportunities." *Organization Science* 11, no. 4: 448–469.

———. 2003. *A General Theory of Entrepreneurship: The Individual-Opportunity Nexus.* Cheltenham: Edward Elgar Publishing.

Shane, Scott, and Jonathan T. Eckhardt. 2003. "The Individual Opportunity Nexus." In *Handbook of Entrepreneurship Research: An Interdisciplinary Survey and Introduction,* vol. I, edited by Z. J. Acs and D. B. Audretsch, 141–160. Dordrecht: Kluwer.

Shane, Scott, and Sankaran Venkataraman. 2000. "The Promise of Entrepreneurship as a Field of Research." *Academy of Management Review* 25, no. 1: 217–226.

Shaver, Kelly G. 1995. "The Entrepreneurial Personality Myth." *Business and Economic Review* 41, no. 3: 20–23.

Shaver, Kelly G., and Linda R. Scott. 1991. "Person, Process, Choice: the Psychology of New Venture Creation." *Entrepreneurship, Theory and Practice* 16, no. 2: 23–45.

Shepherd, Dean A., and Dawn R. DeTienne. 2005. "Prior Knowledge, Potential Financial Reward, and Opportunity Identification." *Entrepreneurship Theory and Practice* 29, no. 1: 91–112.

Singh, Robert P. 2000. *Entrepreneurial Opportunity Recognition Through Social Networks.* New York: Garland.

Singh, Robert P., Gerald E. Hills, G. T. Lumpkin. 1999. "Examining the Role of Self-Perceived Entrepreneurial Alertness in the Opportunity Recognition Process." Working paper, presented at the 13th UIC/AMA Symposium on Marketing and Entrepreneurship Interface, Nice, June.

Sigrist, B. 1999. "Entrepreneurial Opportunity Recognition." Working Paper, presented at the annual UIC/AMA Symposium on Marketing/Entrepreneurship Interface, Sofia-Antipolis.

Starr, Jennifer A., and Ian MacMillan. 1990. "Resource Cooptation via Social Contracting: Resource Acquisition Strategies for New Ventures." *Strategic Management Journal* 11: 79–92.

Stevenson, Howard H., and J. Carlos Jarillo. 1990. "A Paradigm of Entrepreneurship: Entrepreneurial Management." *Strategic Management Journal* 11, no. 5: 17–27.

Stevenson, Howard H., and William A. Sahlman. 1989. "The Entrepreneurial Process." In *Small Business and Entrepreneurship,* edited by P. Burns and J. Dewhurst, 94–157. Basingstoke: Macmillan.

Sykes, Hollister B., and Zenas Block. 1989. "Corporate Venturing Obstacles: Sources and Solutions." *Journal of Business Venturing* 4, no. 3: 159–167.

Thorelli, Hans B. 1986. "Networks: Between Markets and Hierarchies." *Strategic Management Journal* 7, no. 1: 37–51.

Tidd, Joe, John Bessant, and Keith Pavitt. 1997. *Managing Innovation; Integrating Technological, Market and Organizational Change.* Chichester: John Wiley and Sons.

Timmons, Jeffry A., and Stephen Spinelli. 1994. *New Venture Creation: Entrepreneurship for the 21st Century.* Boston: Irwin

Tushman, Michael L., and Philip Anderson. 1986. "Technological Discontinuities and Organizational Environments." *Administrative Science Quarterly* 31, no. 3: 439–465.

Utterback, James M. 1974. "Innovation in Industry and the Diffusion of Technology." *Science* 183, no. 4125: 620–626.

Van Praag, Mirjam C., and Peter H. Versloot. 2007. "What is the Value of Entrepreneurship? A Review of Recent Research." *Small Business Economics* 29, no. 4: 351–382.

Venkataraman, Sankaran. 1997. "The Distinctive Domain of Entrepreneurship Research: An Editor's Perspective." In *Advances in Entrepreneurship, Firm Emergence, and Growth,* vol. 3, edited by J. Katz and R. Brockhaus, 119–138. Greenwich: JAI Press.

Von Hippel, Eric. 1988. *The Sources of Innovation.* Oxford: Oxford University Press.

———. 1994. "Sticky Information and the Locus of Problem Solving: Implications for Innovation." *Management Science,* vol. 40, no. 4: 429–439.

Westhead, Paul, Deniz Ucbasaran, Mike Wright, and Martin Binks. 2005. "Novice, Serial and Portfolio Entrepreneur Behaviour and Contributions." *Small Business Economics* 25, no. 2: 109–132.

Westhead, Paul, and Mike Wright. 1998. "Novice, Portfolio, and Serial Founders: Are They Different?" *Journal of Business Venturing* 13, no. 3: 173–204.

Williamson, Oliver E. 1975. *Markets and Hierarchies: Analysis and Antitrust Implications.* New York: Free Press.

———. 1985. *The Economic Institutions of Capitalism.* New York: The Free Press.

Woodman, Richard W., John E. Sawyer, and Ricky W. Griffin. 1993. "Toward a Theory of Organizational Creativity." *Academy of Management Review* 18, no. 2: 293–321.

Wright, Mike, Ken Robbie, and Christine Ennew. 1997. "Serial Entrepreneurs." *British Journal of Management* 8, no. 3: 251–268.

Zahra, Shaker A. 1991. "Predictors and Financial Outcomes of Corporate Entrepreneurship: An Exploratory Study." *Journal of Business Venturing* 6: 259–285.

———. 1993. "Environment, Corporate Entrepreneurship, and Financial Performance: A Taxonomic Approach." *Journal of Business Venturing* 8, no. 4: 319–340.

Zahra, Shaker A., and Jeffrey G. Covin. 1995. "Contextual Influences on the Corporate Entrepreneurship-Performance Relationship: A Longitudinal Analysis." *Journal of Business Venturing* 10, no. 1: 43–58.

Zahra, Shaker A., Anders Parup Nielsen, and William C. Bogner. 1999. "Corporate Entrepreneurship, Knowledge, and Competence Development." *Entrepreneurship Theory and Practice* 23, no. 2: 69–189.

Appendix D
Internationalization

Traditionally, innovation and *internationalization* have been considered as alternative growth options, occurring occasionally in the case of innovation, and incrementally in internationalization (Ansoff, 1957; Johanson and Vahlne, 1977; Vernon, 1966). Nowadays, especially for technology-based firms, entrepreneurship and internationalization are more likely to be instantaneous, fast, and inter-related. Both processes are driven and influenced by the exploration and exploitation of new knowledge, which is embedded in different locations and may rely on different social and inter-organizational ties scattered across the globe (Doz, Santos, and Williamson, 2001; Gereffi and Korzeniewicz, 1994; Powell et al., 2005).

This creates novel challenges for an organization's survival and success. The context in which business decisions are made today is far more complicated than in the past and requires entrepreneurs and managers to adopt effective managerial tools. Specifically, the ability to successfully internationalize is a must. Therefore, in this Appendix, we walk you through the international business studies and provide some insights into the most recent approaches that meld together internationalization and entrepreneurship. In particular, we first give you an overview of the early studies the international business theories have been founded on. Thereafter we introduce you to the main international theories in the field (economic-based approaches vs. behavioral theories) and the more recent domain of International Entrepreneurship (McDougall and Oviatt, 2000a) that results from the overlap between international business and entrepreneurship research.

D.1 INTERNATIONALIZATION THEORIES: HISTORY AND BACKGROUND

Both entrepreneurship and international business are fields of research that have seen an increasing number of studies during the last decade (McDougall and Oviatt, 1996, 2003; Zahra and Garvis, 2000). Entrepreneurship and international business are strictly interrelated because entering and venturing into foreign markets is frequently considered in the literature (Lumpkin and Dess, 1996; Zahra and George, 2002; Zahra, Ireland, and Hitt, 2000) as an entrepreneurial action.

The internationalization phenomenon has been studied for a long time, and a series of definitions have been introduced. In general, internationalization is the growth of the firm outside the national boundaries. More precisely, internationalization assumes the company's growth and development in foreign markets. This phenomenon does not only imply that the company operates abroad, but also determines a gradual opening to different cultures and a growing standardization of product characteristics and operational procedures that leads managers all over the world to run their business in an increasingly similar way (Levitt, 1993).

The modern theory of the internationalization of the firm can be dated back to the 1960s, when a greater number of researchers started to analyze, from different points of view, the subject of the international development of firms. Nevertheless it must be pointed out that the first theoretical frameworks about international business have their roots in the studies of Adam Smith and David Ricardo.

In 1776 Adam Smith underlined the *national specialization* as an element of advantage. According to Smith, each nation should specialize in the production of goods in which it demonstrates higher competences and resources. Therefore it should export part of the national production and receive in exchange other goods it is not able to manufacture.

David Ricardo (1817), starting from Smith's theory of absolute advantage, introduced the concept of *comparative advantage,* i.e., the ability of a country to produce goods more efficiently than others. According to Ricardo, a country should focus on the activities for which it has a greater comparative advantage and import the goods in which its comparative advantage is lower.

Smith and Ricardo adopted a country-perspective, whereas the recent international business studies have been focusing more on firms. The goal today is to explain why and how companies enter international markets.

The first theories in the field of international business can be divided into two main categories: the Economic Decision-Based approaches to internationalization and the Evolutionary/Behavioral approaches to internationalization (Benito and Welch, 1994).

The first and most important economic-based theories are the market imperfection theory by Hymer (1976),[1] the International Product Life Cycle theory (PLC) (Vernon, 1966; 1979) and the Eclectic Paradigm (Dunning, 1980), while the main evolutionary theories are the Uppsala Model (Johanson and Vahlne, 1977) and the Network theory.

The original behavioral models portrayed internationalization as an incremental and gradual process. In the current environment, the increased regional and global integration, on the one hand, and accelerating technological progress, on the other hand, enable internationalization processes that are faster and more geographically extended. In particular, researchers have found more and more evidence of new ventures that have shown an intense internation-alization since inception (McDougall, Shane, and Oviatt, 1994). This new category of ventures engaged in early internationalization[2] have been vari-ously referred to as "international new ventures" (McDougall et al., 1994), "born global" (Knight and Cavusgil, 1996; Madsen and Servais, 1997), "infant multinationals" (Lindqvist, 1991), "instant international" (Preece, Miles, and Baetz, 1998), "instant multinationals" (Andersen, 1993; Brush, 1992; Rennie, 1993), and "global start-ups" (Oviatt and McDougall, 1994).

In the following paragraphs we guide you into the main international theories the literature has proposed thus far.

D.1.1 Economic Decision-Based Approaches to Internationalization

In this section we present the main traditional theories and models of inter-nationalization known as *Economic Decision-Based approaches*. They focus on large sized companies that make *foreign direct investments* (FDI) and benefit of monopolistic and oligopolistic advantages. The main research question is to understand the reasons firms enter into foreign markets.

The Market Imperfection Theory

Studying the distinctive features of FDIs and reasons behind the internation-alization strategies of American multinational corporations (MNCs) is the main goal of Hymer's research published in 1960.[3] According to Hymer, the main factors driving internationalization are, on the one hand, the limited growth opportunities and intense competition on the domestic market and, on the other hand, the ownership of firm-specific advantages. Once an orga-nization has developed its firm-specific advantages, it can try to exploit them on the foreign markets, even if at higher costs compared to local competitors.

Hymer stresses the difficulties that a company faces operating abroad. Foreign firms have to deal with more adverse market conditions compared to the local firms. The latter knows the market, the language, the legal sys-tem and the consumers' preferences. Last but not least, government and consumer discrimination have to be considered. For these reasons, foreign enterprises sustain additional costs to those of the domestic companies.

Firms "despite the disadvantages find it profitable to have foreign opera-tions" (Hymer, 1960). Typically a company initially focuses on the domestic market. As the local market becomes mature, it starts looking abroad for new markets to be exploited. According to Hymer, the existence of *firm ownership advantages* is a prerequisite for offsetting the disadvantage of being foreign.

Being located in diverse countries (i.e., being multinational/international) may also provide advantages: a larger size (the multinational scale); the abil-ity to benefit from scale economies; the access to markets and raw materials not available to competitors; and the exclusive ownership of intangible assets, including additional knowledge and skills.

Hymer assumes that all these advantages, instead of being exploited through third parties, are exploited internally, through FDIs. As mentioned, Hymer's theory focused on foreign direct investments that were the prevalent way companies went international. His theory is based on several assumptions that need to be highlighted: a leadership position established on the home market, the maturity of the domestic market, a large size, the availability of the resources and capabilities required to gather and evaluate information about foreign markets, and the ownership of competitive advantages suitable to be exploited abroad.

The International Product Life Cycle (Vernon)

Vernon (1966) analyzes the Product Life Cycle model (Levitt, 1965) from an international perspective. His goal is to explain the trade flow between the US and Europe after the Second World War. Specifically, he aims at understanding why and how American firms exploit their products on the international markets (mostly in developing countries) through foreign direct investments. In the sixties, the time Vernon wrote his theory, the United States was the world's leading economy and the main source of product innovation. New products were initially developed for the large US domestic market and thereafter introduced to other countries.

Vernon identifies four stages companies follow to become international: introduction, growth, maturity, and decline.

During the *introduction* phase, the production is home-based and the target market is domestic. At this stage there is no need to go abroad for either sales or production. The company benefits from a sort of monopolist position since it markets a completely new product with high growth potential and limited competition. The focus here is to penetrate the domestic market.

In the second stage (*growth*), the product is largely accepted by consumers. Sales grow not only in the domestic market, but also abroad. Products are exported abroad where they gain market shares.

During the *maturity* phase, the company starts facing price competition from local competitors that have entered the market attracted by the high demand. Exporting products from the country of origin is no longer possible. This situation requires making foreign direct investments in production facilities to benefit from the lower local production costs.

In the last stage (*decline*), the company has to deal with limited demand, increasing production costs (due to the growth of the countries of destination), and intense competition. Available options are to find new locations (characterized by lower production costs) to place the production, further innovate/differentiate the product, or abandon the market.

During the seventies, Vernon was aware that his model was going to become obsolete. International markets were seeing the emergence of new economies such as Japan and Europe. In this situation most of new technologies were coming from countries other than the United States. In 1974, Vernon introduces a revised version of his Product Life Cycle model that factors a scenario of oligopolistic competition.[4]

The Eclectic Paradigm

During the eighties, John Dunning developed a general framework that put together different prior theoretical approaches.[5] According to Dunning, companies have several paths of growth (not necessarily alternative): they can diversify by adding new products/business lines or integrate activities both upwards and downwards. They can also expand internationally, by entering new markets. Choosing the last option, they become international enterprises, which are defined as "firms servicing foreign markets."

According to the *Eclectic Paradigm*, successful international companies must rely on one or more of the three advantages described below: ownership-specific advantages (defined as "O advantages"), location-specific advantages ("L advantages"), or internalization-incentive advantages ("I advantages").

The *ownership-specific advantages* are idiosyncratic, firm-specific assets that are able to differentiate the company from competitors. Dunning defines these kinds of assets as "advantages that stem from the exclusive privileged possession of or access to particular generating income assets" (Dunning, 1980). MNCs can utilize or transfer these advantages. The O-advantage can be in different areas, such as, for example, production, marketing, finance, or G&A (general and administrative activities).

Ownership advantages can be divided into two main categories: the asset ownership advantages and transactional ownership advantages.

The *asset ownership advantages* arise from the proprietary ownership of specific assets. They can be either material or immaterial, such as privileged access to markets (i.e., proximity to markets), ownership of scarce natural resources, technology and knowledge, patent rights, and regulatory advantages (particular laws or policies that may give the company an advantage). Certainly, this typology of advantage is an asset that a firm can take advantage of, independently from the internationalization process.

The *transactional ownership advantages* arise from the governance of a network of assets spread throughout various locations. In this sense being multinational provides an additional advantage over the (domestic) competitors. Examples are economies of large size (advantages of common governance) such as economies of learning, economies of scale and scope and larger bargaining power, those with broader access to financial capital, and those with advantages from international diversification of assets and risks. Different from the first type mentioned above, these advantages depend on the fact that the company operates internationally.

MNCs use some foreign factors in connection with their native ownership-specific advantages. The *location-specific advantages* are assets specific to certain locations that a firm might find convenient to exploit through localization decisions. Examples of these country-specific advantages are low cost production factors (such as labor, energy, or materials), political incentives (such as government policies that influence inward FDIs and intercompany trade), and regulatory barriers (such as import restrictions that hamper exports to the foreign market). International growth, from this point of view, originates from the research of location advantages. These advantages are key in determining which will become host countries during the internalization process.

The *internalization-incentive advantages* are advantages from performing some activities internally. The MNCs have several choices of entry mode into foreign markets, ranking from the market (transactions) to the hierarchy (subsidiary). They choose internalization where the market does not effectively work so that transaction expenses are higher than internal organizational costs. According to Dunning, ownership and internalization advantages are closely interrelated: internal production abroad is utilized anytime the transaction costs of contracting-out to foreign third-party companies exceed the cost of coordinating the production and the exchange of these products within the firm.

MNCs, by internalizing activities in foreign markets, may also generate new ownership advantages and further increase the benefits of internalizing. The main incentive of a firm to internalize activities is to avoid the disadvantages—or capitalize on the imperfections—of the market; for example wherever transaction costs are high, information about the product or service to be marketed are not readily available or costly to acquire (Williamson, 1981), and so on.

D.1.2   The Evolutionary Approaches to Internationalization

The *Evolutionary* (also known as *Behavioral*) *theory of internationalization* therefore assumes that international expansion can be described as a process in which a firm goes through incremental steps to reduce the uncertainty embedded in cross-border activity (Aharoni, 1966). This approach refers mainly to two models: the Stage Theory and the Network Approach. Both models are built upon the concept of market knowledge.

The *Stage Theory* is based on the accrual of progressive experiential knowledge through a gradual international commitment that reduces the firm's perception of the risk associated to the internationalization process. The companies first accrue experience in the domestic market before they move to foreign markets and start their internationalization process from culturally and/or geographically close countries before they move to more distant countries.

The *Network Approach* indicates that the internationalization process of the firm is driven by the development of cooperative relationships with customers, suppliers, and/or other business partners.

The Uppsala Model (the Stage Model of Internationalization)

The *Uppsala Model* (also known as stage model or process model) of internationalization is based on the work by Johanson and Wiedersheim-Paul (1975) and Johanson and Vahlne (1977). It includes the concept of gradualism in the internationalization process.[6]

Johanson and Wiedersheim-Paul (1975) discuss how a firm extends its degree of internationalization over time. They introduce a framework (defined as the "*establishment chain*" and represented in Figure D.1) that identifies four stages of internationalization, each representing a higher degree of international involvement.

The levels range from occasional export activities (i.e., minimal commitment for the company) and off-shore manufacturing (i.e., high commitment). It is, however, important to point out that a firm does not have to pass through all the stages. It is possible for a firm to jump from one stage directly to another (the so-called "leapfrog" in the establishment chain) (Figure D.2). Johanson and Wiedersheim-Paul (1975) believe that firms internationalize stepwise, extending their international presence and operations gradually.

The way the internationalization process is structured depends also on the characteristic of the foreign markets: there are markets that are too small to have high levels of commitment (Johanson and Wiedersheim-Paul, 1975).

Figure D.1   The Traditional Establishment Chain
Source: Johanson and Wiedersheim-Paul (1975)

Figure D.2   An Example of Leapfrog in the Establishment Chain
Source: Johanson and Wiedersheim-Paul (1975)

The firm in the initial stage of the establishment chain does not accrue any international experience, since the internationalization decisions mostly are occasional and passive. As the firm reaches the second stage, it starts gathering some initial—although superficial—information about the foreign market conditions. The subsequent stages of the internationalization process lead to a more articulated and wide market experience (Johanson and Vahlne, 1990).

The more experience companies accrue, the far they go. Distance is not only geographic, but, according to Johanson and Vahlne (1977, 1990), also *psychic*. By psychic distance the authors refer to factors preventing or disturbing the flow of information between a firm and the foreign market, such as the language, culture, education, accepted business practices, law system, and industrial development (Johanson and Vahlne, 1977).

The more experience companies accrue, the more intensive and demanding operation modes (i.e., from export to FDIs) they use.

According to the Uppsala model, the internationalization process is not the output of a process aimed at optimum resource allocation; rather it is the result of incremental adjustments to changes at both the environment and firm levels—hence a dynamic model of internationalization where certain decisions trigger other decisions.

The model is based on four concepts (*market commitment, market knowledge, current activities,* and *commitment decisions*) and distinguishes between state aspects and change aspects. The *state aspects* include foreign market commitment (i.e., resource commitment) and market knowledge (i.e., knowledge about foreign markets and activities). The *change aspects* include the current activities and decisions to commit resources and engage in foreign activities, as described below.

The four concepts are interrelated. The level of experience and commitment accrued by the company at a given time affects the way current activities are performed as well as the decisions to commit resources to foreign markets. Current activities and commitment decisions, in turn, have an effect on market knowledge and market commitment (Andersen, 1993).

The Network Model

The network model of internationalization (Johanson and Mattsson, 1988) allows for the influence of external actors or organizations on the internationalization of the firm. "The development of cooperative relationships with customers, suppliers or other business partners may be critical," as Holm et al. (1999: 1049) point out. The internationalization of a company is then the result of its positioning within a network of firms and their relationships. Johanson and Mattsson (1988), the main authors behind this approach, instead of considering internationalization as an interaction only between the firm and the foreign market(s), underline the relevance of networks. According to their model, internationalization depends on network relationships rather than on firm-specific advantages or geographic/psychic distance from the target market. Individuals/external actors, who have experience in the target markets, are able to generate experiential knowledge of the firm and trigger the internationalization process.[7] Then, the degree of internationalization of the network affects the internationalization process of a particular firm, which means that firms cannot be analyzed separately. Therefore, by analyzing the network a firm is part of and identifying the roles and the strengths of the different actors within it, it is possible to understand its internationalization process and the potential constraints and opportunities (Johanson and Vahlne, 1992).

Johanson and Mattsson (1988) use the network framework to categorize four international situations: the Early Starter, the Late Starter, the Lonely International, and the International among Others. The four positions are graphically represented in the matrix included in Table D.1 where they are classified based on the degree of internationalization of both the firm and the network it belongs to.

The *Early Starter* firm has a low degree of internationalization. The model describes how the firm's internationalization situation can influence its level of knowledge. Since the Early Starter has a scarce presence (commitment) on the foreign markets, it has only weak channels of contact with foreign networks. This negatively affects the level of information feedback from the foreign markets.

Table D.1   The Internationalization Matrix (Network Model)

		Degree of Internationalization of the Network	
		Low	High
Degree of Internationalization of the Firm	Low	*The Early Starter*	*The Late Starter*
	High	*The Lonely International*	*The International among Others*

Different from the Stage Model by Johanson and Vahlne, where market knowledge can only be acquired through direct interaction with the market, the firm can accrue knowledge through other actors of the network. The network may also influence the firm's decision-making process.

The Early Starter's lack of current activities involving foreign actors as well as the lowly internationalized position of the network hinders the acquisition of knowledge and the internationalization process. Then, in comparison to the other three firm types, the Early Starter has the lowest level of internationalization and foreign business knowledge.

Similar to the Early Starter, the *Late Starter* has a low degree of internationalization, but is positioned within a highly internationalized market. The Late Starter is characterized by a low level of activities (commitment) in international markets, low direct international experience, and limited direct international relationships (Johanson and Mattsson, 1988).

However, the Late Starter can leverage the participation in its highly internationalized network. Therefore, being part of a highly internationalized network may provide an "inexperienced" firm with experiential knowledge (different from the Early Starter that is an inexperienced firm in an internationally inexperienced network).

Although the *Lonely International* firm is part of on an internationally inexperienced network, its high degree of commitment to the internationalization process provides the firm with a greater level of experiential knowledge compared to the Early Starter and the Late Starter.[8] This is due to the advantage of being a more highly internationalized firm. On the other hand, the circumstance of not residing in a highly internationalized network diminishes its foreign business knowledge.

Johanson and Mattsson describe the *International among Others* as a firm characterized by a high degree of internationalization and having an established presence in foreign markets. Additionally, it can exploit its highly internationalized network, from where it can source its high level of business knowledge.

We can then argue that the International among Others shows the highest levels of internationalization and foreign business knowledge.

D.1.3   The Knowledge-Based Theories

The basic assumption of *knowledge-based theories* (Conner, 1991; Conner and Prahalad, 1996; Madhok, 1996; Nahapiet and Ghoshal, 1998) is that firms grow based on their ability to create new knowledge and transfer this knowledge in order to expand their market.

Empirical studies on technology transfer support the proposition that the characteristics of knowledge determine the cost and mode of transfer. Most of the knowledge is tacit knowledge that is difficult to codify and transfer. It is cheaper and easier to transfer such knowledge to wholly owned subsidiaries than to third parties. Kogut and Zander (1993) find that MNCs are efficient vehicles to transfer knowledge across borders.[9] They create knowledge, transfer knowledge to subsidiaries, get knowledge from their subsidiaries, and evolve. Subsidiaries are therefore considered learning platforms that recombine the firm's knowledge previously acquired within its home market with the new knowledge gradually learned in the foreign one. As the recombination process evolves,[10] the knowledge acquired from the foreign market is transferred internationally and influences the accumulation and recombination of knowledge, including the home market.

D.2   INTERNATIONAL ENTREPRENEURSHIP STUDIES

In the previous parts of this Appendix, we have described the main international approaches in international business studies. Most of these models focus on MNCs (and FDIs) with the goal to understand why firms started to internationalize their operations. Moreover, recent studies (Bloodgood et al., 1996; Coviello and Munro, 1997; Preece et al., 1999; McDougall et al., 1994; Sullivan and Bauerschmidt, 1990; Turnbull, 1987) have shown that the stage theory is inadequate in predicting and explaining the internationalization processes of a significant number of firms.

Recently, the focus on the internationalization of the small firms and young companies has resulted in a growing overlap of interests between international business and entrepreneurship research (McDougall and Oviatt, 2000b). In the remaining part of this Appendix, we walk you through the domain of International Entrepreneurship (IE) to understand how new ventures go international.

D.2.1   International Entrepreneurship: Definition and Main Features

Morrow (1988) introduces the term *"International Entrepreneurship"* in describing the evolving technological and cultural international environment that was opening previously untapped foreign markets to new ventures. Since the beginning of the nineties, studies on the subject have had an impressive growth, ranging from contributions on the role of national culture (McGrath,

MacMillan and Scheinberg, 1992; Wright and Ricks, 1994) to the practice of alliances and inter-firm cooperation (Steensma, Marino, Weaver, and Dickson, 2000), the entrepreneurial attitude and background of top management teams (Reuber and Fischer, 1997), and the role of venture financing (Roure, Keeley and Keller, 1992).

Besides, the publication of several additional studies—such as research on SMEs[11] (Lu and Beamish, 2001), entry modes (Zacharakis, 1997) and corporate entrepreneurship (Birkinshaw, 1997)—the appearance of special issues in various journals,[12] and the organization of forums on international entrepreneurship have all helped to increase the interest in the field.

One of the first empirical studies in the International Entrepreneurship area is McDougall's (1989) work on new ventures' international sales. McDougall (1989, p. 394) defines International Entrepreneurship "as the development of international new ventures or start-ups that, from their inception, engage in international business, thus viewing their operating domain as international from the initial stages of the firm's operation."

In the early nineties, McDougall and Oviatt further developed the study on the so-called "*born-global* venture" defined as ". . . a business organization that, from inception, seeks to derive significant competitive advantage from the use of resources and sale of outputs in multiple countries"(Oviatt and Mc Dougall, 1994, p. 49).

The boundaries of the International Entrepreneurship have been discussed by many researchers: while some authors identify its domain in the new international ventures, others emphasize the construct of the entrepreneurial behavior, which can be observed in very different kinds of organizations. Zahra (1993), for example, points out that the study of International Entrepreneurship should encompass new firms as well as established companies, defining International Entrepreneurship as "the study of the nature and consequences of a firm's risk-taking behaviour as it ventures into international markets." Wright and Ricks (1994) suggest that International Entrepreneurship focuses on the relationship between businesses and the international environments in which they operate. In addition, other authors recognize that a firm's business environment plays an important role in influencing the expression of entrepreneurial activities (Zahra, 1993) as well as their returns (Zahra and Covin, 1995). The importance of national cultures as "loci" for different expressions of International Entrepreneurship and the specific influence of the business environment emphasize the need for comparative studies as one of the areas of interest in International Entrepreneurship.

In 2000, Oviatt and McDougall introduce a broader definition of International Entrepreneurship that includes the study of established companies and the recognition of comparative (cross-national) analysis. They define this field as "a combination of innovative, proactive, and risk-seeking behaviour that crosses or is compared across national borders and is intended to create value in business organizations" (McDougall and Oviatt, 2000b, p. 903).

This definition considers Miller's (1983) definition of entrepreneurship as a phenomenon at the organizational level that focuses on innovation, risk taking, and proactive behavior. It also focuses on the entrepreneurial behavior of these firms rather than studying only the characteristics and intentions of the individual entrepreneurs. The key dimensions of entrepreneurship—innovativeness, proactiveness, and risk propensity—can be found and developed at the organizational level.

Innovativeness reflects the attitude to support new ideas, experimentation, and new processes, whereas *proactiveness* refers to the capacity to anticipate and act on future needs and desires. Lastly, *risk-taking* conduct indicates the will to commit resources together with the awareness of the potential risk of failure.

Including established companies in the study allows for the assumption that well-established companies can also be innovative and risk-taking, correcting an oversight in the entrepreneurship field. Many highly regarded well-established companies work hard to foster innovation, support venturing, and encourage risk-taking behaviors.

The process supporting international entrepreneurial orientation is described by Shane and Venkataraman (2002) as a process of discovery, and this seems to correspond to what Weick (1995) describes as enactment.

Consequently, the definitions of International Entrepreneurship and the object of analysis have moved from specific subjects (given typologies of firms, industries, and markets) to organizational attributes, grounded on the entrepreneurship literature, and firm resources and capabilities.

The evolution of these definitions suggests that an expression of international entrepreneurship is not the entry per se into a foreign market, but it is a combination of attitudes at the individual and organizational level (proactiveness, innovativeness, risk-seeking) and of actions over time, along an evolutionary and potentially discontinuous process.

Table D.2 provides a comparison between the main different definitions of International Entrepreneurship over the last 15 years. It confirms the enlargement—mentioned above—of the research field in terms of object of analysis (categories of firms),[13] but it also discloses other emerging research perspectives: entrepreneurial attitudes and actions, events and processes, and individual and organizational resources and capabilities.

D.2.2   Typologies of International Entrepreneurial Organizations

There are many international entrepreneurial firms that internationalize steadily, although at a relatively slow pace. However, academic researchers have observed accelerated internationalization among some of the smallest and newest SME organizations (Oviatt and McDougall, 1999). The international entrepreneurship scholars identify three main categories of

Table D.2 Main International Entrepreneurship Definitions

Author, date	Definition of International Entrepreneurship
McDougall, 1989	International Entrepreneurship is defined in this study as the development of international new ventures or startups that, from their inception, engage in international business, thus viewing their operating domain as international from the initial stages of the firm's operation.
Zahra, 1993	The study of the nature and consequences of a firm's risk-taking behavior as it ventures into international markets.
Oviatt and McDougall, 1994	A business organization that, from inception, seeks to derive significant competitive advantage from the use of resources and sale of outputs in multiple countries.
McDougall and Oviatt, 1996	New and innovative activities that have the goal of value creation and growth in business organization across national borders.
Oviatt and McDougall, 2000	A combination of innovative, proactive, and risk-seeking behavior that crosses or is compared across national borders and is intended to create value in business organizations.
Knight, 2000	It is associated with opportunity seeking, risk-taking, and decision action catalyzed by a strong leader or an organization.
Knight, 2001	International entrepreneurial orientation reflects the firm's overall proactiveness and aggressiveness in its pursuit of international markets.
McDougall, Oviatt and Shrader, 2003	International Entrepreneurship is the discovery, enactment, evaluation, and exploitation of opportunities—across national borders—to create future goods and services.
Jones and Coviello, 2005	An evolutionary and potentially discontinuous process determined by innovation, and influenced by environmental change and human volition, action or decision.
Mathews and Zander, 2007	Entrepreneurial processes that stretch across the discovery of new business opportunities in an international context to aspects of exploitation including the redeployment of resources and the ultimate engagement with competitors.

international entrepreneurial firms that face, at the same time, the liability of smallness, foreignness, and newness:

- *Born globals*—[14] i.e., SMEs with the potential for accelerated internationalization and a global market vision.

- *Born-again globals*—i.e., companies that focus on their domestic market for many years before beginning rapid and dedicated internationalization (Bell, McNaughton, and Young, 2001).
- Subsidiaries of Multinational Corporations.

All these types of firms have common characteristics, since they are showing proactive behavior, willingness to confront uncertainty, committing resources in different (and distant) markets, and leveraging their networks to access/enact worldwide opportunities (Autio, Sapienza, and Almeida, 2000; Bell, 1995; Bell and McNaughton, 2000; Bloodgood, Sapienza, and Almeida, 1996; Burgel and Murray, 2000; Coviello and Munro, 1995, 1997; Crick and Jones, 1999; Knight and Cavusgil, 1996; Larimo, 2003; Madsen, Rasmussen, and Servais, 2000; Madsen and Servais,1997; Moen, 1999; Petersen and Pedersen, 2002; Zahra, Ireland, and Hitt, 2000).

International New Ventures and Born Globals

Born global firms are dynamic and newly established small firms that become international right at inception or a very short time after foundation. The growing importance of this new phenomenon seems to challenge most of the already established theories on internationalization, and, in particular, the process/stage internationalization path theorized by the Uppsala School. This model—which defines internationalization as a process of gradual commitment and assumes companies go international in a relatively long period of time passing through a certain number of stages—does not fit with firms that originate internationally. These firms do not slowly evolve to doing business internationally. By contrast, they immediately develop strategies to expand themselves abroad, also in countries that are really far (both psychically and geographically) from the country of origin.

The born global literature, especially in the initial phase, has been focused on high-tech business, since the effects of globalization were particularly apparent in these fields. Nonetheless, some researchers have shown that the Born Global phenomenon is not limited to the high-tech business. Indeed, several empirical studies (Zucchella and Scabini, 2007) have shown that the phenomenon also occurs in more traditional sectors, such as the footwear industries. Consistent with this view, Zucchella (2001) points out that "the 'high-tech bias' may lead research to indicate the industry/product as a qualifying feature of born-global firms, while it is only one of their possible attributes."

Diverse definitions for born global companies have been offered by different authors. We summarized the main one in Table D.3.

The Table D.3 shows how different authors from different countries come out with heterogeneous conclusions, specifically regarding the parameters (time from foundation to internationalization, international sales contribution to overall revenue, and so on) to be used to identify the born globals. The criteria proposed by the American researchers ("25% export to total sales ratio in three years since inception") has been adopted by many researchers.

Table D.3   Definition of Born Global Firms

Author	Vision	Time from Establishment to Internationalization	International Sales (% of Revenue)
Oviatt and McDougall, 1994	A business organization that, from inception, seeks to derive significant competitive advantage from the use of resources and the sale of outputs in multiple countries.	—	—
McKinsey & Company, 1993; Rennie, 1993	Management views the world as their market place from the outset.	Began exporting, as an average, within 2 years after foundation.	Achieved 76% of their total sales through exports at an average age of 14 years.
Knight and Cavusgil, 1996	Management views the world as its marketplace from the outset.	Began exporting one or several products within 2 years from establishment.	Tend to export at least a quarter of total production.
Chetty and Campbell-Hunt, 2004	—	Within 2 years from inception.	80% of sales outside New Zealand; markets are worldwide.
Luostarinen and Gabrielsson, 2006	Global vision and/or at global growth path.	Entered global markets at the outset.	Make over 50% of their sales outside home continent. Established after 1985.
Servais et al., 2006	—	Within 3 years of establishment.	More than 25% of foreign sales or sourcing outside home continent.

In this regard it is really difficult to identify universally accepted parameters, also because the internationalization decisions of the companies are heavily impacted by various exogenous factors, such as the home market potential, the target market receptivity, and the characteristics of the product/service offered. What, at the end, distinguishes the born global companies is the fact that the entrepreneurial and management team views the world as their marketplace.[15] This view—or better attitude—inform the company's strategy and, as a consequence, the internationalization decisions.

The Born-Again Globals

The born-again globals are typically small to medium firms "that have been well established in their domestic markets, with apparently no great motivation to internationalize, but which have suddenly embraced rapid and dedicated internationalization" (Bell, McNaughton, Young, 2001). They are different from born globals (because they do not develop international activities from their foundation) and subsidiaries (because they are not linked to any multinational enterprise). Nevertheless, they demonstrate a proactive entrepreneurial behavior, they own knowledge-based resources, and show a receptive attitude to international opportunities, which are all common characteristics of the two other typologies of international entrepreneurial firms.

MNCs' Subsidiaries

The traditional role assigned to subsidiaries refers to the adaptation of the product to local markets. Its role is, on the one hand, to execute the overall MNC's strategy at the local level and, on the other hand, recognize changes in the local demand and to convey this information to headquarters (Bartlett and Goshal, 1989; Doz, 1986; Harzing, 2000; Perlmutter, 1969; Porter, 1986; Stopford and Wells, 1972). Recent research[16] recognized that subsidiaries also have unique capabilities of their own and, most importantly, they develop critical relationships with local customers and suppliers. According to Birkinshaw (1997), the subsidiaries must play a more proactive role with the goal of identifying and exploiting new resources and opportunities. In this perspective they have to assume a more entrepreneurial and international approach.

D.2.3   The Phase Model for Born Global Firms

As mentioned above, born global firms are characterized by *international or global precocity,* where we refer to the speed of the international growth (Nayyar and Bantel, 1994), the pace of internationalization (Eisenhardt and Brown, 1998), or the early start of the international expansion (Zucchella and Scabini, 2007). It is therefore important to focus on their evolution over time. In this regard. Gabrielsson et al. (2008) theorize that born global firms evolve through three phases.

In the *introductory phase* (phase 1) the born global firm has limited resources and an underdeveloped organizational structure. Its most valuable resources are the founder/s and other key people. They have accrued in previous employment or prior ventures international business experience and built an international network of contacts. Based on their empirical case evidence, Gabrielsson et al. (2008) assume that the born global needs to position itself in relevant channels/networks in order to compensate for its own resource shortfalls. In this regard they can use different channels: MNCs (acting as systems integrators or distributors for their products), other companies with an international presence, or even the Internet.

In phase 1, the intensity of the growth depends strictly on the selected channel.

In phase 2 (*growth and resource accumulation*) the born global company learns from its channel partners and uses it to offset its resource paucity in R&D, marketing, sourcing. or financing. The length of Phase 2 depends on two main factors: the potential to become a global industry (which is dependent on the types of products/services it provides) and the firm's attitude toward globalization (i.e., the resources and organizational learning) (Solberg, 2005).

During phase 3 (*break-out*), the born global firms leverage the organizational learning and experience accumulated in the prior phases. This allows them to get a global market positioning of their own, which can be totally or partially independent of the original key customers.

In Figure D.3 shows the main differentiators for born global companies.

Trigger: The main driver of a born global company is the global vision of the founders, which often, but not always, stems from their background.

Commitment: The founders play a key role. They believe strongly that their new companies will become market leaders and commit all their efforts to the company.

Export activities: They are immediate, because the born global firm relies on channels and networks that allow rapid global growth.

Learning: As mentioned above, as market knowledge increases, the traditional SME is ready to take on new challenges, to develop established positions further, and then to commit resources accordingly. For born global companies, organizational learning happens differently. They leverage channels/networks and large initial customers. The pace of learning is increased by the network.

Specific investments: The traditional SME commits resources as its market knowledge increases. born global companies commit resources from day one, prior to receiving positive feedback from the market. Obviously the risk profile is higher, since they are dealing with both new markets and new products.

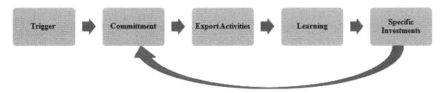

Figure D.3   Commitment in Born Global Internationalization

Source: Gabrielsson et al. (2008).

D.2.4   The Drivers of International Entrepreneurship

The drivers for born global firms are far from being completely explored; they range from "environmental" factors—such as world market globalization—to industry- and business-specific factors, and from location-specific to entrepreneur-specific elements.

A key driver in the internationalization process of born global firms is the entrepreneur (Autio, Sapienza and Almeida, 2000) or the entrepreneurial/founding team. It requires a widespread innovative, proactive, and risk-taking approach (McDougall and Oviatt, 2000b). This approach should be shared by the top management team. According to Harverston, Kedia and Davis (2000), founders and managers in born global firms have, to a great extent, experience with international settings, international contacts and—generally—a more positive attitude toward internationalization, which influences the firm's international path.

Beyond attitude, the prior international experience of the entrepreneur and the top management is key. Recent research (Cannone et al., 2012; Onetti et al., 2010; Presutti, Onetti, and Odorici, 2008) shows that prior experience can play a role in the early internationalization process of born global firms: the market experience, which new established companies don't have, is surrogated by the experience owned by the entrepreneurial and management team.

Coviello and Munro (1995) highlight the importance of the network as a driver for small-firm internationalization. It is also an important factor for the selection of the target foreign market and the modes of entry. The social and inter-organizational networks, as well as dyadic alliances, are actually gatekeepers to opportunity exploration and exploitation. Their role is fundamental for firms that are characterized both by the liability of newness and foreignness (Zucchella and Scabini, 2007).

Moreover, the firm's local environment and its geographical location influence the internationalization process of born global firms. Studies conducted in Italy (Maccarini, Scabini, and Zucchella, 2003), Portugal (Sopas, 2001) and New Zealand (Brown and Bell, 2001) show that born globals arise from local clusters and industrial districts (Zucchella and Scabini, 2007). Table D.4 below summarizes the main drivers for international or global precocity.

Table D.4 The Drivers for International Entrepreneurship

		Issues	Author
Context	**Global Environment**	Shrinking transportation and communication costs	Holstein, 1992
		Better accessibility to knowledge, enhanced knowledge creation and exploitation	Czinkota, Ronkaininen, 1995; Nordstrom, 1991; Dunning, 2000
		Role of ICT	Kobrin, 1991; Dunning and Wymbs, 2001
		Enhanced opportunities to create value and to manage international value chains	Brandenburger and Nalebuff, 1998
		Enhanced speed of growth and value creation processes	Einsenhardt, 1989; Zaheer and Manrakhan, 2001
Drivers	**Business-specific**	From industries to spaces where myriads of Born Global niches either exist or can be created by entrepreneurs (see also entrepreneurial drivers)	Hamel and Prahalad, 1994
		Knowledge intensive industries and high tech businesses as natural arena of Born Global behaviour	Lindqvist, 1991; Preece et al., 1998
		Growing niche orientation both in mature and in innovative businesses	McKinsey, 1993; Zucchella, 2001; Madsen and Servais, 1997
	Location-specific (Clusters and Districts)	The role of local networking	Johanson, 1994; Lindmark, 1994
		Co-location effects and local clusters as drivers of fast international growth	Solvell, Zander, 1995; Dunning, 2000; Markusen, 1996; Porter, 1998; Brown, Bell 2001; Porter, 1990; Servais and Rasmussen, 1999
		Industrial districts as a natural locus for international entrepreneurial orientation	Storper, 1992; Sopas, 2001; Saxenian, 1994; Leamer, Storper, 2001; Maccarini, Scabini and Zucchella, 2003

(Continued)

Table D.4 (Continued)

	Issues	Author
Networking Attitude	The role of international networking (both personal and inter-organizational) in internationalization	Rasmussen et al., 2001; Nooteboom, 2004; Petersen and Petersen 2002; Chetry et al., 2002; Beamish and Makino, 1999
	The role of partnering with global customers	Majkgård and Sharma, 1998
Entrepreneur-specific	Key features in international entrepreneurship	Sahlman and Stevenson, 1992; Venkataraman, 2002; Brush et al., 2001; Andersson, 2003
	The role of the entrepreneur in Born Global firms	Madsen and Servais, 1997; Rasmussen et al., 2001; Bloodgood et al., 1996; Kandsaami, 1998; Harveston et al., 2000
	Governance issues in international entrepreneurial firms	Oviatt and McDougall, 1994; Preece et al., 1998; Larimo, 2001

Table D.5 Learning Blocks—Appendix D

Foreign Direct Investments (FDI)	Ownership-Specific Advantages (O Advantages)	International Product Life Cycle
Location-Specific Advantages (L Advantages)	Internalization Incentive Advantages (I Advantages)	Market Commitment
Market Knowledge	Early Starter	Late Starter
Lonely International	International Among Others	International Entrepreneurship
Born Global	International New Venture (INV)	Born-Again Global

NOTES

1. See also Kindleberger (1969) and Caves (1971).
2. These ventures are defined as "a business organization that, from inception, seeks to derive significant competitive advantage from the use of resources and the sale of outputs in multiple countries" (Oviatt and McDougall, 1994, p. 49).
3. The date of publication of his Ph.D. thesis.
4. The last stage is called "senescent oligopoly."
5. The Eclectic Paradigm cannot be considered as a general theory, since it mostly represents a summary of the extent literature to date. The aim of the author is expressly to analyze and combine different theoretical threads into a single model and stress points of contact as well as areas of disagreement. Dunning argues and defends in his theory that the previous theories are partially correct as well as partially incorrect in explaining every instance of FDI, but also they are incomplete: "Precisely because of its generality, the eclectic paradigm only has limited power to explain or predict particular kinds of international production, and even less power to explain the behaviour of individual enterprises" (Dunning, 1980, p. 1).
6. The model is based on two main assumptions: (1) the goal of a firm is long-term profit that is assumed to be equivalent to growth (Williamson, 1966) and (2) the firms are risk-adverse and try to minimize risk as much as possible.
7. The basic assumption of the model is that companies need an accessible knowledge of one another in order to do business. With these relationships in place, externalization of transactions is more likely to happen than internalization. Due to the resulting informal division of labor among the network's members, each firm will become dependent on these external resources to the extent that exchanges are commenced. Companies can then internationalize with the help of partners who offer contacts and help to develop new partners. Thus, internationalization decisions are influenced by the various members of the firm's network.
8. It is suggested that the Late Starter could benefit from the knowledge of its more experienced peers, but this is not considered enough to offset the experience of the Lonely International (Hadley et al., 2003)
9. Technologies that are difficult to codify also represent platforms for expansion into future markets. Because they are not well understood, they are resistant to rapid imitation.

10. "By recombining knowledge, resting upon what we have called a combinative capability that a firm exploits its current knowledge for expansion into new markets" (Kogut and Zander, 1993, p. 636).
11. Small and medium-sized enterprises.
12. Such as Entrepreneurship Theory and Practice in 1996 and Academy of Management Journal in 2000.
13. Not only new ventures but also established organizations.
14. As discussed above, Born Globals (BG) are also defined as International New Ventures (INV), "Global Startups," "Rapid Internationalizers," or "Instant International" companies. Although some authors make further distinctions, we consider the definitions above as synonyms of companies that are international from day one.
15. Gabrielsson et al. (2008), based on eight case studies conducted in four European countries (Norway, Finland, Greece, and Italy), define born global companies as "firms having products with global market potential." "The founder and its global vision at inception are the key factors" for identifying these companies.
16. The proactive role of subsidiaries in MNCs has been progressively subject to attention, from the seminal work of Hedlund (1980, 1986) on heterarchical international organizations as opposed to the traditional hierarchical ones.

REFERENCES AND SUGGESTED READINGS

Aharoni, Yair. 1966. "The Foreign Investment Decision Process." In *The Internationalization of the Firm*, edited by Peter J. Buckley and Pervez N. Ghauri, 413–28. London: Thompson Learning.

Andersen, Otto. 1993. "On the Internationalization Process of Firms: A Critical Analysis." *Journal of International Business Studies* 24, no. 2: 209–231.

Andersson, Svante. 2003. "The Entrepreneur and the Internationalization of the Firm." Paper presented at the 7th Vaasa International Business Conference, Vaasa, Finland, August 14–16.

Ansoff, H. Igor. 1957. "Strategies for Diversification." *Harvard Business Review* 35, no. 5: 113–124.

Autio, Erkko, Harry J. Sapienza, and James G. Almeida. 2000. "Effects of Age at Entry, Knowledge Intensity, and Imitability on International Growth." *Academy of Management Journal* 43, no. 5: 909–924.

Bartlett, Christopher A., and Sumantra Ghoshal. 1989. *Managing Across Borders. The Transnational Solution*. Boston: Harvard Business School Press.

Beamish, Paul W., and Shige Makino. 1999. "Characteristics and Performance of International Joint Ventures with Non-Conventional Ownership Structures." *Journal of International Business Studies* 29, no. 4: 797–818.

Bell, Jim. 1995. "The Internationalization of Small Computer Software Firms: A Further Challenge to 'Stage' Theories." *European Journal of Marketing* 29, no. 8: 60–75.

Bell, Jim, and Rod McNaughton. 2000. "Born Global Firms: A Challenge to Public Policy in Support of Internationalization." Marketing in a Global Economy: 176–185.

Bell, Jim, Rod McNaughton, and Stephen Young. 2001. "'Born-Again Global Firms: An Extension to the 'Born Global' phenomenon." *Journal of International Management* 7, no. 3: 173–189.

Benito, Gabriel R. G., and Lawrence S. Welch. 1994. "Foreign Market Servicing: Beyond Choice of Entry Mode." *Journal of International Marketing*: 7–27.

Birkinshaw, Julian. 1997. "Entrepreneurship in Multinational Corporations: The Characteristics of Subsidiary Initiatives." *Strategic Management Journal* 18, no. 3: 207–229.

Bloodgood, James M., Harry J. Sapienza, and James G. Almeida. 1996. "The Internationalization of New High-Potential US Ventures: Antecedents and Outcomes." *Entrepreneurship Theory and Practice* 20: 61–76.

Brandenburger, Adam M., and Barry J. Nalebuff. 2002. "Use Game Theory to Shape Strategy." *Strategy: Critical Perspectives on Business and Management* 4, no. 4: 260.

Brown, Peter, and Jim Bell. 2001. "Industrial Clusters and Small Firm Internationalization". In *Multinationals in a New Era*, edited by James H. Taggart, Michael C. McDermott, and Maureen Berry, 10–27. Basingstoke: Palgrave Macmillan.

Brush, Candida G. 1992. "Factors Motivating Small Companies to Internationalize: The Effect of Firm Age." PhD dissertation, Boston University.

Burgel, Oliver, and Gordon C. Murray. 2000. "The International Market Entry Choices of Start-Up Companies in High-Technology Industries." *Journal of International Marketing* 8, no. 2: 33–62.

Cannone, Giusy, Gaia Costantino, Alessia Pisoni, and Alberto Onetti. 2012. *Drivers of International Development for Born Global Companies Founded by Italian Entrepreneurs*. No. qf1201. Department of Economics, University of Insubria.

Caves, Richard E. 1971. "International Corporations: The Industrial Economics of Foreign Investment." *Economica* 38, no. 149: 1–27.

Chetty, Sylvie, and Colin Campbell-Hunt. 2004. "A Strategic Approach to Internationalization: A Traditional versus a 'Born-Global' Approach." *Journal of International Marketing* 12, no. 1: 57–81.

Chetty, Sylvie, Kent Eriksson, and Jukka Hohenthal. 2002. "A Cross cultural Comparison of Collaborative Experience in Internationalizing Firms." In *Learning in the Internationalisation Process of Firms*, edited by Anders Blomstermo and Dharma D. Sharma, 56–74. Cheltenham: Edward Elgar.

Conner, Kathleen R. 1991. "A Historical Comparison of Resource-Based Theory and Five Schools of Thought within Industrial Organization Economics: Do We Have a New Theory of the Firm?" *Journal of Management* 17, no. 1: 121–154.

Conner, Kathleen R., and Coimbatore K. Prahalad. 1996. "A Resource-Based Theory of the Firm: Knowledge versus Opportunism." *Organization Science* 7, no. 5: 477–501.

Coviello, Nicole E., and Hugh J. Munro. 1995. "Growing the Entrepreneurial Firm: Networking for International Market Development." *European Journal of Marketing* 29, no. 7: 49–61.

Coviello, Nicole, and Hugh Munro. 1997. "Network Relationships and the Internationalisation Process of Small Software Firms." *International Business Review* 6, no. 4: 361–386.

Crick, Dave, and Marian Jones. 1999. "Design and Innovation Strategies within 'Successful' High-Tech Firms." *Marketing Intelligence & Planning* 17, no. 3: 161–168.

Czinkota, Michael R., Ilkka A. Ronkainen. 1995. *International Marketing*, 4th ed. Forth Worth: The Dryden Press.

Doz, Yves L. 1986. *Strategic Management in Multinational Companies*. New York: Pergamon.

Doz, Yves, Jose Santos, and Peter J. Williamson. 2001. *From Global to Metanational: How Companies Win in the Knowledge Economy*. Boston: Harvard Business Press.

Dunning, John H. 1980. "Toward an Eclectic Theory of International Production: Some Empirical Tests." *Journal of International Business Studies* 11, no. 1: 9–31.

———. 1999. "Trade, Location of Economic Activity and the Multinational Enterprise: A Search for an Eclectic Approach." In *The Internationalization of a*

Firm, edited by Peter J. Buckley and Pervez Ghauri, 61–79. London: Thompson Learning.

Dunning, John H., and Cliff Wymbs. 2001. "The Challenge of Electronic Markets for International Business Theory." *International Journal of the Economics of Business* 8, no. 2: 273–301.

Eisenhardt, Kathleen M., and Shona L. Brown. 1998. "Time Pacing: Competing in Markets That Won't Stand Still." *Harvard Business Review* 76, no. 2: 59.

Gabrielsson, Mika, V. H. Kirpalani, Pavlos Dimitratos, Carl Arthur Solberg, and Antonella Zucchella. 2008. "Born Globals: Propositions to Help Advance the Theory." *International Business Review* 17, no. 4: 385–401.

Gereffi, Gary, and Miguel Korzeniewicz. 1994. *Commodity Chains and Global Capitalism*, no. 149. Westport: ABC-CLIO.

Hadley, Richard D., and Heather IM Wilson. 2003. "The Network Model of Internationalisation and Experiential Knowledge." *International Business Review* 12, no. 6: 697–717.

Harveston, Paula D., Ben L. Kedia, and Peter Davis. 2000. "Internationalization of Born Globals and Gradual Globalising Firms: The Impact of the Manager." *Advances in Competitiveness Research* 8, no. 1: 92–9.

Harzing, Anne-Wil. 2000. "An Empirical Analysis and Extension of the Bartlett and Ghoshal Typology of Multinational Companies." *Journal of International Business Studies* 31, no. 1: 101–120.

Hedlund, Gunnar. 1980. "The Role of Foreign Subsidiaries in Strategic Decision-Making in Swedish Multinational Corporations." *Strategic Management Journal* 1, no. 1: 23–36.

———. 1986. "The Hypermodern MNC—A Heterarchy?" *Human Resource Management* 25, no. 1: 9–35.

Holm, Desiree B., Kent Eriksson, and Jan Johanson. 1999. "Creating Value through Mutual Commitment to Business Network Relationships." *Strategic Management Journal* 20, no. 5: 467–486.

Holstein, William J., and Kevin Kelly. 1992. "Little Companies, Big Exports." *Business Week* 1: 70–72.

Hymer, Stephen. 1976. *The International Operations of National Firms: A Study of Direct Foreign Investment*. Boston: MIT Press.

Johanson, Jan, and Lars-Gunnar Mattsson. 1988. "Internationalization in Industrial Systems—A Network Approach." In *Strategies in Global Competition,* edited by Neil Hood and Jan-Erik Vahlne, 303–321. New York: Croom Helm.

Johanson, Jan, and Jan-Erik Vahlne. 1977. "The Internationalization Process of the Firm—A Model of Knowledge Development and Increasing Foreign Market Commitments." *Journal of International Business Studies* 8, no. 1: 23–32.

———. 1990. "The Mechanism of Internationalization." *International Marketing Review* 7, no. 4: 11–24.

———. 1992. "Management of Foreign Market Entry." *Scandinavian International Business Review* 1, no. 3: 9–27.

Johanson, Jan, and Finn Wiedersheim-Paul. 1975. "The Internationalization of The Firm—Four Swedish Cases 1." *Journal of Management Studies* 12, no. 3: 305–323.

Jones, Marian V., and Nicole E. Coviello. 2005. "Internationalisation: Conceptualising an Entrepreneurial Process of Behaviour in Time." *Journal of International Business Studies* 36, no. 3: 284–303.

Kandsaami, Selvi. 1998 "Internationalization of Small and Medium Sized Born Global Firms: A Conceptual Model." Presented at the 43rd ICSB Conference, Singapore, June 17–19.

Kindleberger, Charles P. 1969. "American Business Abroad." *The International Executive* 11, no. 2: 11–12.

Knight, Gary A. 2000. "Entrepreneurship and Marketing Strategy: the SME Under Globalization." *Journal of International Marketing*, 8, no. 2: 12–32.

———. 2001. "Entrepreneurship and Strategy in the International SME." *Journal of International Management* 7, no. 3: 155–71.

Knight, Gary A., and S. Tamar Cavusgil. 1996. "The Born Global Firm: A Challenge to Traditional Internationalization Theory." *Advances in International Marketing* 8: 11–26.

Kobrin, Stephen J. 1991. "An Empirical Analysis of the Determinants of Global Integration." *Strategic Management Journal* 12, no. S1: 17–31.

Kogut, Bruce, and Udo Zander. 1993. "Knowledge of the Firm and the Evolutionary Theory of the Multinational Corporation." *Journal of International Business Studies* 24, no. 4: 625–645.

Larimo, Jorma. 2003. "Internationalisation of SMEs: Two Case Studies of Finnish Born Global Firms." In *Learning in the Internationalization Process of Firms*, edited by Anders Blomstermo and D. Deo Sharma, 258. Cheltenham: Edward Ellis Publishing.

Leamer, E. E., and M. Storper. 2001. "The Economic Geography of the Internet Age." *Journal of International Business Studies* 32, no. 4: 641–665.

Levitt, Theodore. 1965. "Exploit the Product Life Cycle," *Harvard Business Review* 43, November–December: 81–94.

———. 1993. "The Globalization of Markets." *Harvard Business Review* 70, no. 3: 92–102.

Lindmark, Leif. 1994. *Småföretagens Internationalization—En Nordisk Jämförande Studie*. Norway: Nordrefo.

Lindqvist, Maria. 1991. "Infant Multinationals: The Internationalization of Young, Technology-Based Swedish Firms." PhD diss., Stockholm School of Economics.

Lu, Jane W., and Paul W. Beamish. 2001. "The Internationalization and Performance of SMEs." *Strategic Management Journal* 22, no. 6–7: 565–586.

Lumpkin, Tom G., and Gregory G. Dess. 1996. "Clarifying the Entrepreneurial Orientation Construct and Linking It to Performance. " *Academy of Management Review* 21, no. 1: 135–172.

Luostarinen, Reijo, and Mika Gabrielsson. 2006. "Globalization and Marketing Strategies of Born Globals in SMOPECs." *Thunderbird International Business Review* 48, no. 6: 773–801.

Maccarini, Maurizio Ettore, Paolo Scabini, and Antonella Zuchella. 2003. "Internationalization Strategies in Italian District-Based Firms: Theoretical Modeling and Empirical Evidence." Paper presented at the Conference on Cluster, Industrial Districts and Firms, Modena, Italy, September 12–13.

Madhok, Anoop. 1996. "Crossroads—The Organization of Economic Activity: Transaction Costs, Firm Capabilities, and the Nature of Governance." *Organization Science* 7, no. 5: 577–590.

Madsen, Tage Koed, Erik S. Rasmussen, and Per Servais. 2000. "Differences and Similarities between Born Globals and Types of Exporters." *Advances in International Marketing* 10: 247 265.

Madsen, Tage Koed, and Per Servais. 1997. "The Internationalization of Born Globals: An Evolutionary Process?" *International Business Review* 6, no. 6: 561–583.

Majkgard, Anders, and Deo D. Sharma. 1998. "Service Quality by International Relationships: Service Firms in the Global Market." In *Globalization, Privatization and the Free Market Economy*, edited by Chatrathi P. Rao. Westport: Quorum Books.

Markusen, Ann. 1996. "Sticky Places in Slippery Space: A Typology of Industrial Districts." *Economic Geography* 72, no. 3: 293–313.

Mathews, John A., and Ivo Zander. 2007. "The International Entrepreneurial Dynamics of Accelerated Internationalisation." *Journal of International Business Studies* 38, no. 3: 387–403.

McDougall, Patricia P. 1989. "International versus Domestic Entrepreneurship: New Venture Strategic Behavior and Industry Structure." *Journal of Business Venturing* 4, no. 6: 387–400.

McDougall, Patricia Phillips, and Benjamin M. Oviatt. 1996. "New Venture Internationalization, Strategic Change, and Performance: A Follow-Up Study." *Journal of Business Venturing* 11, no. 1: 23–40.

McDougall, Patricia P., and Benjamin M. Oviatt. 2000a. "International Entrepreneurship Literature in the 1990s and Directions for Future Research." *Entrepreneurship* 3: 291–320.

McDougall, Patricia Phillips, and Benjamin M. Oviatt. 2000b. "International Entrepreneurship: The Intersection of Two Research Paths." *Academy of Management Journal* 43, no. 5: 902–906.

McDougall, Patricia P., and Benjamin M. Oviatt. 2003. "Some Fundamental Issues in International Entrepreneurship." *Entrepreneurship Theory & Practice* 18: 27.

McDougall, Patricia P., Benjamin M. Oviatt, and Rodney C. Shrader. 2003. "A Comparison of International and Domestic New Ventures." *Journal of International Entrepreneurship* 1, no. 1: 59–82.

McDougall, Patricia Phillips, Scott Shane, and Benjamin M. Oviatt. 1994. "Explaining the Formation of International New Ventures: The Limits of Theories From International Business Research." *Journal of Business Venturing* 9: 469–487.

McGrath, Rita Gunther, Ian C. MacMillan, and Sari Scheinberg. 1992. "Elitists, Risk-Takers, and Rugged Individualists? An Exploratory Analysis of Cultural Differences Between Entrepreneurs and Non-Entrepreneurs." *Journal of Business Venturing* 7, no. 2: 115–135.

McKinsey & Co. 1993. "Emerging Exporters: Australia's High Value-added Manufacturing Exporter." Presented at the Australian Manufacturing Council, Melbourne, Australia, June.

Miller, Danny. 1983. "The Correlates of Entrepreneurship in Three Types of Firms." *Management Science* 29, no. 7: 770–791.

Moen, Øystein. 1999. "The Relationship between Firm Size, Competitive Advantages and Export Performance Revisited." *International Small Business Journal* 18, no. 1: 53–72.

Morrow, John F. 1988. "International Entrepreneurship: A New Growth Opportunity." *New Management* 3, no. 5: 59–61.

Nahapiet, Janine, and Sumantra Ghoshal. 1998. "Social Capital, Intellectual Capital, and the Organizational Advantage." *Academy of Management Review* 23, no. 2: 242–266.

Nayyar, Praveen R., and Karen A. Bantel. 1994. "Competitive Agility: A Source of Competitive Advantage Based On Speed and Variety." *Advances in Strategic Management* 10, no. A: 193–222.

Nooteboom, Bart. 2003. *Inter-Firm Collaboration, Learning and Networks: An Integrated Approach*. London: Routledge.

Nordstrom, Kjell A. 1991. "The Internationalization Process of the Firm: Searching for New Patterns and Explanations." PhD diss., Stockholm Institute of International Business.

Onetti, Alberto, Marco Talaia, Vincenza Odorici, Manuela Presutti, and Sameer Verma. 2010. "The Role Of Serial Entrepreneurs in the Internationalization of Global Start-Ups. A Business Case." *Journal of Strategic Management Education* 6, no. 1: 79–94

Oviatt, Benjamin M., and Patricia Phillips McDougall. 1994. "Toward a Theory of International New Ventures." *Journal of International Business Studies* 25, no. 1: 45–64.

Oviatt, Benjamin M., and Patricia P. McDougall. 1999. "A Framework for Understanding Accelerated International Entrepreneurship." *Research in Global Strategic Management* 7: 23–40.

———. 2005. "Defining International Entrepreneurship and Modeling the Speed of Internationalization." *Entrepreneurship Theory and Practice* 29, no. 5: 537–554.

Perlmutter, Howard V. 1969. *The Tortuous Evolution of the Multinational Corporation*. London: Routledge.

Petersen, Bent, and Torben Pedersen. 2002. "Coping with Liability of Foreignness: Different Learning Engagements of Entrant Firms." *Journal of International Management* 8, no. 3: 339–350.

Porter, Michael E. 1986. "Competition In Global Industries: A Conceptual Framework." In *Competition in Global Industries*, edited by Michael E. Porter. Boston: Harvard Business Scholl Press.

———. 1990. *The Competitive Advantage of Nations*. New York: Free Press.

———. 1998. *On Competition*. Boston: Harvard Business School Press.

Powell, Walter W., Douglas R. White, Kenneth W. Koput, and Jason Owen-Smith. 2005. "Network Dynamics and Field Evolution: The Growth of Interorganizational Collaboration in the Life Sciences." *American Journal of Sociology* 110, no. 4: 1132–1205.

Preece, Stephen B., Grant Miles, and Mark C. Baetz. 1999. "Explaining the International Intensity and Global Diversity of Early-Stage Technology-Based Firms." *Journal of Business Venturing* 14, no. 3: 259–281.

Presutti, Manuela, Alberto Onetti, and Vincenza Odorici. 2008. "Serial Entrepreneurship and Born-Global New-Ventures. A Case Study." *International Journal of Entrepreneurship Education* 6: 255–278

Rasmussan, Erik S., Tage Koed Madsen, and Felicitas Evangelista. 2001. "The Founding of the Born Global Company in Denmark and Australia: Sensemaking and Networking." *Asia Pacific Journal of Marketing and Logistics* 13, no. 3: 75–107.

Rennie, Michael. 1993. "Global Competitiveness: Born Global." *McKinsey Quarterly* 4: 45–52.

Reuber, Rebecca A., and Eileen Fischer. 1997. "The Influence of the Management Team's International Experience on the Internationalization Behaviors of SMEs." *Journal of International Business Studies*: 807–825.

Ricardo, David. 1980. *Principles of Political Economy and Taxation*. London: Penguin. (Original work published 1817.)

Roure, Juan B., Robert Keeley, and Thomas Keller. 1992. "Venture Capital Strategies in Europe and the US Adapting to the 1990's." In *Frontiers of Entrepreneurship Research*, edited by Neil C. Churchill, 345–359. Babson Park, MA: Babson College.

Sahlman, William, and Howard Stevenson. 1992. *The Entrepreneurial Venture*. Boston: Harvard Business School.

Servais, Per, Tage K. Madsen, and Erik S. Rasmussen. 2006. "Small Manufacturing Firms. Involvment in International E-business Activities." *Advances in International Marketing* 17: 297–317.

Servais, Per, and Erik S. Rasmussen. 2000. "Different Types of International New Ventures." Presented at the Academy of International Business (AIB) Annual Meeting, Phoenix, Arizona, November 17–20.

Shane, Scott, and Sankaran Venkataraman. 2001. "Entrepreneurship as a Field of Research: A Response to Zahra and Dess, Singh, and Erikson." *Academy of Management Review* 26, no. 1: 13–16.

Solberg, Carl Arthur. 2005. "Two Factors Impacting on Firm Strategy. Presentation in Panel on Born Globals: How to Reach New Business Space." Paper presented at the 31st EIBA Conference, Oslo, Norway, December 11.

Sölvell, Orjan, and Ivo Zander. 1995. "Organization of the Dynamic Multinational Enterprise." *International Studies of Management and Organization* 25: 17–34.

Sopas, Lenor. 2000. "Born Exporting in Regional Clusters: Preliminary Empirical Evidence." Paper presented at the 27th Annual Conference UK Chapter, Glasgow, UK, April 14–15.

Steensma, H. Kevin, Louis Marino, Mark K. Weaver, and Pat H. Dickson. 2000. "The Influence of National Culture on the Formation of Technology Alliances by Entrepreneurial Firms." *Academy of Management Journal* 43, no. 5: 951–973.

Stopford, John M., and Louis T. Wells, Jr. 1972. *Managing the MNE: Organization of the Firm and Ownership of the Subsidiaries*. New York: Basic Books.

Storper, Michael. 1992. "The Limits to Globalization: Technology Districts and International Trade." *Economic Geography* 68, no. 1: 60–93.

Sullivan, Daniel, and Alan Bauerschmidt. 1990. "Incremental Internationalization: A Test of Johanson and Vahlne's Thesis." *MIR: Management International Review* 30, no. 1: 19–30.

Turnbull, Peter W. 1987. "A Challenge to the Stages Theory of the Internationalization Process." In *Managing Export Entry and Expansion,* edited by Philip J. Rosson and Stanley D. Reid, 21–40. Santa Barbara, CA: Praeger.

Venkataraman, Sankaran. 2002. *The Distinctive Domain of Entrepreneurship Research*. Cheltenham: Edward Elgar Press.

Vernon, Raymond. 1966. "International Investment and International Trade in the Product Cycle." *The Quarterly Journal of Economics* 80, no. 2: 190–207.

Vernon, Raymond. 1979. "The Product Cycle Hypothesis in a New International Environment." *Oxford Bulletin of Economics And Statistics* 41, no. 4: 255–267.

Weick, Karl E. 1995. *Sensemaking in Organization,* vol. 3. Thousand Oaks: Sage Publications.

Williamson, Oliver E. 1981. "The Economics of Organization: The Transaction Cost Approach." *American Journal of Sociology* 87, no. 3: 548–577.

Wright, Richard W., and David A. Ricks. 1994. "Trends in International Business Research: Twenty-Five Years Later." *Journal of International Business Studies:* 687–701.

Zacharakis, Andrew. 1997. "Entrepreneurial Entry into Foreign Markets: A Transaction Cost Perspective." *Entrepreneurship Theory and Practice* 21, no. 3: 23.

Zaheer, Srilata, and Shalini Manrakhan. 2001. "Concentration and Dispersion in Global Industries: Remote Electronic Access and the Location of Economic Activities." *Journal of International Business Studies* 32, no. 4: 667–686.

Zahra, Shaker A. 1993. "A Conceptual Model of Entrepreneurship as Firm Behavior: A Critique and Extension." *Entrepreneurship Theory and Practice* 17, no. 4: 5–21.

Zahra, Shaker A., and Jeffrey G. Covin. 1995. "Contextual Influences on the Corporate Entrepreneurship-Performance Relationship: A Longitudinal Analysis." *Journal of Business Venturing* 10, no. 1: 43–58.

Zahra, Shaker A., and Dennis M. Garvis. 2000. "International Corporate Entrepreneurship and Firm Performance: The Moderating Effect of International Environmental Hostility." *Journal of Business Venturing* 15, no. 5: 469–492.

Zahra, Shaker A., and Gerard George. 2002. "International Entrepreneurship: The Current Status of the Field and Future Research Agenda." In *Strategic Entrepreneurship: Creating a New Mindset,* edited by Michael A. Hitt, 255–288. Oxford: Wiley-Blackwell

Zahra, Shaker A., R. Duane Ireland, and Michael A. Hitt. 2000. "International Expansion by New Venture Firms: International Diversity, Mode of Market Entry, Technological Learning, and Performance." *Academy of Management Journal* 43, no. 5: 925–950.

Zucchella, Antonella. 2001. "The Internationalization of SMEs: Alternative Hypotheses and Empirical Survey." In *Multinationals in a New Era,* edited by James H. Taggart, Michael C. McDermott, and Maureen Berry, 47–66. Basingstoke: Palgrave Macmillan.

Zucchella, Antonella, and Paolo Scabini. 2007. *International Entrepreneurship Theoretical Foundations and Practices*. Basingstoke: Palgrave Macmillan.

Author Bios

ALBERTO ONETTI

Forward-looking, dividing his time between Italy and the United States, Alberto Onetti works to bridge technology and business.

Professor of Business Administration and Innovation Management at the University of Insubria in Varese, Alberto has dedicated himself to research in entrepreneurship and corporate strategy. He has authored and co-authored more than 100 publications.

Alberto graduated from the University of Pavia in 1994, before completing his Master's studies in International Finance and a Ph.D. in Corporate Strategy. His academic career is divided between Italy—where he teaches Management and Entrepreneurship at the University of Insubria in Varese and LUISS in Rome, and serves as head of the Research Centre for Innovation and Life Sciences Management (CrESIT)—and the United States, where he is a visiting faculty member at the College of Business at San Francisco State University since 2006. In 2009, he was appointed to chair the Californian Mind the Bridge Foundation, which has as its mission to inspire, educate and stimulate a new generation of young European entrepreneurs and create startups inspired by the methods and successes achieved in the Silicon Valley. Through the seed venture fund Mind the Seed, where he serves as partner, Alberto concretely invests in the best startups to create successful international ventures.

He is a seasoned serial entrepreneur with core competences in corporate strategy and finance. He founded—together with Fabrizio Capobianco—Funambol, Inc., a mobile personal cloud company based in Foster City, CA. He also acts as consultant and advisor for leading banking groups and Italian and multinational companies, and sits on the board of several private companies and startups.

Alberto regularly blogs and writes for newspapers. Follow him on Twitter @aonetti.

ANTONELLA ZUCCHELLA

Antonella Zucchella is Professor of Marketing and International Entrepreneurship at the Faculty of Economics of University of Pavia. She earned her doctorate in strategic management from the University of Pavia, and she has been Visiting Professor at the School of Management of Universitè Robert Schuman—Strasbourg since 2003 and at Universitè Jean Moulin Lyon 3 since 2009.

Her research focuses mostly on innovation, entrepreneurship and international business. Antonella has authored more than 100 articles and essays, as well as several books.

She serves as Director of the Department of Economics and Management and President of the Centre for International Business and the International Economy at the University of Pavia. Antonella is a board member of several academies and foundations.

VALERIA LORENZI

Valeria Lorenzi has travelled a lot since she was a kid. With a sibling living in Boston, she used to spend her summer holidays in the States, attending English schools, summer camps and doing volunteer work in public museums, hospitals and companies.

A Ph.D. candidate in Marketing and Business Management at the University of Milan Bicocca, she collaborates in several international research projects with the Department of Economics and Management at the University of Pavia. She is a Visiting Fellow at SPRU (Science and Technology Policy Research, University of Sussex) and at Harvard Business School, where she conducts researches on business development in the biopharmaceutical industry.

During her study and research career, Valeria has been received scholarships and grants, along with the recognition and esteem of senior colleagues and corporate managers. After some experience in a private consultancy company, she decided to continue her work in the business arena, supporting recently established companies in business planning and marketing.

Index

Made in the USA
Monee, IL
08 November 2021